REPUTATION, CELEBRITY AND DEFAMATION LAW

To Simon Bensley

Reputation, Celebrity and Defamation Law

DAVID ROLPH
University of Sydney, Australia

ASHGATE

Published by
Ashgate Publishing Limited
Gower House
Croft Road
Aldershot
Hampshire GU11 3HR
England

Ashgate Publishing Company
Suite 420
101 Cherry Street
Burlington, VT 05401-4405
USA

www.ashgate.com

British Library Cataloguing in Publication Data
Rolph, David
Reputation, celebrity and defamation law
1. Libel and slander - Australia 2. Reputation (Law) - Australia
I. Title
346.9'4034

Library of Congress Cataloging-in-Publication Data
Rolph, David.
Reputation, celebrity and defamation law / by David Rolph.
p. cm.
Includes bibliographical references and index.
ISBN 978-0-7546-7124-4
1. Reputation (Law) 2. Libel and slander. I. Title.

K5210.R65 2008
346.03'4--dc22

2008017888

ISBN 978 0 7546 7124 4

Mixed Sources
Product group from well-managed forests and other controlled sources
www.fsc.org Cert no. SA-COC-1565
© 1996 Forest Stewardship Council
FSC

Printed and bound in Great Britain by
MPG Books Ltd, Bodmin, Cornwall.

Contents

Table of Cases

Australia

United Kingdom

New Zealand

Canada

United States

Table of Legislation

Foreword

The Hon Justice Michael Kirby AC CMG
Justice of the High Court of Australia

Article 19 of the *International Covenant on Civil and Political Rights* attempts to strike a sensitive balance between the stated basic rights that are in competition. It asserts that everyone shall have the right to 'hold opinions without interference' and 'to freedom of expression'. However, so far as the latter is concerned, it recognises that the right 'carries with it special duties and responsibilities' and may be 'subject to certain restrictions'. Such restrictions must be provided by law and must be only such as are necessary (primarily) for 'respect of the rights or *reputations* of others'.

Defamation proceedings constitute the principal remedy afforded by our legal system for defending an individual's reputation. Yet, as this valuable and original text demonstrates, there is comparatively little detailed analysis in the cases about exactly what 'reputation' entails. Moreover, the action at law for damages for defamation is often self-defeating as a medium to repair a damaged reputation. The inevitable publicity of court proceedings and the way they often re-expose the plaintiff to ridicule and re-agitate the insult, frequently makes the remedy inapt for the harm.

This book begins with an attempt to stamp a conceptual classification upon the various attributes of a person's reputation that are apt for legal protection. The author accepts the taxonomy proposed in 1986 by Professor Robert Post, now of the Yale Law School. He classifies the protectable interests in reputation as being concerned with the individual's property rights, honour and dignity. The heart of the book is an explanation, by reference to the cases, of the ways in which these three purposes of the law have been served, or frustrated, by defamation proceedings, old and new.

In an amazing examination of ancient and venerable decisions, traced back to English law from the beginning of the thirteenth century, Dr Rolph examines the way in which, virtually from the start, reputation and character have been seen as intertwined and how sexual and intimate conduct has been closely linked with both. Lady Joan Gray brought proceedings in 1290 in an attempt to vindicate her reputation against rumours of adultery. Assertions of fornication, false speaking and 'covert crimes' mark many of the early cases of defamation in the ecclesiastical courts and in the Star Chamber. Reading of these contests, far away and long ago, demonstrates how comparatively little changes in the gossip and fascinations of human society. The topics of hurtful calumny remain astonishingly stable.

Paraded before us in this book are the heroes, heroines and villains of recent defamation proceedings, brought to vindicate an injured reputation. Junie Morosi, Jim Cairns, Tony Abbott, Peter Costello, Rene Rivkin, Liberace, Tom Cruise, Jason Donovan, Andrew Ettingshausen. They and many others appear in this book to play their litigious parts and to help to understand the purposes of the law of defamation and the imperfect way in which the action seeks to achieve those purposes. It is useful to start the enquiry with a realisation that protection of 'reputations' is recognised and upheld in international human rights law. In a sense, it is integral to the notion of human dignity. To the extent that our legal system fails to protect this element of human personality, it is therefore a serious failing. Yet most readers will come away from this book convinced that the action of defamation is a most imperfect vehicle for achieving its purported objectives.

As Dr Rolph points out, this is not only by reason of the openness of court proceedings and the consequential reportage of defamation trials. It is also connected with the modern media of communications. Not only do radio and television bring reputational controversies and stories of court proceedings to the notice of millions. The Internet and the capacity of search engines will track down elements of old gossip and falsehoods that once would have been lost in inaccessible files and fallible human memories. Anyone who enters the public domain today knows that this is so and that, basically, there is not much they can do about it.

Someone once (probably as a jest) claimed that, during my service as President of the New South Wales Court of Appeal, I helped my partner in the early morning hours to deliver newspapers for his then business. The story was totally false. His business was far from the reported sightings. Denials got us nowhere. Now, the story has entered the realm of apparent truth. When people congratulate me on these 'endearing' acts of loyalty and support, I no longer bother to set them right. In the Internet, we are all reduced to victims of other people's falsehoods or misperceptions. Expecting a defamation action to restore truth about reputations may thus be as foolish as the beliefs of King Canute's courtiers that he had the power to turn back the waves.

The need to adapt defamation law still further to match the realities of contemporary electronic communications was mentioned in the High Court of Australia in *Channel Seven Adelaide Ltd v Manock* [2007] HCA 60 at [162]. But the new technology creates infotainment and celebrities who are expected to play out their roles as members of the 'mediacracy'. Having signed up to the Faustian pact with fame, they are expected to be 'good sports' when some of the communications about them expose their reputations to insult, ridicule, falsehood and harm. Anyone in doubt about the celebrity culture needs to look at the popular magazines displayed by their dentist or hairdresser. They are jam-packed with characters, some of whom wander across the stage of this book in search of a remedy when false or hurtful statements are published about them. Many, perhaps most, play the game, ignore the hurt and ascribe this conduct to the fact that defamation proceedings rarely, if ever, succeed in restoring a damaged reputation. Yet, if this is so, and if protection of reputation is a basic human right, this conclusion should give us pause to consider better, quicker, cheaper and more appropriate ways to vindicate serious harm from the manner in which the modern world perceives individuals. They do have some rights to privacy. They can be harmed by false words or images that wound. But is there any remedy against such wrongs in the current age?

In its 1979 report, proposing reform of the law of defamation, the Australian Law Reform Commission suggested the introduction into our law of rights of correction and rights of reply, as supplements, or alternatives, to damages in defamation proceedings. The Commission also proposed a limited protection for privacy in the place of the requirement to prove 'public benefit' or 'public interest' to justify a publication that had damaged a person's reputation. The recent advent of *Uniform Defamation Acts* throughout Australia has achieved one of the objectives of this report. But it has done so without reform of the remedies or the grant of privacy protections. As Dr Rolph points out, some of the cases described in this book were more concerned with invasions of privacy than assaults on reputation, as such. Defamation law reform in Australia thus remains a work-in-progress.

Further progress will be made with the aid of the conceptual thinking evident in these pages. If we can appreciate the multi-textured elements of 'reputation', we may be in a better position to protect this value in a deserving case. The great strength of this work is that it is founded upon centuries of historical examples; stimulated by clear conceptual analysis; and illustrated by references to many recent cases. By pointing to the impact of new technology and the phenomena of infotainment and celebrities, the analysis is well and truly situated in the real world of defamation law as it is now commonly practised. One leaves these pages with the nagging doubt that the ordinary person whose reputation is damaged in Australia will have a real remedy. If that is so, it probably puts Australia in breach of the guarantee promised in the *International Covenant*. But does anyone care? Given the powerful players in this aspect of the law, will anything be done?

I congratulate Dr Rolph and the publisher for a book that is at once sound in legal analysis and illustrated by many highly readable instances. This mixture of theory and empiricism constitutes a fine example of legal publishing. At once, useful, fascinating and disturbing.

Michael Kirby
7 February 2008
High Court of Australia, Canberra

Acknowledgements

This book would not have been possible without the unstinting love and support of my parents, Ken and Jan Rolph, and my sister, Emma. The friendship and support of current and former academic colleagues at the University of Sydney Faculty of Law – Assoc. Prof. Barbara McDonald, Assoc. Prof. Patricia Loughlan, Prof. Joellen Riley and Prof. Elisabeth Peden – have been particularly valuable to me during the writing of this book. I would also like to thank Kate Peterson and Hugh Atkin for their excellent research assistance. Special thanks to Katherine Biber, who encouraged me to pursue this research and who is always a magnificent interlocutor – stimulating and insightful. Finally, I would like to thank my friends, Michelle Arrow, Richard Ackland, Simon Bensley, Nerida Campbell, Valentyna Jurkiw, Beth Kilner, Andrew Murray and Fran Smithard, for their kindness, their patience and their support.

The use of material from D. Rolph, 'Dirty Pictures: Defamation, Reputation and Nudity', in (2006) 10 *Law Text Culture* 101–36 in Chapter 7, Reputation as Dignity, is reproduced here with kind permission.

Introduction

> Fame is a shuttlecock. If it be struck only at one end of the room, it will soon fall to the ground. To keep it up, it must be struck at both ends.
>
> (*Samuel Johnson* in Boswell, *The Journal of a Tour of the Hebrides* 1984, 408)

Why Analyse Reputation?

A reputation may be protected, vindicated, made, acquired, deserved (or undeserved), damaged, injured, diminished or traduced. Each of these ways of affecting a reputation implies something different about the concept of reputation itself and the value to be ascribed to it. There are many competing and often contradictory discourses surrounding the concept of reputation in defamation. Given the rich and sometimes evocative ways in which reputation can be described and acted upon, one might have expected to encounter a substantial body of jurisprudence analysing the concept of reputation in defamation law. However, there has been scant attention given to this crucial concept.

This omission is surprising, given the centrality of reputation to defamation law. It is uncontroversial to state that the tort of defamation protects reputation. Indeed, it is clear that reputation is the sole interest directly protected by the law of defamation (Watterson 1993, 812–13; Barendt 1999, 112–14; Beverley-Smith 2002, 249–50; Rogers 2002, 12.1). It is equally uncontroversial to state that the common law claims to value freedom of speech. Consequently, it is axiomatic that the tort of defamation purports to strike a balance between freedom of speech and the protection of reputation.

What is meant by the concept of freedom of speech generally and what is meant by it specifically in the context of defamation law have been extensively analysed from a variety of legal and critical perspectives (Barendt 2005, 205–26; Peonidis 1998; Cottrell 1999; Stone and Williams 2000; Magnusson 2001). Similarly, the appropriate balance between freedom of expression and the protection of reputation in defamation, and the way in which that balance should be implemented, have also been the subject of detailed, scholarly consideration (Schaffner 1990; Boivin 1997; Tingley 1999).

There are a number of likely reasons for this focus: firstly, the influence of the First Amendment of the United States Constitution, guaranteeing freedom of speech, *inter alia*, the constitutionalisation of American defamation law in *New York Times v Sullivan* 376 US 254; 84 S Ct 710 (1964) and the resulting jurisprudence;[1] secondly, the recent development of enforceable, rights-based jurisprudence, in their various constitutional and statutory forms, in Canada, New Zealand and the United Kingdom and its subsequent impact on defamation law in those countries;[2] and thirdly, in Australia, the recognition of the implied freedom of political communication, arising from the text and structure of the Commonwealth Constitution, and its subsequent impact on defamation law, coupled with the political resistance to the introduction of constitutional or statutory regimes to protect individual rights (Potter 1998; Stone 1998; Chesterman 2000; Butler 2000a; Meagher 2005).[3]

In stark contrast, the concept of reputation itself remains relatively unexamined. The meaning and importance of reputation is largely assumed. General texts on tort law and specialist texts on defamation law tend not even to address what is meant by reputation, instead commencing their analyses of the law of defamation by examining what is defamatory. (However, see now George 2006, 74–86.) Those textbooks which acknowledge the need to define the central interest of reputation tend to do so perfunctorily. This lack of analysis of the concept of reputation has been noted by judges and academics alike (see, for example, *Hill v Church of Scientology* (1995) 126 DLR (4th) 129 at 160 per Cory J; Levine 2002, 8; Tingley 1999, 632; Walker 1994, 732–3; Kenyon 1998, 76; Barendt 1996, 114; Beverley-Smith 2002, 250).

One consequence of this lack of analysis is that assumptions are implicitly made about the concept of reputation. For example, it is assumed that there is a single, coherent, immutable concept of reputation protected by defamation law. It is assumed that the plaintiff's reputation exists and that the defendant's publication adversely affects it (Gibbons 1996, 587). Yet these assumptions are surely contestable.

1 See for example *Rosenblatt v Baer* 383 US 75; 86 S Ct 669 (1966); *Curtis Publishing Co v Butts* 388 US 130; 87 S Ct 1975 (1967); *Gertz v Robert Welch Inc* 418 US 323; 94 S Ct 2997 (1974); *Dun & Bradstreet Inc v Greenmoss Builders Inc* 472 US 749; 105 S Ct 2939 (1985); *Milkovich v Lorain Journal Co* 497 US 1; 110 S Ct 2695 (1990); *Masson v New Yorker Magazine Inc* 501 US 496; 111 S Ct 2419 (1991); Anderson 2004.

2 See, for example, in relation to Great Britain, *Reynolds v Times Newspapers* [2001] 2 AC 127; [1999] 4 All ER 609; [1999] 3 WLR 1010. See, for example, in relation to New Zealand, *Lange v Atkinson* [2000] 1 NZLR 257; *Lange v Atkinson* [2000] 3 NZLR 385. See, for example, in relation to Canada, *Hill v Church of Scientology* (1995) 126 DLR (4th) 129. See generally Stone and Williams 2000.

3 The leading cases in relation to the implied freedom of political communication are *Nationwide News Pty Ltd v Wills* (1992) 177 CLR 1; 108 ALR 681; 66 ALJR 658; *Australian Capital Television Pty Ltd v Commonwealth (No 2)* (1992) 177 CLR 106; 108 ALR 577; 66 ALJR 695; *Theophanous v Herald & Weekly Times Ltd* (1994) 182 CLR 104; 124 ALR 1; 68 ALJR 713; *Lange v Australian Broadcasting Corporation* (1997) 189 CLR 520; 145 ALR 96; 71 ALJR 818; *Levy v State of Victoria* (1997) 189 CLR 579; 146 ALR 248; 71 ALJR 837; *Coleman v Power* (2004) 220 CLR 1; 209 ALR 182; 78 ALJR 1166.

More importantly, another consequence is that it is difficult to assess the validity of central claims made about defamation law. The question of how effective the existing principles of defamation law are in providing protection for a plaintiff's reputation cannot be adequately assessed without an understanding of what reputation actually is. Likewise, the issue of how appropriate the existing balance between freedom of expression and protection of reputation struck in defamation law is, and whether any recalibration is required, can only be properly evaluated if there is an understanding of what is in fact meant by reputation (Post 1986, 692; Walker 1994, 733).

The Meaning of Reputation

It is important to start by attempting to define the term, 'reputation'. Those scholars who engage with the problem of defining reputation readily admit the difficulty of the task. According to Post, reputation is 'a mysterious thing' (Post 1986, 692). Balkin and Davis characterise reputation as 'highly prized but intangible' (Balkin and Davis 2004, [17.3]). Explaining why they chose not to include defamation in their textbook on torts, Luntz and Hambly describe reputation as 'nebulous, yet much cherished' (Luntz and Hambly 2002, [1.4.6]). Perhaps, as Watterson suggests, it is misguided to view reputation as 'one of the few safe harbours in the law of defamation' (Watterson 1993, 812). As another scholar has observed, 'pinning down a definition of reputation is a difficult task' (Calvert 1995, 939; cf. Levine 2002, 5).

A useful starting-point is to examine how the term 'reputation' is ordinarily defined for non-legal purposes. Indeed, Prosser and Keeton have stated that reputation, for the purposes of defamation law, is understood 'in the popular sense' (Keeton et al. 1984, 773; Spencer Bower 1990, 243).

The *Oxford English Dictionary* (1989, 678) defines 'reputation', thus:

1. Opinion, supposition; also the opinion or view *of* one about something …
2. The common or general estimate of a person with respect to character or other qualities; the relative estimation or esteem in which a person or thing is held.
3. The condition, quality, or fact of being highly regarded or esteemed; credit, note, or distinction; also respectability, good report.
4. The honour or credit *of* a particular person or thing; one's good name, good report, or fame in general.
5. The estimation, credit, or ascription *of* being or possessing something.

The unifying feature of all these definitions of 'reputation' is the dependence of an individual's reputation on the recognition of others (Post 1986, 692).

Beyond certain, incidental judicial assertions about the nature of reputation, the common law has generally eschewed engagement with the problem of defining reputation. For instance, recently, in *Rogers v Nationwide News Pty Ltd* (2003)

216 CLR 327; (2003) 201 ALR 184; 77 ALJR 1739; Aust Torts Reports ¶81-713, Hayne J (at 349; 199) has stated that 'reputation is not a commodity having a market value'. However, in *Dixon v Holden* (1869) 7 LR Eq 488, Malins V-C stated (at 492) that '[o]ne man has property in lands, another in goods, another in business, another in skill, another in reputation' and further observed that 'his reputation … is his property'. It is difficult to reconcile these apparently conflicting statements about reputation. Is it a proprietary or a purely personal interest (Boivin 1997, 290–91)? Is reputation an economic or a dignitary interest (Beverley-Smith 2002, 251)? Is it possible for it to be both (Linden 2001, 683)? If so, why do judges disagree about the nature of reputation? These incidental assertions about reputation do not help define the concept of reputation so much as highlight its underdevelopment in defamation jurisprudence.

To the extent that the law of defamation has engaged with the problem of defining the term, 'reputation', it has contented itself with generalities. The classic statement of what constitutes reputation for the purposes of defamation law is taken from Lord Denning's judgment in *Plato Films Ltd v Speidel* [1961] AC 1090:

> A man's 'character', it is sometimes said, is *what he in fact is*, whereas his 'reputation' is *what other people think he is*. If this be the sense in which you are using the words, then a libel action is concerned only with a man's reputation, that is, with what people think of him: and it is for damage to his reputation, that is, to his esteem in the eyes of others, that he can sue, and not for damage to his own personality or disposition. ([1961] AC 1090at 1138 (original emphasis))[4]

Lord Denning's definition of 'reputation' is problematic for several reasons. Firstly, the case law, old and new, is replete with references wherein the terms, 'character' and 'reputation', are used interchangeably.[5] Indeed, Lord Denning himself recognises this precise problem (at 1138).

4 Lord Denning's distinction between reputation and character has been subsequently endorsed. See, for example, *Re T and Director of Youth & Community Services* [1980] 1 NSWLR 392 at 395 per Waddell J; *Melbourne v R* (1999) 198 CLR 1 at 15–16; 164 ALR 465; 73 ALJR 1097 per McHugh J; *O'Hagan v Nationwide News Pty Ltd* (2001) 53 NSWLR 89 at 91 per Meagher JA; Levine 2002, 5; Veeder 1904, 33; Pound 1915, 447.

5 For examples of older authorities, see, for example, *De Crespigny v Wellesley* (1829) 5 Bing 392 at 405–6; 130 ER 1112 at 117–18 per Best CJ; *Toogood v Spyring* (1834) 1 CM & R 181 at 193; (1834) 149 ER 1044 at 1049 per Parke B; *Smith v McQuiggan* (1863) 2 SCR(NSW) (L) 268 at 270 per Stephen CJ; *Bryce v Rusden* (1886) 2 TLR 435 at 439 per Huddleston B; *Pullman v Walter Hill & Co Ltd* [1891] 1 QB 524 at 527 per Lord Esher MR. For examples of more recent authorities, see, for example, *Slim v Daily Telegraph Ltd* [1968] 2 QB 157 at 171–2 per Diplock LJ; *Delaney v News Media Ownership Ltd* [1976] 1 NZLR 322 at 326–8; *Gorman v Barber* (2004) 61 NSWLR 543 at 550 per Mason P. See further Spencer Bower 1990, 242.

Moreover, it is perhaps important not to overstate the distinction between reputation and character so as to posit a false dichotomy between the two. Reputation and character are different, but not absolutely distinct, concepts. There is surely a necessary interdependence between what an individual in fact is and what other people think an individual is. What other people think of an individual is intimately connected with what other people know about the individual. Other people know about an individual through that individual's interaction with them. In that interaction, the individual has control over what aspects of his or her character are or are not disclosed. Ideally, perhaps, reputation and character would be identical but, because reputation is socially mediated, whereas character is innate, there is invariably some discrepancy between the two. In turn, what an individual thinks about himself or herself is, to varying degrees, informed and affirmed by what others think about that individual. Reputation and character cannot, or perhaps should not, be so neatly divided.

The common law of defamation is ambivalent about whether reputation and character can, or ought, be co-extensive (Spencer Bower 1990, 243). On the one hand, the rationale stated for the defence of truth, which, at common law, is a complete defence to a claim for defamation, is that:

> [A]s the object of civil proceedings is to clear the character of the plaintiff, no wrong is done to him by telling the truth about him. The presumption is that, by telling the truth about a man, his reputation is not lowered beyond its proper level, but is merely brought down to it. (*Rofe v Smith's Newspaper Ltd* (1924) 25 SR(NSW) 4 at 21–22; (1924) 42 WN(NSW) 3 per Street ACJ; Spencer Bower 1990, 242)

According to Windeyer J, 'the law does not protect the reputation that a man has, but only the reputation that he deserves' (*Uren v John Fairfax & Sons Pty Ltd* (1966) 117 CLR 118 at 150; see also *M'Pherson v Daniels* (1829) 10 B & C 263 at 272; 109 ER 448 at 451 per Littledale J). In theory, perhaps, reputation and character should be co-extensive and defamation law assists in calibrating them.

Yet, this is not necessarily borne out in practice. It is well-known that the case law is replete with undeserving plaintiffs receiving compensation for injured reputations, reinforcing the notion that, in reality, reputation and character are not co-extensive. George describes defamation law as 'controversial' precisely because 'it has provided protection to criminals and the corrupt, to rogues and villains, preventing exposure of their true characters and maintaining their undeserved reputations' (George 2006, 3). Like George, Barendt names few names but journalist Evan Whitton demonstrates no such reticence, identifying Liberace and Australian political figures, Junie Morosi and Jim Cairns, *inter alia*, as examples of such plaintiffs (Barendt 1999, 115; Whitton 2004. See Chapters 5 and 6).

Nonetheless, what Lord Denning's definition makes tolerably clear is that reputation is not simply the plaintiff's subjective sense of self (Keeton et al. 1984, 773). Defamation is a social tort and the interest it protects, reputation, has been described as analogous to a relational interest (Skolnick 1986, 677; Bellah 1986,

744; Keeton et al. 1984, 773). For good or ill, the common law of defamation has made damage to the plaintiff's reputation, not the insult experienced by the plaintiff, the gist of the action (Pollock 1929, 249; *Dow Jones & Co Inc v Gutnick* (2002) 210 CLR 575 at 600 per Gleeson CJ, McHugh, Gummow and Hayne JJ; 194 ALR 433; 77 ALJR 255; Aust Torts Reports ¶81-682). Watterson has argued that reputation tends to be associated with personal characteristics, such as honesty and integrity, not with physical characteristics, such as gender or ethnicity (Watterson 1993, 812). Thus, reputation is derived from the exhibition of these personal characteristics in interactions with others, reinforcing its social nature. There is therefore an indelibly social aspect to reputation. However, whilst reputation has this indelibly social aspect to it, the personal aspect of reputation, the plaintiff's subjective response to a defamatory publication and its impact on his or her sense of self, is not wholly irrelevant. Reputation is a complex concept, difficult to define, because it is an interest that is at once both purely personal to the plaintiff and inherently social. The implications of this recognition require exposition.

The Importance of Reputation

Judges and Academics on Reputation

Whilst the meaning of reputation is somewhat elusive, the importance ascribed to it is not. The importance of reputation is often glibly and grandly stated by judges and academics alike. The examples are innumerable; a selection will suffice. For instance, in *De Libellis Famosis* (1605) 5 Co Rep 125a at 125b; 77 ER 250 at 251, Sir Edward Coke opined that a man's 'good name … ought to be more precious to him than his life'. In the mid-nineteenth century, in *De Crespigny v Wellesley* (1829) 5 Bing 392 at 406; 130 ER 1112 at 1118, Best CJ boldly claimed that 'if we reflect on the degree of suffering occasioned by loss of character, and compare it with that occasioned by loss of property, the amount of the former injury far exceeds that of the latter.' More recently, in *Hill v Church of Scientology* (1995) 126 DLR (4th) 129 at 160, a decision of the Supreme Court of Canada, Cory J stated that, 'to most people, their good reputation is to be cherished above all.' (See also *R v Lucas* (1998) 157 DLR (4th) 423 at 456 per Cory J: 'This is the attribute which is most highly sought after, prized and cherished by most individuals. The enjoyment of a good reputation in the community is to be valued beyond riches.')

Judges are not alone in their endorsement of the importance of reputation; academics have been similarly effusive. The eminent torts scholar, Sir Frederick Pollock, opined that '[r]eputation and honour are no less precious to good men than bodily safety and freedom. In some cases they may be dearer than life itself' (Pollock 1929, 242). To similar effect, the late John Fleming described reputation as 'perhaps the most dearly prized attribute of civilised man' (Fleming 1998, 580). The legal historian, J.H. Baker, opined that '[w]ords can be more harmful than deeds, and in some circumstances honour may be more tender than personal safety' (Baker 2002, 437).

Shakespeare on Reputation

The importance and value of reputation is often asserted shorthand through the deployment of an evocative Shakespearean quote (Post 1986, 692; Walker 1994, 733). One of the most popular quotes from the Shakespearean corpus is taken from *Othello*:

> Good name in man and woman, my dear lord,
> Is the immediate jewel of their souls.
> Who steals my purse steals trash; 'tis something, nothing;
> 'Twas mine, 'tis his, and has been slave to thousands.
> But he that filches from me my good name
> Robs me of that which not enriches him
> And makes me poor indeed. (III.iii.160–66)

Writing extra-curially, Heerey J of the Federal Court of Australia observed that it was routine practice for counsel for the plaintiff in defamation cases to rely on this passage from *Othello* in support of the importance of reputation (Heerey 2000, 8). In a number of cases, judges too have uncritically cited this passage in their reasoning and some scholars too.[6] It is important, however, not to rely too heavily on this Shakespearean quotation to establish the importance of reputation, particularly by emphasising the sentiment out of context (Spencer Bower 1990, 241–2; Brown 1994, 8; Barendt 1999, 114). It is certainly an elegant statement of the importance of reputation and demonstrates the erudition of the advocate, judge or academic citing it. However, it forecloses debate on a worthwhile point.

6 See Post 1986, 692 (and cases cited therein); *Thomas v Canadian Broadcasting Corporation* [1981] 4 WWR 289 at 339 per Disbery J; *Milkovich v Lorain Journal Co* 497 US 1; 110 S Ct 2695, 2702 (1990) (Rehnquist CJ); *National Life Insurance Co v Phillips Publishing Inc* 793 F Supp 627, 642 n 28 (1992) (Northrop J); *Lewis v McGraw-Hill Broadcasting Co Inc* 832 P 2d 1118, 1125 (1992) (Dubofsky J); *Bernson v Browning-Ferris Industries of California Inc* 873 P 2d 613; 30 Cal Rptr 2d 440, 447 (1994) (Arabian J); *Newman v Delahunty* 681 A 2d 671, 687 (1994) (Piscal J); *Mucci v Dayton Newspapers Inc* 654 NE 2d 1068, 1074–1075 (1995) (Froelich J); *Pressler v Lethbridge* (1997) 153 DLR (4th) 537 at 554 per Owen-Flood J; *R v Lucas* (1998) 157 DLR (4th) 423 at 456–7 per Cory J; *Howlett v Saggers* (unreported, SC(NSW), 20783/95, Donovan AJ, 24 April 1998) at 59–60; *Guildford Transportation Industries Inc v Wilner* 760 A 2d 580, 595 (2000) (Schwelb AJ); *Nassa v Hook-Superx Inc.* 790 A 2d 368, 374 n 12 (2002) (Flanders J); *W.J.L.A.-T.V. v Levin* 264 Va 140; 564 SE 2d 383, 396 n 8 (2002) (Koontz J); *Knievel v ESPN* 393 F 3d 1068, 1079 (2005) (Bea J (dissenting)); *Ramsey v Fox News Network LLC* 351 F Supp 2d 1145, 1153 (2005) (Figa J); Carter-Ruck and Starte 1997, 1; Linden 2001, 683; Levine 2002, 4; George 2006, 11.

As Donovan AJ observed in *Howlett v Saggers* (unreported, SC(NSW), 20783/95, Donovan AJ, 24 April 1998) (at 60), Shakespeare 'puts these lines into the mouth of the most mendacious man in the panoply of people in his plays', Iago (see also Barendt 1996, 114). In the previous act (II, iii), in response to Cassio's declaration: 'Reputation, reputation, reputation – O, I ha' lost my reputation, I ha' lost the immortal part of myself, and what remains is bestial! My reputation, Iago, my reputation.' Iago counters with the following statements: 'As I am an honest man, I thought you had received some bodily wound. There is more sense in that than in reputation.' Iago then observes to Cassio that '[r]eputation is an idle and most false imposition, oft got without merit and lost without deserving.'

Another passage from Shakespeare, which is also relied upon by judges, advocates and academics, is the sentiments expressed by Thomas Mowbray, Duke of Norfolk, in the opening scene of *Richard II*:

> The purest treasure mortal times afford
> Is spotless reputation; that away,
> Men are but gilded loam, or painted clay …
> Mine honour is my life. Both grow in one.
> Take honour from me, and my life is done. (I.i.177–9, 182–3)[7]

Whilst Shakespeare allows that the concept of reputation is complex and its value is controvertible, judges, advocates and academics have been less willing to engage with the vexed problem of defining reputation and the related issue of the importance to be ascribed to it.

The Continuing Historical Importance of Reputation

Another justification for ascribing importance to the concept of reputation is that it is a value universally recognised. There is certainly a venerable literary tradition lauding the importance of reputation. For instance, the wisdom literature of the Old Testament emphatically endorses the importance of a good reputation, stating in one place that '[a] good name is to be chosen rather than great riches'[8] and, in another place, that '[a] good name is better than precious ointment' (Ecclesiastes 7:1). There is an equally well-established legal tradition protecting reputation against attack. For example, in Roman law, an individual's reputation was protected by the

---

7 See, for example, *Australian Consolidated Press Ltd v Ettingshausen* (unreported, CA40079/93, CA(NSW), Gleeson CJ, Kirby P, Clarke JA, 13 October 1993) at 41 per Kirby P; *Barella v Exchange Bank* 101 Cal Rptr 2d 167, 169 (2001) (Rivera J); *Nassa v Hook-Superx Inc* 790 A 2d 368, 372 (Flanders J); Kux 2004a; Post 1986, 701; Carter-Ruck and Starte 1997, 2; Levine 2002, 4; George 2006, 11–12.

8 Proverbs 22:1; as cited in *Pullum v Johnson* 647 So 2d 254, 256 n 4 (1994) (Van Nortwick J); *Mucci v Dayton Newspapers Inc* 654 NE 2d 1068, 1074 (1995) (Froelich J); *Barella v Exchange Bank* 101 Cal Rptr 2d 167, 169 (2001) (Rivera J).

delict of *iniuria*,[9] with the gist of the action being the insult or affront to the dignity of the individual. Several commentators have observed that all major civilisations and cultures, and their legal systems, appear to have afforded some protection to the reputations of individuals (Brown 1994, 4; Carter-Ruck and Starte 1997, 1–2; Pound 1915, 448–50; see also *Hill v Church of Scientology* (1995) 126 DLR (4th) 129 at 160–62 per Cory J).

It would appear that an individual's reputation continues to be important and that the protection of reputation remains a legitimate goal of the legal system. For example, in *Hill v Church of Scientology* (1995) 126 DLR (4th) 129 at 162, Cory J observes that, whilst the original purpose of defamation law was to provide 'a bulwark against the duel and blood feud', defamation law remains relevant, protecting the reputations of individuals. According to his Honour (at 160, 162), a good reputation is part of the innate dignity of the individual, which, in turn, is the constituent element of a democratic society. In *Reynolds v Times Newspapers* [2001] 2 AC 127 at 201; [1999] 4 All ER 609; [1999] 3 WLR 1010, Lord Nicholls of Birkenhead agrees with Cory J's identification of a connection between reputation and dignity, but differs slightly from Cory J's assessment of the role of reputation in a democratic society. His Lordship (at 201) views reputation not only as part of the inherent dignity of the individual but also as a public good, informing everyday decisions about community life.

There is, however, no real explanation in the judgments of Cory J and Lord Nicholls of Birkenhead as to the historical processes by which a body of law which developed in the ecclesiastical courts of medieval England and the royal courts and the Star Chamber of Tudor and Stuart England, a body of law designed to protect rank, status and the public perception of Christian virtue, transformed itself into an integral part of the rights of the individual in a modern, Western liberal democracy. This reflects the fundamentally ahistorical approach to the concept of reputation that is evident in defamation law.

Like the use of a Shakespearean quote, the assertion of the continuing historical importance of reputation forecloses debate and investigation of the meaning and the value that should be ascribed to reputation. Moreover, it suggests that the meaning and the importance of reputation is immutable, transcending time and culture – a position that seems highly debatable, if not untenable. This book contends that placing reputation in its historical context will illuminate what meaning, and, more significantly, what value should be ascribed to reputation in contemporary defamation law.

IMPT

9 Justinian, *The Digest of Justinian* (rev. edn) (ed. Alan Watson), Vol. 2, University of Pennsylvania Press, Philadelphia (PA), 1998, 47.10; Justinian, *Institutes* (transl. Peter Birks and Grant McLeod), Duckworth, London, 1994, 4.4; Nicholas 1962, 215–17.

Dissenting Views on the Importance of Reputation

Yet this view of the importance of reputation and the need for a high level of protection through defamation law is not incontrovertible. For example, an American lawyer, writing in the early twentieth century, sought to challenge the importance both judges and lawyers place upon the protection of reputation:

> Those who resort to such suits nowadays are not persons of distinction or high standing, but are generally adventurers, having more cupidity than good character, and who, vulgarly speaking, are down in the heel and wish to make a raise without labor. The ancient presumption that every plaintiff bringing suit for slander or libel has a good character is far from the truth under present conditions. Nowadays seldom do persons of high standing resort to these actions to vindicate a good name. (Courtney 1902, 554)

Likewise, an American scholar, David A. Anderson, writing more recently, encouraged scepticism about the claims made about the meaning and value of reputation:

> Many of our ideas about reputation are products of a simpler era. When most people spent their entire lives in one community, and the community value system was narrowly drawn and widely shared, good reputation was painstakingly earned, easily lost, and not readily rebuilt. Today most of us move from one community to another, not only geographically, but also socially and professionally. Whatever reputation we have in each of those communities may be recently acquired and shallowly based.
>
> In today's pluralistic society, much is tolerated and little is universally condemned. A congressman can be the subject of a sex scandal one year and win an election the next. An entertainer can pursue drug abuse to the brink of death and return more popular than ever. Behavior (sic) that outrages adults can make a musician the idol of millions of teenagers. Even if one's reputation is harmed, the victim is not condemned automatically to live out his life in disgrace. The mobility and anonymity of modern society make rehabilitation much easier. (Anderson 1984, 777–8)

In part, these assessments might be explicable on the basis that the authors are writing from an American perspective. With its First Amendment, US defamation jurisprudence is more sceptical than Anglo-Australian defamation jurisprudence about intrusions on freedom of speech and consequently about claims made about the importance of reputation (Barendt 2005, 198).

However, commentators outside the United States have also challenged the importance placed upon reputation by defamation law. For example, the Canadian defamation scholar, Raymond E. Brown, criticised the right to reputation in the following terms:

> Reputation is a flawed value. It is only a snapshot of the plaintiff's character, quite often doctored to portray something that has little or no basis in reality. A person may have

> a right to project an image of himself that does not exist; he does not have a right to prevent others from exposing what is merely an illusion. (Brown 1994, 8)

More recently, Australian author, John Birmingham, has lambasted defamation laws, writing that '[d]efamation laws were framed to protect the reputations of 19th-century gentlemen hypocrites. It does very well at protecting the reputations of new-millennium hypocrites as well' (Knox 2003a; 2003b; Rimmer 2004, 48–50).

Even more recently, in *Saffron v John Fairfax Publications Pty Ltd* [2004] NSWCA 254, the New South Wales Court of Appeal has found that it was not perverse or unreasonable of a jury to find that an imputation that the plaintiff had an unsavoury reputation was not defamatory.[10] The Court justified its decision on the basis that the ordinary, reasonable reader might suspend his or her judgment on the plaintiff's reputation, rather than deferring to the opinion proffered that the plaintiff had an unsavoury reputation (*Saffron v John Fairfax Publications Pty Ltd* [2004] NSWCA 254 at [17]). Alternatively, the Court reasoned that the imputation was 'an historical commentary' – that a plaintiff may have had an unsavoury reputation in the past but has since been rehabilitated and now enjoys a more savoury reputation (at [19]). Ultimately, Sheller JA held (at [17]) that 'to describe a person's reputation as unsavoury may not be regarded as something that, in itself, harms that reputation.'

There is therefore a countervailing view about the importance of reputation, albeit a minority one. Perhaps a good reputation is not as important as it once was. Perhaps defamation law is an inadequate vehicle for protecting a good reputation. These concerns can only be adequately addressed when it becomes clear what is meant by reputation for the purposes of defamation law.

10 As to the jury verdict, see *Saffron v John Fairfax Publications Pty Ltd* [2004] NSWCA 254 at [11]–[12] per Sheller JA. Described by *The Sydney Morning Herald* as 'the legendary Mr Sin', the late Abe Saffron, a 'colourful Sydney identity', was vigorous in defending his reputation, such as it was. Saffron sued the publisher of *The Gold Coast Bulletin* over a clue to a crossword puzzle printed in the 2 January 2004 edition of the newspaper. The answer to the clue – 'Sydney underworld figure, nicknamed Mr Sin (3, 7)' – was revealed the following day as 'Abe Saffron'. Counsel for Saffron, Clive Evatt, observed to *The Sydney Morning Herald* that the case 'reads like a law school exam paper'. See Pelly 2004; Kux 2005a. He also sued two Melbourne journalists and their book publishers over his inclusion in a book entitled *TOUGH: 101 Australian Gangsters*. See Kux 2005b. Saffron also threatened defamation proceedings against the City of Sydney Council, having taken exception to a proposed footpath plaque commemorating his role in Kings Cross history. The plaque was in the following terms: 'Abe Saffron. Publican and nightclub owner from 1946. Convictions and court appearances from 1938. Friends in high places.' See Cornford 2004. As to Saffron's history and reputation generally, see McNab 2005; Reeves 2007.

The Outline of the Book

This book seeks to identify how the concept of reputation is embedded in the history, principles and practice of Anglo-Australian defamation law. It seeks to explore how the concept or, perhaps more correctly, concepts, of reputation, central to the law of defamation, manifest themselves. This book contends that the meaning of reputation is not immutable. It argues, rather, that the concept of reputation changes historically, reflecting social, political, economic, cultural and, most importantly, technological changes. As a consequence, this book also suggests that the value of a good reputation is not immutable.

This book is divided into three parts. The first part provides the framework for the subsequent analysis. In this part, an historical and a doctrinal approach to the concept of reputation is adopted. The starting-point for this book is necessarily Robert Post's seminal article, 'The Social Foundations of Reputation and the Constitution' (Post 1986). Over two decades after its publication, it remains the most important, and indeed the only sustained, analysis of the concept of reputation in defamation law. Adopting a sociological approach, Post identified three concepts of reputation in United States defamation law – reputation as property; reputation as honour; and reputation as dignity. Chapter 1 seeks to introduce Post's typology of reputational interests and, more importantly, to provide a critique of it.

Chapter 2 then analyses the history of English defamation law – which is the formative part of the defamation law of many common law countries – through the prism of reputation. It argues that the reason there is no unitary concept of reputation at the centre of defamation law is explained by the fact that defamation law itself has heterogeneous origins. Defamation law is derived from a number of sources, each jurisdiction providing protection for different reputational interests in different ways. Importantly, this chapter highlights the arrested historical development of defamation law.

Chapter 3 then analyses the basic principles of liability for defamation – defamatory capacity and meaning; identification; and publication – as well as the available heads of damages and the principles and purposes which govern their application, again through the prism of reputation.

The cumulative effect of this analysis of the history and doctrines of defamation law then informs the second part of the book. This part seeks to illuminate the various concepts of reputation through a series of case studies drawn from recent Australian defamation law. Although drawn from Australian defamation law, it is to be hoped that the insights gained as to the nature of reputation are applicable more generally, as well as the cases being intrinsically interesting. Each chapter in this part seeks to highlight a particular concept of reputation. Chapter 4 examines reputation as property by analysing cases relating to allegations of professional dishonesty and incompetence and cases involving corporate reputation. Chapters 5 and 6 examine reputation as honour, the former by exploring cases involving cases of 'unchastity', including imputations of adultery and pre-marital sex, the latter by exploring cases involving imputations of homosexuality. Chapter 7 examines reputation as dignity by dealing with cases where the plaintiff has been exposed to ridicule by having naked photographs published without his or her permission. Whilst each chapter takes a particular concept of reputation as the starting-point of its analysis, the discussion is not confined to that concept alone. What becomes apparent through these case studies is that frequently a single case, and a single plaintiff's reputation, will manifest multiple concepts of reputation.

An important feature of the analysis adopted in the case studies is the desire to locate the cases and, more importantly, the plaintiff's reputation, in their broader, non-legal context. In particular, these case studies seek to identify how the plaintiff's reputation existed in the media, if at all, before, during and after the defamation litigation and to assess what impact, adverse or positive, such litigation had upon the reputation sought to be protected or vindicated. This book suggests that reputation, as it is sought to be protected in the courtroom, is not always the same as reputation outside the courtroom. What a number of these case studies suggest is that defamation litigation as a means of protecting or vindicating a plaintiff's reputation can be an effective or equally ineffective means of achieving these goals. Moreover, the defamation litigation itself can become part of the plaintiff's reputation, for good or ill.

The insights provided by these case studies then furnish the basis for the third and final part of the book. In Chapter 8, it is suggested that, in addition to the recognition of reputation as an economic construct – reputation as property – and reputation as a social construct – reputation as honour and dignity – reputation can also be conceptualised as a media construct – reputation as celebrity. It is submitted that such a concept specifically accounts for the mediated nature of reputation and the damage done to it characteristic of an era of mass communications. Drawing particularly upon the approaches to celebrity in media and cultural studies scholarship, this chapter expounds the concept of reputation as celebrity. Just as the concepts of reputation identified by Post do not manifest themselves in relation to each and every reputation, so celebrity is not raised in each and every case. However, as the case studies amply demonstrate, certain cases, and certain reputations, are explicable only by an acknowledgement of the element of celebrity. It is a truism that we live in a celebrity-obsessed age. This book will seek to demonstrate that reputation as celebrity is of great contemporary relevance at this point in the history of defamation law.

The Scope of the Book

Given the comparative lack of analysis of this topic, as well as the constraints of space, this book does not purport to provide a comprehensive analysis of the concept of reputation in defamation law. It will not deal in detail with how the concept or concepts of reputation inhere in the defences to defamation (see, for example, Slaughter 1992, 362ff; Gillooly 2004). Some defences to defamation clearly raise the question of the plaintiff's reputation. The defence of unlikelihood of harm or triviality is one example.[11] However, other defences raise the question of the appropriate balance between freedom of expression and the protection of reputation. To avoid entering into this debate, a debate that has been well-served by the academic literature, this book concentrates on meaning and liability for defamation and the basic principles relevant to the assessment of damages for defamation. Nor will it be possible, again due to constraints of space, to undertake an extensive analysis of the ways in which competing concepts of reputation inhere in the complex principles and procedural rules pertaining to the assessment of defamation damages.

In addition, this book, whilst drawing many of its examples from Australian law, focuses on the principles of defamation law which are, in significant respects, common to jurisdictions based on English law. Certain legal doctrines, such as the 'public figure' doctrine, which are unique to the United States and to its First Amendment jurisprudence, will therefore not be considered here.

Defamation law is, of course, not the only area of law which affords protection to reputation. Clearly, other areas of law, such as the tort of passing off and injurious falsehood, provide direct protection of a plaintiff's interest in its reputation. Other areas of law, such as false imprisonment, negligence and breach of contract may provide a measure of indirect protection for a plaintiff's reputation.[12] This book will also not analyse the manner in which reputation

---

11 See, for example, *Civil Law (Wrongs) Act* 2002 (ACT) s 139D; *Defamation Act* 2006 (NT) s 30; *Defamation Act* 2005 (NSW) s 33; *Defamation Act* 2005 (Qld) s 33; *Defamation Act* 2005 (SA) s 33; *Defamation Act* 2005 (Tas) s 33; *Defamation Act* 2005 (Vic) s 33; *Defamation Act* 2005 (WA) s 33; *Morosi v Mirror Newspapers* [1977] 2 NSWLR 749; *Singleton v John Fairfax & Sons Ltd [No 1]* [1983] 2 NSWLR 722; *Chappell v Mirror Newspapers* (1984) Aust Torts Reports ¶80-691; *King and Mergen Holdings Pty Ltd v McKenzie* (1991) 24 NSWLR 305; *Jones v Sutton* [2004] NSWCA 439; (2004) 61 NSWLR 614.

12 See, for example, *Walter v Alltools Ltd* (1944) 171 LT 371; 61 TLR 39; [1944] WN 214 at 214 per Lawrence LJ; *Myer Stores Ltd v Soo* [1991] 2 VR 597 at 603–4; (1991) Aust Torts Reports ¶81-077 at 68,624 per Murphy J; *Sattin v Nationwide News Pty Ltd* (1996) 39 NSWLR 32 at 34ff per Levine J; *Wade v State of Victoria* [1999] 1 VR 121; *Sullivan v Moody* (2001) 207 CLR 562 at 580–81; 183 ALR 404; 75 ALJR 1570; Aust Torts Reports ¶81-622 *per curiam*; *Tame v New South Wales* (2002) 211 CLR 317 at 335 per Gleeson CJ, at 342 per Gaudron J, at 361 per McHugh J, at 425 per Callinan J; 191 ALR 449; 76 ALJR 1348; Aust Torts Reports ¶81-672; *Cornwall v Rowan* [2004] SASC 384 at [684]–[696]; *Spring v Guardian Assurance plc* [1995] 2 AC 296; [1994] 3 All ER 129; [1994] 3 WLR 354; *Bell-Booth Group Ltd v Attorney-General* [1989] 3 NZLR 148; *Balfour v Attorney-General* [1991] 1 NZLR 519; *Midland Metals Overseas Pty Ltd v The Christchurch Press Co Ltd* [2002] 2 NZLR 289; *Fulton v Globe & Mail Ltd* (1997) 152 DLR (4th) 377; Butler 2000b; *Foaminol Laboratories Ltd v British Artid Plastics Ltd* [1941] 2 All ER 393 at 399

is protected by other areas of law. It proceeds on the basis that the concept of reputation has been insufficiently analysed in the context of defamation law such that an exclusive focus on this area of law is justified.

per Hallett J; *Malik v Bank of Credit & Commerce International SA (in liq)* [1998] AC 20; [1997] 3 All ER 1; [1997] 3 WLR 95; *Gambotto v John Fairfax Publications Pty Ltd* (2001) 104 IR 303 at 312 per Peterson J; Enonchong 1996.

PART I

Chapter 1
Post on Reputation

Introduction

Despite the fact that it is the central interest directly protected by defamation law, there has been insufficient detailed academic consideration of the concept of reputation in defamation law. The most significant and detailed piece of legal scholarship analysing the concept of reputation remains Robert C. Post's seminal article, 'The Social Foundations of Defamation Law: Reputation and the Constitution' (Post 1986). In his article, Post presents a taxonomy of reputation – reputation as property; reputation as honour; and reputation as dignity (Post 1986, 693). Post's approach is avowedly sociological. He presents these concepts of reputation as ideal types – analytically distinct but actually co-existing or overlapping (Post 1986, 693). However, Post acknowledges that it is possible to analyse reputation from other critical or theoretical perspectives. He does not suggest that a sociological approach is the only possible one. Indeed, Post specifically mentions that an historical approach to reputation might yield further insights – a task he himself does not undertake (Post 1986, 693). Nor does he suggest that his conceptions of reputation are the only possible ones (Post 1986, 720). The categories of reputation are not closed.

Any analysis of the concept of reputation in defamation needs to engage with Post's schema of reputational interests. This book adopts, and ultimately adapts, Post's framework and seeks to apply it to Australian defamation law in particular. In order to establish the parameters of the subsequent analysis, this chapter outlines Post's framework and provides a critique of it.

Reputation as Property

Post on Reputation as Property

The first concept of reputation Post introduces is reputation as property. According to Post, this conception of reputation is the 'most easily available to contemporary observers', one with which they are 'intimately comfortable' (Post 1986, 693, 726). It is, he asserts, the least problematic of the three concepts of reputation (Post 1986, 727). For Post, reputation as property means 'reputation in the marketplace' and is thus akin to goodwill (Post 1986, 693). He gives as examples of reputation as property 'the merchant who works hard to become known as creditworthy' and 'the carpenter who strives to achieve a name for quality workmanship' (Post 1986,

693). Indeed, in the historical development of the law of defamation, this type of reputation – professional reputation – received early recognition and protection (see for example Slaughter 1992, 358).

Post then quotes at length from nineteenth-century jurist, Thomas Starkie, on reputation:

> Reputation itself, considered as the object of injury, owes its being and importance chiefly to the various artificial relations which are created as society advances.
>
> The numerous gradations of rank and authority, the honours and distinctions extended to the exertion of talent in the learned professions, the emoluments acquired by mechanical skill and ingenuity under the numerous subdivisions of labour, the increase of commerce, and particularly the substitution of symbols for property in commercial intercourse – all, in different degrees, connect themselves with credit and character, affixing to them a value, not merely ideal, but capable of pecuniary admeasurement, and consequently recommending them as the proper objects of legal protection. (Post 1986, 694)

Adopting a Lockean view of property, Post states that reputation as property acknowledges that an individual may form a reputation for himself or herself through labour – through 'the exertion of talent' or 'mechanical skill and ingenuity' (Slaughter 1992, 358; Post 1986, 694). Such a professional reputation acquired through labour is therefore a form of property. Consequently, to defame a professional person is to destroy a valuable right and interest, namely the product of that person's skill, labour and effort (Post 1986, 694). The damage to reputation, like all other forms of property loss, is therefore 'capable of pecuniary admeasurement' (Post 1986, 694).

Post does not limit this analysis of reputation as property to instances of professional reputation but extends it to instances of purely personal or private reputation. He argues that personal or private reputations can be equally characterised as property because they are earned. A good reputation can be created and cultivated through exertions in social relations (Post 1986, 694–5).

Acknowledging that reputation is inherently social and arguing that, as such, each concept of reputation is premised upon an image of society, Post then seeks to identify the image of society that informs the concept of reputation as property (Post 1986, 692). Post argues that the concept of reputation as property is premised upon an image or a notion of a market society, that individuals are connected to each other through the mechanism of the marketplace (Post 1986, 695). He then identifies three features of reputation as property in a market society.

Firstly, Post argues that the concept of reputation as property acknowledges that a reputation is contingent in the sense that, notwithstanding the current reputation of an individual, that individual possesses the ability to create a new reputation into the future (Post 1986, 695–6). This means that an individual's personal identity is 'distinct from and anterior to' his or her social identity (Post 1986, 696). As such, reputation as property suggests that '[i]ndividuals are not constituted by the social regard with which they are apprehended by others' (Post 1986, 696).

Secondly, Post states that reputation as property acknowledges that the value of an individual's reputation will fluctuate with the market and, importantly, the individual's participation in the market. Again, reputation as property presupposes the contingency of an individual's reputation but additionally suggests that such movements are not 'a matter of either honor or dishonor' (Post 1986, 696).

Thirdly, Post argues that reputation as property assumes that all persons are participants in the market; that all participants are equal in that they are all subject to the market; that no person enjoys a right to reputation outside what Post styles 'the evaluative processes of the market'; and that there are no barriers to entry and participation in the market for reputations (Post 1986, 696).

Post ultimately contends that the concept of reputation as property is firmly entrenched in defamation law (Post 1986, 696–7). According to Post, certain forms of reputation protected by defamation law, notably corporate reputation, are only explicable on the basis of an underlying conception of reputation as property (Post 1986, 696).

The Limitations of the Concept of Reputation as Property

Post himself states there are several limitations to the concept of reputation as property that should be noted. He observes that the concept of reputation as property does not explain key doctrines of defamation law, such as the requirement that a publication be deemed defamatory before liability will be established and, more importantly, the presumption of damage to reputation in the overwhelming majority of defamation cases.

There are further criticisms that may be made of the concept of reputation as property. Firstly, one of the common characteristics or indicia of property is alienability. Property can be alienated, transferred, disposed of, traded or sold. Yet, whilst a natural person can commodify part of his or her reputation and trade or sell it, he or she cannot wholly alienate it (see *Rogers v Nationwide News Pty Ltd* (2003) 216 CLR 327 at 349–51 per Hayne J). Reputation inheres in the person of the plaintiff. Post grapples with this problem, arguing that reputation is alienable, and therefore a form of property, because corporations can buy and sell their goodwill. Rather than addressing the impossibility of extending this to personal reputations, Post instead emphasises the features of reputation as the result of individual exertions and the assessment of the value of a reputation by the marketplace (Post 1986, 695). An earlier theorist of the concept of reputation, George Spencer Bower, acknowledged that the reputation of individuals was not alienable and that this might detract from its characterisation as property. Nevertheless, Spencer Bower advocated an understanding of reputation as property, albeit of 'a somewhat peculiar description' (Spencer Bower 1990, 240–41). Spencer Bower is perhaps more forthright about the limitation of his analysis but ultimately reaches the same, somewhat unsatisfactory conclusion.

A related problem with the concept of reputation as property is that there is no real marketplace for reputations. The value of a plaintiff's reputation is not determined in an open marketplace; it is determined in a court. Such a marketplace as exists for reputations is closed, controlled and artificial; it exists solely in the verdicts of juries and, more recently, judges. Yet, even describing this as a 'marketplace' is difficult because judges eschew any real and necessary relationship between awards of damages in defamation cases, let alone between awards of damages in defamation and other types of cases (see *Crampton v Nugawela* (1996) 41 NSWLR 176 at 191 per Mahoney ACJ; *Rogers v Nationwide News Pty Ltd* (2003) 216 CLR 327 at 349–51 per Hayne J. See also George 2006, 75).

Ultimately, the major limitation of the concept of reputation as property, at least in its application to Australian defamation law, is that Australian judges have consistently rejected the treatment of reputation as property. Whilst there is a line of authority in English defamation cases asserting that reputation is a form of property, or at least a quasi-proprietary right, the prevailing view in Australian defamation jurisprudence is against such a characterisation (see also Gibbons 1996, 594).

Indeed, the English authorities providing explicit support for the notion of reputation as property all emanate from the nineteenth century, indicating perhaps more the judicial temper of the time, rather than the nature of reputation properly understood. For example, in *M'Pherson v Daniels* (1829) 10 B & C 263; (1829) 109 ER 448, Park J asked rhetorically (at 276; 453), 'every injury to property is the subject of a civil action. Upon what principle can it be said that a wrong done to the good name and reputation of another is not equally so?'

Likewise, in *Dixon v Holden* (1869) 7 LR Eq 488, in an equally rhetorical vein, Sir Richard Malins V.-C. asked (at 492):

> What is property? One man has property in lands, another in goods, another in a business, another in skill, another in reputation; and whatever may have the effect of destroying property in any one of these things (even in a man's good name) is, in my opinion, destroying property of a most valuable description.

Indeed, the Vice-Chancellor went further, opining that, for a merchant, 'his reputation, which is his property' is 'if possible, more valuable than other property'.

The contemporary Australian authorities stand in marked contrast to their nineteenth-century English counterparts. For instance, in *Uren v John Fairfax & Sons Ltd* (1966) 117 CLR 118, Windeyer J observed (at 150):

> [a] man's reputation, his good name, the estimation in which he is held in the opinion of others, is not a possession of his as a chattel is. Damage to it cannot be measured as harm to a tangible thing is measured. Apart from special damages strictly so called and damages for a loss of clients or customers, money and reputation are not commensurables.

To similar effect, Brennan J stated (at 70) in *Carson v John Fairfax & Sons Ltd* (1993) 178 CLR 44 that, '[a]lthough damages are awarded to vindicate the plaintiff's reputation, damages are not awarded as compensation for the loss in value of a plaintiff's reputation as though that reputation were itself a tangible asset or a physical attribute which, once damaged, is worth less than it was before.'

Most recently, Hayne J in *Rogers v Nationwide News Pty Ltd* (2003) 216 CLR 327 stated (at 349) that 'a plaintiff's reputation is not a commodity having a market value.' (See also George 2006, 74–5.)

Equally, some academic commentators have suggested that reputation as property is not as useful an understanding of reputation as reputation as honour. The eminent American jurist, Roscoe Pound, argued that it is possible to overstate the extent to which individuals acquire a reputation as an asset through interaction with others, suggesting instead that reputation as honour is the preferable view (Pound 1915, 447). According to the sociologist, Robert N. Bellah, 'reputation is not a property or possession of individuals – it is a relation between persons' (Bellah 1986, 743). Dealing with the issue of an individual's professional reputation, Bellah suggests that such a reputation may seem like an asset of its owner, but it is preferable to conceive of it as 'a public good, not merely a private possession' (Bellah 1986, 744, 745). More recently, David A. Anderson stated that '[d]efamation is a dignitary tort; attempting to reduce it to a remedy for economic loss would be historically unfaithful, doctrinally radical, and destructive of important cultural values' (Anderson 2006, 1047).

However, Post is clearly correct to observe that certain aspects of defamation law are only explicable on the basis that the common law provides protection for reputation as property. The extension of defamation law to protect corporate reputation is the most obvious example of this, as Post himself contends. Nevertheless, it is clear that reputation as property can only provide a partial explanation of reputation in defamation law and, moreover, Post's assertion that reputation as property is the most readily apparent understanding of reputation is not accepted as a concept informing Australian defamation law.

Reputation as Honour

Post on Reputation as Honour

The second concept of reputation Post introduces is reputation as honour. Post commences his analysis of the concept of reputation as honour by identifying the venerable tradition that treats reputation as transcending monetary value (Post 1986, 699). As examples of this tradition, Post cites the Old Testament and Shakespeare. Post concludes that the notion of reputation underpinning this tradition is inconsistent with the notion of reputation as property (Post 1986, 699).

Post defines honour as 'a form of reputation in which an individual personally identifies with the normative characteristics of a particular social role and in return personally receives from others the regard and estimation that society accords to that role' (Post 1986, 699–700).

Unlike reputation as property, reputation as honour cannot be earned but is rather ascribed. It is not a product of exertion but is rather a right that attaches to a social role (Post 1986, 700). According to Post, an individual is ascribed to or identifies with a social role; certain attributes are ascribed to that social role; and the individual ascribed to or identifying with that social role is then expected to embody and exemplify those attributes (Post 1986, 700). Therefore, reputation as honour connotes a reciprocity of responsibilities between an individual and his or her society.

Post then defines reputation as honour through a detailed contrast with reputation as property. For instance, whilst reputation as property is premised upon the equality of all individuals before the marketplace, reputation as honour is premised upon inequality. Because individuals occupy different roles and their honour is a reflection of their respective roles, individuals (and, by extension, their reputations) are inherently unequal (Post 1986, 700).

In addition, whilst the value of reputation as property fluctuates according to individual exertions and market conditions, the value of reputation as honour is fixed (Post 1986, 700). This is because honour is linked to social roles, the order of which and the value attending each is preordained. Unlike reputation as property, reputation as honour 'cannot be converted into a medium of exchange' – there can be no marketplace for reputations; reputation is inalienable and unquantifiable. According to Post, it is possible to lose but impossible to gain honour (Post 1986, 700, 701).

Finally, whilst reputation as property presupposes that an individual's personal identity is distinct from and anterior to his or her social identity, reputation as honour is premised upon the complete identification of an individual's personal and social identities. The reputation of the plaintiff is based on and consumes the whole of the plaintiff's life. Thus, such a concept of reputation views a defamatory publication as depriving a plaintiff not merely of an asset but more seriously of the loss of self (Post 1986, 701).

Again, acknowledging that reputation is inherently social, Post then considers what image of society informs the concept of reputation as honour. According to Post, the image of society underpinning the concept of reputation as honour is one in which social roles are 'pervasive and well-established' and, more importantly, provide the 'normative standards of personal conduct' (Post 1986, 701). Post describes this image of society as 'deference society' (Post 1986, 702).

Post then contrasts reputation's place in a market society and a deference society. For instance, in a market society, reputation as property is a private possession. The state's interest in protecting reputation is therefore the same rationale for the protection of all forms of private property (Post 1986, 702). By contrast, in a deference society, reputation as honour is premised upon agreed understandings about social roles. In such a society, reputation becomes a public good and the state's interest in protecting reputation becomes an interest in maintaining the social structure (Post 1986, 702). According to Post, defamation law in a deference society has the dual functions of defining and enforcing social roles and their attendant status (Post 1986, 702). In its service of these functions, defamation law is buttressed by public power, and, as such, may be viewed as authoritative (Post 1986, 703).

Post then contrasts the rationale and effectiveness of remedies for defamation in market and deference societies. In a market society, reputation is an asset and thus damage to it can be comprehended as, in the words of Thomas Starkie, 'capable of pecuniary admeasurement' (in Post 1986, 694). In a deference society, reputation is equated with a social role and a social status and thus damage to it involves harm that cannot be quantified (Post 1986, 703). Consequently, Post argues that the notion of reputation as honour explains the importance of defamation in the vindication and restoration of the plaintiff's honour (Post 1986, 703–4).

However, Post argues that there are aspects of defamation law which make an understanding of reputation as honour problematic. For instance, Post suggests that the award of damages in a civil defamation action is most consistent with a notion of reputation as property, but can be reconciled with the notion of reputation as honour if it is viewed as part of the process by which the plaintiff's reputation is vindicated and restored (Post 1986, 705). Post also views the fact that, at common law, truth is a complete defence to a civil defamation action, as a limitation to the applicability of reputation as honour, as it connotes a movement in the purpose of defamation law away from avenging (with its close connection to vindication) to justification (with its more tenuous connection to vindication) (Post 1986, 704–5).

Nevertheless, Post argues that the concept of reputation as honour is consistent with many aspects of defamation law and, importantly, is consistent with doctrines which are otherwise inconsistent with the concept of reputation as property. He cites as two examples the requirement that a publication be deemed defamatory before liability is established and the presumption of damage (Post 1986, 706).

The Limitations of the Concept of Reputation as Honour

Again, Post identifies some limitations to the utility of the concept of reputation as honour as an interpretive tool. His principal criticism is that the image of society informing the concept of reputation as honour, a deference society, has not actually existed in Western countries since the demise of feudalism. Since at least the sixteenth century, there has been a loosening of rigid, hierarchical social structures. Because the image of society underpinning the concept of reputation as honour has fundamentally altered, Post reasons that the continuing viability of the concept itself must have diminished as well. Post's essential criticism is that the pervasiveness and ideological appeal of egalitarianism has rendered a hierarchical concept like honour obsolete (Post 1986, 722). Other scholars, such as Barendt, agree with Post's assessment that, in contemporary Western society, the concept of reputation as honour forms an incidental part, at most, in contemporary defamation law (Barendt 1999, 116). Nevertheless, Post suggests that there are vestiges of reputation as honour in contemporary Western society in resolutely hierarchical institutions, such as the armed forces (Post 1986, 707).

Notwithstanding Post's own observations about its contemporary relevance, there appears to remain more than vestiges of the concept of reputation as honour in Australian defamation law. The concept of reputation as honour has explicitly found favour in contemporary Australian defamation jurisprudence. The three High Court judges cited as specifically eschewing an understanding of reputation as property – Windeyer J in *Uren* (1966) 117 CLR 118; Brennan J in *Carson* (1993) 178 CLR 44; and Hayne J in *Rogers* (2003) 216 CLR 327 at 349–51 – instead endorsed an understanding of reputation as honour. Moreover, in *Crampton v Nugawela* (1996) 41 NSWLR 176, Mahoney ACJ stated (at 193) that, in cases of professional reputation, 'a person's reputation is, in a relevant sense, his whole life'. This is clearly consistent with the notion of reputation as honour, as defined by Post (Post 1986, 701). Finally and most importantly, the centrality of vindication as a purpose in the assessment and award of defamation damages reinforces the resilience and ongoing relevance of reputation as honour in defamation law (Barendt 1999, 116).

It is obvious that the social structures of Western societies have changed dramatically since the decline of feudalism, moving decisively away from rigid hierarchies towards greater social mobility, from, in Post's terminology, a deference society to a communitarian society. Although these changes have occurred, social roles and their attendant expectations in social organisations remain important. In many respects, it remains the case that a high public profile or standing carries with it a presumption of an equally high reputation. Likewise, there remain social roles that also carry with them a presumption of good reputation. One of the central insights provided by Post's analysis of the concept of reputation as honour is that defamation law affirms and produces 'normative standards of personal conduct' (Post 1986, 701; see also Bar-Am 2000, 297).

Understood in this sense, the case studies dealing with reputation as honour demonstrate the continuing importance of such a concept in contemporary Australian defamation law, particularly defamation law's dual function of defining and upholding social roles and identities. For example, the case study dealing with defamation judgments involving imputations of adultery clearly suggest that the role of a spouse still carries with it the social expectation of, and therefore the presumption of a good reputation for, fidelity and sexual propriety. Similarly, the case study discussing defamation cases dealing with imputations of homosexuality suggest that the ideal citizen is presumptively heterosexual – and that it can be damaging to one's reputation to be thought or perceived otherwise. It is argued that the prevailing judicial view in Australia, namely that such an imputation is capable of being defamatory, entails the creation and enforcement of '[hetero-] normative standards of personal conduct' (Post 1986, 701), with consequences for the ideal of a good reputation. This book, therefore, defines the concept of reputation as honour differently to Post, emphasising a broadly normative, rather than a rigidly hierarchical concept. However, as these case studies will demonstrate, the extent to which these social roles and identities and their attendant expectations, even in this normative sense, can remain intact has been and will continue to be challenged by the liberalisation of social attitudes towards sexual matters, a process initiated in the 1960s, and the recognition of the existence of a pluralistic society, again with consequences for what is viewed as a good reputation in these matters. Nonetheless, this book contends that Australian defamation law currently encodes and protects notions of reputation as honour in this normative sense, rather than a traditional, hierarchical sense.

For the purposes of this book, and particularly for the historical, as opposed to sociological, analysis, the concept of dignity will also need to be re-defined. The interaction between reputation as honour and reputation as dignity historically needs to be explored. In order to refine and re-define these key terms and to analyse their relationship, it is, however, necessary first to introduce the concept of reputation as dignity.

Reputation as Dignity

Post on Reputation as Dignity

The third concept of reputation Post introduces is reputation as dignity. For Post, the concept of reputation as dignity is problematic. He notes that the concept of reputation as dignity has been emphatically endorsed in purely personal and private terms by Stewart J in *Rosenblatt v Baer* 383 US 75; 86 S Ct 669 (1966), yet this is inconsistent with his starting-point that reputation is a social and a public phenomenon. Dignity, as a personal and private concept, is therefore not readily accommodated within Post's understanding of reputation. For Post, there is a 'gulf' between 'dignity' and 'reputation', 'between the private and public aspects of the self' (Post 1986, 708).

Post bridges this 'gulf' by reference to the symbolic interactionist school of American sociology, in particular to the works of Charles H. Cooley, George Herbert Mead and Erving Goffman (Post 1986; cf. Gibbons 1996, 595). Post particularly draws upon the work of Goffman to provide the 'implicit theory' of defamation law (Goffman 1967, 56; Post 1986, 709). In his work, *Interaction Ritual*, Goffman argues that an individual's identity is constantly constituted through social interactions. According to Goffman, these interactions are bound by rules of deference and demeanour. The rules of deference are the acts by which an individual indicates his or her appreciation '*to* a recipient *of* a recipient, or of something of which this recipient is taken as a symbol, extension, or agent' (Goffman 1967, 56). The rules of demeanour are the acts by which the recipient indicates to the individual whether he or she is acceptable or unacceptable.

The purpose of the rules of deference and demeanour are to bind the individual participants of the particular social interaction together and, more generally, to bind society together. Goffman suggests that each individual presents both a demeanour image of himself or herself and a deference image to others (Post 1986, 709). In this way, Goffman argues that the self is created by an individual and his or her community working together, to create 'a product of joint ceremonial labor' (Post 1986, 710).

Thus, Post notes that the dignity of the individual is contingent – it requires all members of the community to perform their 'ceremonial labor' – and can be imperilled by any break in the 'chain of ceremony', as a consequence of which the 'complete man' may fail to be 'socially constituted' (Post 1986, 710). Therefore, he suggests that 'our own sense of intrinsic self-worth, stored in the deepest recesses of our "private personality", is perpetually dependent upon the ceremonial observance by those around us of rules of deference and demeanor' (Post 1986, 710).

Post concludes that defamation law may be viewed as a means by which a society 'polices breaches of its rules of deference and demeanor, thereby protecting the dignity of its members' (Post 1986, 710). He articulates the dual functions of defamation law, envisaged by the concept of reputation as dignity, as being the protection of the individual's interest in his or her own dignity and the protection of society's own interest in maintaining its own rules of civility and thus its own constitution (Post 1986, 710). The individual's interest is clearly private; the society's interest is properly understood as public (Post 1986, 712, 713). Thus, for Post, reputation as dignity entails the interaction of public and private interests.

Moreover, according to Post, the defamation trial itself serves as an important venue in which the dispute over the plaintiff's reputation can be resolved:

> Defamation law is an excellent vehicle for … confirmation [of community membership], because it provides an occasion for a court to resolve the ambiguity created when rules of civility are violated. A defamation trial can from this perspective be viewed as an arena in which the parties are free to present 'competing interpretations of behavior': the plaintiff contending that the defamation should be explained by the social incompetence and inappropriate behavior of the defendant; the defendant urging that the lack of respect implied by the defamation should be understood as justified by the plaintiff's conduct. The plaintiff's dignity is rehabilitated if the court authoritatively determines that the defendant's departure from the rules of civility was unjustified. In effect the court, speaking for the community at large, designates the plaintiff as worthy of respect, thereby confirming his membership within the community. (Post 1986, 712–13)

Having thus defined reputation as dignity in sociological terms, Post then seeks to apply this understanding to existing principles of defamation law. In order for defamation law to operate, it requires publication of a defamatory matter to a third party. Yet, Goffman's notion of rules of deference and demeanour are premised on face-to-face interactions, on 'purely dyadic' exchanges (Post 1986, 710). Post overcomes this objection by pointing out that a breach of the rules of deference and demeanour between two people is likely to be of 'equivocal significance' (Post 1986, 711). It is only when such a breach occurs in the presence of a third party that there are likely to be clear, adverse consequences to an individual's reputation. If the third party condones or endorses the breach of the rules of demeanour, the individual is 'discredited and stigmatized as a person unworthy of civility' and is thereby excluded from membership of the community (Post 1986, 711).

Post also considers the impact of reputation as dignity on the underlying purposes of defamation law. He concludes that the compensatory purpose of defamation law is not consistent with reputation as dignity. The award of damages for injury to reputation is more consistent with reputation as property (Post 1986, 712). Post also concludes that reputation as dignity does not explain the vindicatory purpose of defamation law, arguing that the means of defending one's honour, such as duels, are not designed to protect one's dignity (Post 1986, 712). Instead, Post argues that reputation as dignity suggests a further purpose of defamation law, a rehabilitative one. Defamation law thus entails the confirmation of the plaintiff's community membership, if he or she is successful, or the exclusion of the plaintiff from the community, if he or she is unsuccessful (Post 1986, 712).

Post then considers the image of society informing the concept of reputation as dignity, designating it as the communitarian society (Post 1986, 716). In order to illuminate the particular features of a communitarian society, Post contrasts reputation as dignity in a communitarian society with reputation as property in a market society. He states that both forms of reputation are premised on an equality of the individual but identify the purpose of that equality differently (Post 1986, 716). In a market society, equality underpins access to the marketplace, whereas in a communitarian society, equality is directed towards community membership (Post 1986, 716). Reputation in a market society is a purely private good, whereas reputation in a communitarian society, as in a deference society, is at once both a public and a private good (Post 1986, 716). In a market society, an individual may create his or her own reputation, whereas, in a communitarian society, as in a deference society, reputation constitutes both social and individual identity (Post 1986, 716–17). The value of a reputation in a market society is assessed by the mechanism of the market, whereas reputation in a communitarian society, as in a deference society, is not amenable to 'pecuniary admeasurement' (Post 1986, 716–17). Implicit then in Post's exposition of reputation as dignity is some similarity between the concepts of reputation as honour and reputation as dignity.

Ultimately, even though Post acknowledges the importance of reputation to the 'private personality' and 'intrinsic self-worth' of the individual, he emphasises the social and public aspects of reputation in his exposition of reputation as dignity, consistent with his view of reputation as the public self of the plaintiff and defamation as a remedy functioning as the protection and vindication of that self.

The Limitations of the Concept of Reputation as Dignity

There are a number of related difficulties with the concept of reputation as dignity, as expounded by Post. Firstly, it does not fully engage with the definitional problems of the concept of dignity. Secondly, the subsequent development of a significant rights-based jurisprudence in common law countries, such as Canada, the United Kingdom and New Zealand, has manifested a concern for individual reputation as a dignitary right in a manner divergent from Post's analysis. In addition, an historical, rather than a sociological, approach may assist in illuminating the relationship between the concepts of honour and dignity. These criticisms need to be examined in turn.

The meaning of dignity One of the difficulties with the concept of reputation as dignity, as Post and other scholars have recognised, is that dignity itself is a problematic term (Post 1986, 715; Feldman 1999, 682). Historically, 'dignity', deriving from the Latin word, '*dignitas*', has been used as a synonym for rank, status or honour (Post 1986, 715–16). The *Oxford English Dictionary*'s (1989, 656–7) definition of 'dignity' confirms its usage as a synonym for 'honour':

1. The quality of being worthy or honourable; worthiness, worth, nobleness, excellence. b. The quality of being worthy of something; desert, merit.
2. Honourable or high estate, position, or estimation; honour; degree of estimation, rank. b. Persons of high estate or rank (cf. the quality).
3. An honourable office, rank, or title; a high official or titular position. b. A person holding a high office or position; a dignitary.
4. Nobility or befitting elevation of aspect, manner, or style; becoming or fit stateliness, gravity.

Yet, with the burgeoning of human rights jurisprudence in the late twentieth century, emanating from both international instruments and national constitutions, 'dignity' has assumed a meaning of the intrinsic self-worth of the individual – all individuals. 'Dignity', with its original connotations of rank and status, has been democratised and universalised.

In his two-part article, 'Human Dignity as a Legal Value', David Feldman notes the complexity of dignity as a concept, that 'dignity' has been used in a variety of legal contexts and can be ascribed to different types of legal entities. For example, Feldman observes that it is possible to discuss state dignity and human dignity. Under the rubric of the human dignity, Feldman identifies at least three further broad senses in which dignity may be understood: the dignity of the species, the dignity of groups and the dignity of individuals. Feldman notes that the extent to which each of these forms of human dignity can be characterised as objective or subjective varies. The dignity of the species is primarily objective; the dignity of groups is partly objective and partly subjective. Importantly, the value ascribed to the dignity of individuals is primarily subjective (Feldman 1999, 684).

It is the dignity of individuals that informs Post's concept of reputation as dignity. This presents a difficulty for Post, given that his concept of reputation is largely a social phenomenon, whilst the contemporary understanding of dignity is subjective and personal.

Reputation as a dignitary interest in international and domestic law The recognition of reputation as a human right in international instruments further underscores an understanding of reputation not as a purely social phenomenon but as an integral aspect of the individual. For example, the *Universal Declaration of Human Rights* is premised on the 'recognition of the inherent dignity and of the equal and inalienable rights of all members of the human family', as the Preamble states. One of these rights expressly provided for is the right of individuals not to be subjected to 'unlawful attacks' on their honour or reputation. The relevant article of the *Universal Declaration of Human Rights* further provides that all people are entitled to the protection of the law against such attacks. Importantly, in this article, the protection of reputation is linked with the sanctity of privacy, family, home and correspondence, suggesting that reputation is conceptualised as part of the private sphere (Article 12).

The *International Covenant on Civil and Political Rights* (ICCPR) is likewise predicated on the 'inherent dignity of the human person', as is evidenced by its Preamble. One of the human rights derived from the inherent dignity of the individual is the right to reputation. Article 17 of the ICCPR provides protection for reputation in near-identical terms to Article 12 of the *Universal Declaration of Human Rights*. Again, in the ICCPR, as in the *Universal Declaration of Human Rights*, the protection of reputation is associated with the sanctity of privacy, family, home and correspondence, again seemingly casting reputation as a primarily private interest. Nonetheless, by enshrining the right of the individual to possess and protect his or her reputation, these international instruments affirm the importance of a good reputation to the dignity of the individual.

At a national level, many legal systems provide constitutional or statutory protections of individual rights. Unlike the international instruments referred to above, few national legal systems confer specific protection to the individual's right to reputation. Nevertheless, courts have been willing to infer such a right to reputation, grounded in a concern for the dignity of the individual.

For example, the United States Constitution contains no guarantee of a right to reputation in its Bill of Rights. Yet, in the United States, with its well-established, rights-based constitutional jurisprudence, Stewart J in the United States Supreme Court decision in *Rosenblatt v Baer* 383 US 75; 86 S Ct 669 (1966) could expressly state that the basis for the right to reputation is 'the essential dignity and worth of every human being – a concept at the root of any decent system of ordered liberty' and 'a basic of our [the United States] constitutional system', notwithstanding the fact that the 'protection of private personality' was a matter for State governments (at 92, 679). Indeed, this was the starting-point for Post's analysis of the concept of reputation as dignity (Post 1986, 707). The *dictum* of Stewart J in *Rosenblatt v*

Baer 383 US 75; 86 S Ct 669 (1966) was endorsed by the United States Supreme Court decision in *Gertz v Robert Welch Inc* 418 US 323, 341; 94 S Ct 2997, 3008 (1974) per Powell J. The importance of reputation as a dignitary interest for individuals and its implicit constitutional protection have been affirmed and applied in subsequent cases.[1]

More recently, a similar approach has been adopted in Canada. The right to reputation is not specifically mentioned in the *Canadian Charter of Rights and Freedoms*, yet Cory J, in *Hill v Church of Scientology of Toronto* (1995) 126 DLR (4th) 129, expressed the view that 'the good reputation of the individual represents and reflects the innate dignity of the individual' (at 163). His Honour further stated (at 160) that '[a] good reputation is closely related to the innate worthiness and dignity of the individual.' According to Cory J (at 162), the purpose of defamation law is the facilitation of 'fostering our self-image and sense of self-worth'. His Honour even claimed (at 159) that '[f]alse and injurious statement cannot enhance self-development'. In turn, the dignity of the individual underscored the rights contained in the Charter specifically and democracy more broadly (per Cory J at 154, 163).

Cory J went further, explaining why the dignity of the individual, and therefore the reputation of the individual, was important and warranted legal protection. His Honour reasoned that the dignity of the individual is fundamentally important to democracy. As such, a democracy has a vested interest in ensuring that its citizens are able to protect their good reputations. His Honour stated (at 160) that the active participation of individuals in community life in a democracy is premised upon their good reputation. In this way, Cory J argued that defamation law is an integral part of the fabric of a modern Western liberal democracy. In doing so, Cory J made an explicit link between the personal, dignitary aspects of reputation and the social, honourable aspects of reputation. Cory J's observations on reputation have been endorsed and applied in subsequent Canadian cases.[2]

Equally, there is no express reference to a right to reputation in the *New Zealand Bill of Rights Act* 1990 (NZ). Nevertheless, New Zealand judges have been willing to infer one, based on analogies to international human rights instruments and the developments in the local law of other common law countries. In *Lange v Atkinson* [1997] 2 NZLR 22, Elias J accepted (at 30) that there was a public interest in the protection of reputation. This public interest was based on a fundamental human right, which Her Honour identified as the '[p]rotection of individual dignity'. The long title of the *New Zealand Bill of Rights Act* 1990 (NZ) indicates that

1 See Post 1986, 707–8; *Kanaga v Gannett Co. Inc.* 687 A 2d 173, 183 (1996) per Veasey CJ; *Lynch v New Jersey Education Association* 735 A 2d 1129, 1136 (1999) per Pollock J.

2 See, for example, *R v Lucas* (1998) 157 DLR (4th) 423 at 444 per Cory J; *Prud'homme v Prud'homme* (2002) 221 DLR (4th) 115 at 137 per L'Heureux-Dube and LeBel JJ; *Neron v Chambredes notaires de Quebec* (2004) 241 DLR (4th) 577 at 603–4 per LeBel J.

the stated purpose of the legislation is to protect and promote human rights and fundamental freedoms in New Zealand and, more specifically, to affirm New Zealand's commitment to the ICCPR. Given that the ICCPR contains a specific protection of the right to reputation as part of the dignity of the individual and that the *New Zealand Bill of Rights Act* 1990 (NZ) is informed by both the specific rights protected as well as the general tenor of the ICCPR, Elias J was prepared to recognise a right to reputation based on the 'inherent dignity of the human person' (at 31).

Under the *European Convention on Human Rights* and, by extension, in its enabling legislation in the United Kingdom, the *Human Rights Act* 1998 (UK), there is no free-standing right to reputation. However, the protection of reputation is listed as one of a number of important limitations on the right to freedom of expression. In the House of Lords' first consideration of the interaction of freedom of expression and protection of reputation in defamation law, Lord Nicholls of Birkenhead stated that '[r]eputation is an integral and important part of the dignity of the individual' (see *Reynolds v Times Newspapers Ltd* [2001] 2 AC 127 at 201). His Lordship states (at 201) that, not only is the protection of reputation in the individual's interest, but it also serves the public good. It is for this reason that, '[c]onsistently with these considerations, human rights conventions recognise that freedom of expression is not an absolute right'.

In Australia, the most likely source of rights-based protection of reputation appears to be the judiciary relying upon international law. The limited constitutional implication ensuring freedom of political communication is unlikely to be such a source.[3] Certain judges have indicated a willingness to develop the common law of Australia by reference to international conventions, although this is, as yet, a decidedly minority position. For instance, in *Dow Jones & Co. Inc. v Gutnick* (2002) 210 CLR 575; 194 ALR 433; 77 ALJR 255; Aust Torts Reports ¶81-682, Kirby J stated (at 626–7) that the common law of Australia needed to develop consistently with the ICCPR and its explicit protection of reputation.

At a federal level, Australia has not developed a rights-based jurisprudence by either constitutional or statutory means – unlike Canada, Great Britain and New Zealand – and it appears unlikely to happen soon. At a State and Territory level, only the Australian Capital Territory and Victoria have passed legislation specifically designed to protect and promote human rights. In March 2004, the ACT Legislative Assembly passed the *Human Rights Act* 2004 (ACT) (for an overview, see Debeljak 2004; Walton 2004; Winterton 2004) and in July 2006,

---

3 *Nationwide News Pty Ltd v Wills* (1992) 177 CLR 1; 108 ALR 681; 66 ALJR 658; *Australian Capital Television Pty Ltd v Commonwealth (No 2)* (1992) 177 CLR 106; 108 ALR 577; 66 ALJR 695; *Theophanous v Herald & Weekly Times Ltd* (1994) 182 CLR 104; 124 ALR 1; 68 ALJR 713; *Lange v Australian Broadcasting Corporation* (1997) 189 CLR 520; 145 ALR 96; 71 ALJR 818; *Levy v State of Victoria* (1997) 189 CLR 579; 146 ALR 248; 71 ALJR 837; *Coleman v Power* (2004) 209 ALR 182; 78 ALJR 1166; see also Lee 2003, 383–411.

the Victorian Parliament passed the *Charter of Human Rights and Responsibilities Act* 2006 (Vic) (for an overview, see Evans and Evans 2006; Williams 2006). The Preamble to the ACT Act commences by stating that '[h]uman rights are necessary for individuals to live lives of dignity and value', whilst the Preamble to the Victorian Act seeks to recognise that 'all people are born free and equal in dignity and rights'. One of the rights expressly protected under s 12 of the ACT Act and s 13 of the Victorian Act is the right to reputation. Notably, both Acts deal with reputation in the same section as privacy, consistent with the concept's treatment in international instruments.

As yet, there has been no detailed judicial consideration of the right to reputation and its interaction with the freedom of expression under this legislation (see *Szuty v Smyth* [2004] ACTSC 77 for an incidental consideration). The ACT Act only commenced on 1 July 2004 and the Victorian Act on 1 January 2007.

There is resistance, in some quarters, in Australia to the introduction of express constitutional or statutory protection of individual rights. The debate in Australia is ongoing and seemingly intractable. (The literature on this point is vast; for a selection of recent contributions see: Daryl Williams 2001; George Williams 2001; Davis and Williams 2002; Charlesworth 2002; Daryl Williams 2003; McClelland 2003; Greig 2003; Ozdowski 2003; Kildea 2003; Behrendt 2003.) Thus, it still seems unlikely that Australian defamation law will manifest a concern for reputation as part of the innate dignity of the individual, emerging from a rights-based jurisprudence, as has recently occurred in Canada, Great Britain and New Zealand.

What this review of the relationship between reputation and dignity in international and national rights-based jurisprudence indicates is that dignity and, by extension, reputation are conceptualised principally as a subjective, personal right, albeit a right reinforced by the state. As such, it does not really conform to the recasting of dignity as largely a social phenomenon.

The relationship between reputation as honour and reputation as dignity Because Post adopts an avowedly sociological approach to the concept of reputation, he does not need to deal with the historical relationship between honour and dignity. His purpose is to provide an exposition of ideal types of reputation. These ideal types reflect markedly different approaches to reputation and, in turn, embody different visions of society. Yet, there must be an explanation for the continuity or disjuncture between these two types of reputation. Therefore, an historical perspective may illuminate the complex relationship between honour and dignity.

Notwithstanding his particular methodological approach, Post does offer some historical explanation for this relationship. Drawing upon Norbert Elias's work on 'the civilizing process', Post asserts that the formerly aristocratic concept of honour and its rules of civility were democratised and disseminated throughout the social strata (Post 1986, 716).

The sociologists, Peter and Brigitte Berger and Hansfried Kellner, whose work is informed by Elias's scholarship and upon whom Post also relies, make a similar point about the decline of honour and the rise of dignity (Berger et al. 1977, 81; Post 1986, 701, 716). According to their account, the decline of honour led firstly to the 'embourgeoisement' of honour, then the emergence of dignity (Berger et al. 1977, 81; cf. O'Malley 1981, 80). They identify the seminal period for this transition as the eighteenth century – the era of the Enlightenment and the French Revolution (Berger et al. 1977, 81). Like Post, Berger et al. acknowledge that the concept of honour persists in contemporary society, through institutions like the royalty, the nobility and the military and through professions such as the law and medicine (Berger et al. 1977, 80). They roundly condemn the concept of honour as one of the 'ideological leftovers in the consciousness of obsolete classes', whilst lauding the concept of dignity as 'most timely' (Berger et al. 1977, 78, 79).

Similarly, M.M. Slaughter attempts to delineate the relationship between honour and dignity. According to Slaughter, reputation as honour was prevalent during the seventeenth and eighteenth centuries (Slaughter 1992, 351). Its importance declined during the eighteenth century and was supplanted by reputation as dignity (Slaughter 1992, 352). For Slaughter, honour and dignity are similar, differing to the extent that they represent distinct forms of society, the former hierarchical, the latter egalitarian (Slaughter 1992, 352). Thus characterising honour and dignity, it is possible for Slaughter to treat them compendiously as 'status dignity' (Slaughter 1992, 351). Importantly, like Berger et al., Slaughter identifies the transitional period from honour to dignity as occurring during the eighteenth century.

Finally, according to Barendt, the concept of reputation as honour 'seems outmoded', suggesting instead that the concept of reputation as dignity provides a more satisfactory contemporary understanding (Barendt 1999, 116). Certainly the concept of dignity seems more consonant with the democratic, egalitarian and socially mobile nature of contemporary Western societies (Barendt 1999, 116; Post 1986, 722). Yet Barendt himself is critical of the concept of reputation as dignity, objecting to the vague, amorphous nature of dignity and self-esteem as the basis for a right to reputation (Barendt 1999, 117).

Implicit in these analyses is the seeming assumption that, because the social and political structures and institutions of Western countries have altered fundamentally, from hierarchy to equality, so as to render honour obsolete and to embrace dignity, defamation law has mirrored closely these developments. It is, however, mistaken so to assume. To do so is to ignore entirely the peculiar history of defamation law. One of the most obvious features of defamation law is its arrested historical development. There is a scholarly consensus that the fundamental principles of defamation law were firmly established by the end of the seventeenth century with later accretions of defences, such as the forms of privilege in the nineteenth century. Unlike almost every other area of common law, defamation law has not been subjected to subsequent rationalisation or revision. As Margaret Simons has pithily observed, the law of defamation is 'fundamentally pre-modern' (Simons 2004, 74). Given then that the contours of liability were shaped in an era when the concept of reputation as honour prevailed and given that the history of defamation law is more properly characterised as one of stasis rather than continuity, it should not be surprising that the concept of reputation as honour persists in the structure and content of defamation law. Similarly, it should not be surprising that the concept of dignity, as articulated by Post, developing as it did after the formative period of the common law of defamation, appears as more of an imposition on defamation law, rather than a manifestation arising from defamation law. Post suggests that, like reputation as property, reputation as dignity is premised on the fundamental equality of all plaintiffs. Yet Australian defamation law proceeds on the basis that not all defamation plaintiffs are created equal. Certain defamation plaintiffs have wider or better reputations than others, a disparity Australian defamation law accepts and reinforces (see *Costello v Random House Australia Pty Ltd* (1999) 137 ACTR 1 at 33; 149 FLR 367; Aust Tort Reports ¶81-503 per Higgins J). Atavistic though it may be, the concept of honour in some form inheres in the principles of defamation law and thus lingers on in practice today.

Redefining Honour and Dignity

In light of this critique of honour and dignity, it is necessary to recast these terms in order to indicate how they will be used in this book. Defamation and the harm caused by it, and indeed the concept of defamation itself, involve the complex interaction of public and private aspects, of objective and subjective elements. Consequently, this book contends that any strict demarcation of the public and private aspects of defamation is not borne out in reality. As Post implies and others have explained, the public and private aspects of defamation are closely linked. For instance, Barendt (1999, 116) observed:

> the esteem in which we are held by others is an integral aspect of our own dignity and self-esteem. As a matter of commonsense, to allege that someone is, say, seriously incompetent or dishonest may well damage the esteem in which he, or she, is held by others and consequently wound his (or her) self-esteem.

Broadly then, in this book, honour and dignity will be used respectively to reflect the public and private aspects of defamation. The concept of reputation as honour will be used to designate those circumstances in which the plaintiff's conduct is being assessed objectively by reference to existing social roles, expectations or norms. It will be used to describe those aspects of defamation law that deal with publicly or socially mediated morality. By contrast, the concept of reputation as dignity will be used to address those aspects of defamation law that deal with the plaintiff's subjective experience of, or response to, a defamatory matter. (#) cf 40

So: honour = public & dig = private
OK, but this needs to be integrated with the redefn of honour at 26-7
AND I'm not sure that he is still close enough to Post that the terms sit well??

A Further Concept of Reputation?

One of the key insights that Post provides about the concept of reputation is that it is inherently relational. Reputation inheres in and is mediated by the mechanisms which connect the plaintiff and others. For instance, the concept of reputation as property suggests that reputation is mediated by the mechanism of the marketplace. The individual offers his or her skill, labour or expertise in the marketplace and others, through the mechanism of the marketplace, make their assessment of that individual. Such a reputation is essentially an economic construct. The concepts of reputation as honour and dignity presuppose that reputation is mediated by the mechanism of society. The individual presents private aspects of himself or herself publicly in society and others make their assessment of that individual. Such a reputation is a social construct. Underpinning Post's concepts of reputation is a recognition of the interconnection between the public and private aspects of reputation and the importance of the mechanism by which that connection is effected.

In his thoughtful critique of Post's article and defamation jurisprudence more generally, Gibbons has argued that the crucial role of the media is largely overlooked (Gibbons 1996, 587). He argues that, in order to provide a meaningful account of defamation law and, more specifically, in order to understand the role of reputation, it is vital to integrate an understanding of how the media operates (Gibbons 1996, 587). Gibbons contends that reputation and the harm done to it by defamation are essentially mediated. In other words, reputation and reputational harm is fundamentally connected to the medium of communication between the plaintiff and the rest of the world. Reputations may be constructed through the mechanism of the mass media and may be likewise damaged. An individual may present himself or herself through the mechanism of the mass media and the audience may make its own assessment of that individual (Gibbons 1996, 591). In Post's terms, the mechanism of the mass media therefore connects a plaintiff and his or her audience, thereby facilitating the formation of reputations. Thus, this book contends that a reputation can be conceptualised not only as a social and an economic construct, but, in this sense, also as a media construct.

Gibbons proceeds to explain some of the potential implications of such a recognition. Whilst the concepts of reputation as honour and dignity are fixed attributes of the plaintiff, a mediated reputation, like reputation as property, is contingent. With its emphasis on vindication and consolation, defamation law is more consonant with a fixed, rather than a contingent, concept of reputation. This leads therefore to a disjunction between the reputations that defamation law purports to protect and the reputations that exist in reality, with Gibbons concluding that defamation law does not protect 'real reputations' (Gibbons 1996, 589, 592).

Accepting Gibbons's critique and seeking to apply it to extend Post's reputational schema, this book contends that it is vital to engage with the media's role in creating and damaging reputations. Indeed, this is the rationale for the approach adopted in the case studies, which attempts to place defamation litigants' reputations in their broader, mediated context, in order to understand defamation litigants' reputations outside the courtroom. During the twentieth century, the forms of mass communications developed to such an extent that a significant proportion of defamation plaintiffs now sue media outlets, be they newspapers, magazines, radio or television. It is also clear that individuals can exploit those same forms of mass communications to build a profile, to construct an image, to attain celebrity. Indeed, internet technologies, with platforms such as MySpace, YouTube and Facebook, now provide individuals with the means to create and sustain a worldwide virtual profile. As such, the development and spread of mass communications has led to the emergence of a distinct form of reputation that should now be recognised in addition to those identified by Post – reputation as celebrity.

However, before examining the emergence of celebrity as a distinct form of reputation and the implications of such a recognition, it is necessary to return to the origins of defamation law to trace the fundamental disjunction between the principles of defamation law and the broader socio-political context of contemporary Australian defamation law.

Chapter 2
The Historical Foundations of the Concept of Reputation

Introduction

The eminent legal historian, Sir William Holdsworth, concluding his account of the history of English defamation law, made the following observation:

> In the law of defamation, as in many other branches of the common law, the outlines of the modern law emerged during the sixteenth and seventeenth centuries. But, owing principally to the great changes effected by the introduction of printing, and to some extent the desire of the common law courts to expand their jurisdiction, this branch of the law is, perhaps, more distinctly than any other, the creation of these two centuries. (Holdsworth 1972, 378; see also Holdsworth 1924a, 303)

More recently, in the Supreme Court of Canada, Cory J commented to a similar effect in *Hill v Church of Scientology* [1995] 2 S.C.R. 1130; (1995) 126 DLR (4th) 129 (at 162) that '[t]he character of the law relating to libel and slander in the 20th century is essentially the product of its historical development up to the 17th century, with a few refinements in relation to available defences.'[1]

Given the historical stasis of defamation law, an understanding of its historical origins is useful (see, for example, *Slim v Daily Telegraph Ltd* [1968] 2 QB 157 per Diplock LJ at 171–2; [1968] 1 All ER 497; [1968] 2 WLR 599). In his seminal article on the concept of reputation in defamation law, in which he proposed a tripartite typology of reputation based on honour, dignity and property, Post suggested that an historical analysis of the origins of reputation in particular may yield further insights into the meaning of reputation and its place in defamation law (Post 1986, 693). This chapter accepts Post's invitation.

The earliest recognition of defamation in England occurred in the ecclesiastical jurisdiction in 1222, reflecting the view that defamation was a spiritual offence. The passage of the Statute of Westminster in 1378, creating the offence of *scandalum magnatum* (the defamation of peers), allowed eminent persons to bring actions for derogation of their status. During the thirteenth and fourteenth centuries, the local courts occasionally provided a remedy for defamation, emulating the ecclesiastical courts, and occasionally refused to provide a remedy, emulating the royal courts at

1 For an excellent analysis of the historical development of the tort of defamation in the eighteenth and particularly the nineteenth centuries, see Mitchell 2005.

the time. The royal courts granted legal redress for injurious words in the sixteenth century but limited the circumstances in which it would be granted. In part due to the limitations placed on recovery for defamation by the royal courts, the Star Chamber began to exercise a jurisdiction over cases involving libel. Following the abolition of the Star Chamber in 1641, the royal courts not only assumed jurisdiction over the types of cases previously adjudicated by the Star Chamber but also integrated significant aspects of the defamation jurisprudence of the Star Chamber into the common law of defamation.

Thus, the tort of defamation has diverse origins: the ecclesiastical courts, the Star Chamber, the local courts, statute and finally the royal courts. The nature and extent of the remedy for injurious words provided by each of these jurisdictions needs to be explored. The interaction of these competing jurisdictions, with the ultimate emergence of the royal courts as the principal engine of the common law, also needs to be traced. The principal focus, however, will remain the types of reputational interests to which English law, in its various *fora*, provided protection. It emerges from this historical analysis that not only does the tort of defamation have diverse origins but also that, over centuries, these diverse origins have afforded protection, under the rubric of defamation, to a variety of reputational interests. Indeed, it is precisely because of these diverse origins that there is no single, coherent concept of reputation in modern defamation law.

In examining the concept of reputation historically, it is important to be aware of a number of major themes. The concept of reputation, being broadly a reflection of what others think of a plaintiff, is necessarily embedded in social relations. Thus, the concept of reputation necessarily changes as social relations change over time. Because reputation is a reflection of what others think of a plaintiff, the means by which that opinion is manifested and expressed is also important. Therefore, a plaintiff's reputation is also necessarily embedded in the modes of communication. Consequently, the concept of reputation changes over time in response to social changes and developments in media technologies. This chapter not only attempts to identify the various reputational interests protected by the law of defamation historically but also begins to trace the impact of such social and media changes on the concept of reputation and the protection provided to it by the law of defamation.

The Ecclesiastical Courts

Introduction

The earliest jurisdiction in which defamation emerged in English law was the ecclesiastical courts (Kiralfy 1951, 117; certain scholars trace the history of English defamation law back even further, see Pollock and Maitland 1898, 536; Veeder 1903, 549; Donnelly 1949; Plucknett 1956, 483; Lovell 1962, 1052–3). In medieval England, defamation was considered a spiritual offence (Helmholz 1971,

255; Milsom 1981, 380). The essence of defamation was the telling of lies about another person. Lying was viewed as a form of immorality, which was properly punishable by the Church (Baker 2002, 436).

The English law of defamation can be traced back to 1222. The foundational text of the ecclesiastical jurisdiction was the Constitution *Auctoritate Dei Patris*, which was passed by the Council of Oxford in that year.[2] There is evidence that the formula provided in the Constitution *Auctoritate Dei Patris* served as a model or was adopted in other dioceses.[3] The Constitution *Auctoritate Dei Patris* was phrased in the following terms:

> *Excommunicamus omnes illos qui gracia odii, lucri, vel favoris, vel alia quacunque de causa maliciose crimen imponunt alicui, cum infamatus non sit apud bonos et graves ut sic saltem ei purgation indicatur vel alio modo gravetur.*
>
> We excommunicate all those who, for the sake of hatred, profit, or favour, or for whatever cause, maliciously impute a crime to any person who is not of ill fame among good and serious men, by means of which at least purgation is awarded to him or he is harmed in some other manner. (Helmholz 1971, 256; Helmholz 1985, xiv)

The Constitution *Auctoritate Dei Patris* was expressly referred to in the pleading of defamation causes before the ecclesiastical courts in medieval and early modern England (see, for example, *Gray v Archdeacon of Buckingham* (1290) 101 SS 1; *Robinson v Rayner* (1424–25) 101 SS 4; *Kingwell v Taylor* (1559) 101 SS 8). It is clear that, even in the absence of express reference to this text or one of its derivatives, it nevertheless provided the elements of the claim (Helmholz 1985, xiv–xv). This is borne out in the extant cases. An early example is provided in *Gray v Archdeacon of Buckingham* (1290) 101 SS 1, a case brought on appeal to Canterbury from the diocese of Lincoln. In this case, Lady Joan Gray alleged that Archdeacon of Buckingham *falsely and maliciously* accused her of the *crime* of adultery with John Harleston. Her Ladyship possessed a good reputation and had never been defamed thus before the Archdeacon's allegation. The accusation by the Archdeacon was made *among good and substantial persons*. For the Archdeacon's maintenance of his baseless allegation, Lady Joan Gray sought his *excommunication* from the Church. The later cases follow this formula closely.

There are a number of features of the Constitution *Auctoritate Dei Patris* which are relevant to the concept of reputation. Firstly, the Constitution *Auctoritate Dei Patris* stipulated the manner in which the claimant's reputation had to be traduced

---

2 The Latin text of the Constitution *Auctoritate Dei Patris* may be found in Powicke and Cheney (1964a, 107). For a detailed account of the history behind the *Auctoritate Dei Patris* and its relationship to canon law, see Helmholz 1985.

3 Powicke and Cheney 1964a, 213 (Coventry), 275 (Lincoln), 332 (London), 357 (Norwich), 387 (Salisbury), 466 (Chichester), 521 (Ely), 626 (Wells), 723 (Winchester); Powicke and Cheney 1964b, 849 (Reading), 906 (Lambeth), 1058 (Exeter). See Helmholz 1985, xiv nn 3, 4.

– the alleged defamer needed to have accused the claimant of a crime (*crimen*). Secondly, the Constitution *Auctoritate Dei Patris* made assumptions about the claimant's reputation. Finally, it also imposed a penalty on the defamer, rather than offering a remedy to the claimant. These aspects of the Constitution *Auctoritate Dei Patris* – crime, reputation and penalty – require close examination.

The Subject Matter of the Jurisdiction: The Imputation of a Crime

Under the Constitution *Auctoritate Dei Patris*, the imputation conveyed about the person defamed was that of the commission of a crime. The Latin word used, '*crimen*', admitted of a broad interpretation. The cases collected by Helmholz demonstrate the range of 'crimes' for which the ecclesiastical courts were willing to provide a remedy in defamation. Common allegations included 'falseness' (see *Topcliff v Greenhode* (1381) 101 SS 2; *Robinson v Rayner* (1424–25) 101 SS 4), theft (see, for example, *Robinson v Rayner* (1424–25) 101 SS 4; *Patrick v Wise* (1441) 101 SS 14; *Fontans v Clover* (1507) 101 SS 20; *Forse v Whytton* (1518) 101 SS 25), adultery (see, for example, *Gray v Archdeacon of Buckingham* (1290) 101 SS 1; *Ex officio c Hancoke* (1464) 101 SS 16; *Johnson v Roper* (1531) 101 SS 26; *James v Harmon* (1514) 101 SS 24) and fornication (see, for example, *Bayly v Harrys* (1507) 101 SS 21; *Hunt v North* (1537) 101 SS 27; *Richardes v Rutter* (1566) 101 SS 30; *Ingram v Knowles* (1593) 101 SS 10). Other examples of defamatory imputations – *crimines* – allowed by ecclesiastical courts include perjury (*Topcliff v Greenhode* (1381) 101 SS 2), prodigality (*Topcliff v Greenhode* (1381) 101 SS 2), heresy (*Moberlay v Morpath* (1509–10) 101 SS 5), witchcraft (*Kingwell v Taylor* (1559) 101 SS 8) and the forging of evidence (*Hervy v Ongle* (1439) 101 SS 13). There are even examples of claims being allowed by ecclesiastical courts for the false allegation of disease, even though this did not amount to an allegation of a crime (*Colmere v Daniel* (1413) 101 SS 3 (leprosy); *Herbert v Garrett* (1540) 101 SS 28 (pox)).

Imputations of adultery and fornication, matters of sexual morality, were clearly within the ecclesiastical jurisdiction. The ecclesiastical jurisdiction over other matters was more complicated. Ecclesiastical wrongs were frequently also temporal wrongs (Milsom 1981, 380). For example, theft was an ecclesiastical and a temporal crime. Other matters, such as heresy, may seem to be clearly within the jurisdiction of the ecclesiastical courts but given the political climate of the reign of Henry VIII and the breaking of ties with Rome, the religious charge of heresy became politically charged. Of course, in an era before the demarcation between Church and State, it was inevitable that there would be conflict about the precise extent of each court's jurisdiction.

It is doubtful that the Constitution *Auctoritate Dei Patris* was intended to deal with both ecclesiastical and temporal wrongs (Milsom 1981, 380). However, in the thirteenth and fourteenth centuries, when the ecclesiastical courts were allowed to deal with defamation cases without interference from the royal courts, which did not recognise a cause of action for defamation, it appears that the ecclesiastical courts dealt indiscriminately with ecclesiastical and temporal wrongs (Milsom 1981, 380). It was only when the royal courts started to develop an interest in defamation that they began to restrict the subject matter of the ecclesiastical courts' defamation jurisdiction. Thus, in the thirteenth and fourteenth centuries, the ecclesiastical courts' jurisdiction over defamation claims was, on one view, expansive – it encompassed a broad range of 'crimes', beyond those which were properly within its purview. However, the requirement of a *crimen* also acted as a limitation. One of the first class of imputations acknowledged by the royal courts when it began allowing claims for defamation in the early sixteenth century was professional incompetence. Even with an expansive interpretation of *crimen*, professional incompetence could not be accommodated within the ecclesiastical jurisdiction.

The Definition of Reputation

The person defamed was presupposed to possess a reputation – and a good reputation. More precisely, under the terms of the *Auctoritate Dei Patris*, the person defamed was not allowed to be of ill-fame (*infamia*). Nevertheless, it appears to have been customary for a litigant to assert his or her own good fame (*bona fama*) (Helmholz 1985, xxxv–xxxvi; or even the good fame of a claimant's own witnesses, *Robinson v Rayner* (1424–25) 101 SS 4). On occasion, this could simply be a statement of the litigant's good fame (*Moberlay v Morpath* (1509–10) 101 SS 5). There is, however, evidence to suggest that the pleading of reputation became formulaic. The litigant would plead that he or she was a man or woman of 'good fame, honest conversation and unblemished reputation' (see *Topcliff v Greenhode* (1381) 101 SS 2). The formula could be varied or augmented, according to the facts of the case. Thus, when Thomas Robinson was accused by John Rayner of being a 'false side-glance thief' and of having beaten Rayner, Robinson emphasised his faithfulness and trustworthiness – he was not the sort of man to lie, to steal or to assault others (*Robinson v Rayner* (1424–25) 101 SS 4 ('*vir fidelis et bone fame et conversationis honeste ac opinionis illese*')). An even stronger example is furnished by *Ingram v Knowles* (1593) 101 SS 10. In this case, Richard Ingram was accused by Elizabeth Knowles of being a whoremaster, a whoremonger and a fornicator. In his claim, Ingram did not only assert that he was a man of good fame, honest conversation and unblemished reputation but added for emphasis that he was 'chaste and never joined in matrimony' – he was certainly not *that* sort of man ('*vir honestus ac castus ac nunquam in matrimonio conjugates bone fame viteque et conversationis honeste*').

The claimant then alleged that his or her reputation was traduced by the defamer's allegations. Yet, in the pleading of their claims, the litigants never used a single word to describe the object injured by the defamer. Rather, the claimants asserted that their '*status, fama et opinio*' was injured by the defamer's accusations (*Robinson v Rayner* (1424–25) 101 SS 4; *Topcliff v Greenhode* (1381) 101 SS 2; *Moberlay v Morpath* (1509–10) 101 SS 5 (*status et fama*); *Kingwell v*

Taylor (1559) 101 SS 8 (*status et bona fama*); *Ingram v Knowles* (1593) 101 SS 10 (*status bona fama et opinio*)). There were reputational interests being protected, not a single, unitary interest. *Opinio*, literally the opinion of others, is the meaning closest to the presumed common law meaning of reputation (Kermode 2001, 133–4). This formula makes clear that the injured parties, bringing their cases to the ecclesiastical courts, were seeking redress not only for damage to the esteem in which they were held by others, the opinion of others, but also for damage to their social position or rank, or the perception of others of same, their *status*. Thus, it emerges clearly from the ecclesiastical case law that early defamation law provided a remedy to preserve not only reputation, in the sense of other people's opinions, but also to preserve rank. Indeed, the notion of reputation that emerges from the ecclesiastical case law is that the opinion of others was inextricably linked to the rank occupied by the injured party in society: a composite form of reputation, which was subject to change or revision.

Combining the assertion of good reputation, compendiously described, and the injury to it, a litigant could emphasise the greatness of their reputation and therefore the injury to their reputation, especially *apud bonos et graves* (among good and serious men). In *Gray v Archdeacon of Buckingham* (1290) 101 SS 1, Lady Joan Gray stressed that the defamatory allegations made about her had not been made before an audience of commoners. Her Ladyship pleaded specifically that the allegations were made before knights and 'great men' ('*magnates*') – she was a great woman and her reputation had been damaged amongst her elevated milieu. Similarly, in *Topcliff v Greenhode* (1381) 101 SS 2, Topcliff was accused of being a wastrel. In his pleading, Topcliff was at pains to emphasise how wealthy he was – he had great wealth and his reputation had been assailed in that respect.

The reputation was traduced *apud bonos et graves* (*Topcliff v Greenhode* (1381) 101 SS 2; *Moberlay v Morpath* (1509–10) 101 SS 5; *Kingwell v Taylor* (1559) 101 SS 8; *Robinson v Rayner* (1424–25) 101 SS 4; *Ingram v Knowles* (1593) 101 SS 10). The hypothetical referees under the Constitution *Auctoritate Dei Patris* therefore were 'good and serious men'. This echoes the test, which still prevails in English and Australian defamation law, though articulated variously, of 'right-thinking members of society'. From its inception in English law, defamation practice was directed towards mediating, establishing and enforcing social norms: what it means to have a 'good reputation' or a 'bad reputation'.

Litigants could geographically demarcate the extent of their reputation. Litigants could also geographically demarcate the extent of the rumour and therefore the damage to their reputation. For instance, in *Gray v Archdeacon of Buckingham* (1290) 101 SS 1, Lady Joan Gray claimed the rumour of her adultery was widely known in the archdeaconry of Buckingham and elsewhere, where she was also known. In *Topcliff v Greenhode* (1381) 101 SS 2, John Topcliff went further. Not only were the rumours acclaimed by 'public voice and fame', they were also 'public, notorious and manifest' (*publica notoria et manifesta*) in the parishes of Ripon and Wakefield, in the diocese of York, as well as in nearby locations. In *Robinson v Rayner* (1424–25) 101 SS 4, Robinson claimed the rumours extended to the town and parish of Cottingham, where he lived, to the city and diocese of York, where he had connections, as well as to other nearby locations.

What becomes clear from this analysis of the extant cases before the ecclesiastical courts is that the law of defamation, at its inception, intended to provide a remedy to reputations damaged within small communities. The extent of the rumour, thus the extent of the damage to reputation, could be demarcated and was circumscribed. The means by which those reputations were formed was by word of mouth; the means by which those reputations were traduced was slander. By the end of the seventeenth century, the impact of social changes and, more importantly, the printing press would change this framework significantly.

The Penalties for Defamation

Defamation proceedings before the ecclesiastical courts were criminal in nature. A litigant bringing such a claim was effectively seeking the punishment of the defamer. The Constitution *Auctoritate Dei Patris* prescribed the penalty for defamation as automatic excommunication. The extant cases indicate that, on occasion, excommunication was sought and imposed (*Robinson v Rayner* (1424–25) 101 SS 4; *Kingwell v Taylor* (1559) 101 SS 8; *Forse v Whytton* (1518) 101 SS 25). However, they also demonstrate that the ecclesiastical courts had a substantial discretion which could be, and was, exercised in the imposition of penalties on defamers. There are examples where an ecclesiastical court suspended the defamer from communion or imposed some lesser form of penance (*Thomson v Faram* (1481) 101 SS 17; *Howie v Smyth* (1513) 101 SS 23; *James v Harmon* (1514) 101 SS 24; *Hall v Haydon* (1556) 101 SS 29). In one case, the punishment imposed in lieu of excommunication was three whippings as penance – the claimant had sought four (*Grewes v Brodehouse* (1416) 101 SS 11). A defamer could confess, publicly seek pardon from the claimant and undertake not to repeat the slander (*Coting v Ward* (1418) 101 SS 12; *Patrick v Wise* (1441) 101 SS 14; *Vane v Skinner* (1441) 101 SS 15; *Hawkyns v Holeherst* (1507) 101 SS 19; *Forse v Whytton* (1518) 101 SS 25; *Hunt v North* (1537) 101 SS 27). There are examples where the litigant withdrew his or her complaint because the parties had agreed to a settlement (*Fontans v Clover* (1507) 101 SS 20; *Bayly v Harrys* (1507) 101 SS 21).

It was possible for an aggrieved party to appeal a decision of an ecclesiastical court to the Pope. Although this did occur, there appear to be no extant cases in which such a course of action succeeded (see *Moberlay v Morpath* (1509–10) 101 SS 5 (appeal lodged); *Robinson v Rayner* (1424–25) 101 SS 4 (appeal dismissed)). The Papacy therefore seemed willing to allow the ecclesiastical courts of England to develop and apply their own defamation jurisprudence.

Importantly, the ecclesiastical courts were unable to award a defamed party damages – a significant limitation (Milsom 1981, 381; Baker 2002, 438). There is evidence that litigants sought an order of costs in defamation proceedings before the ecclesiastical courts and that such requests were, on occasion, granted (*Kingwell v Taylor* (1559) 101 SS 8; *Ingram v Knowles* (1593) 101 SS 10; *Moberlay v*

Morpath (1509–10) 101 SS 5, *Robinson v Rayner* (1424–25) 101 SS 4). However, the power of an ecclesiastical court to award costs against an unsuccessful party was only firmly established in 1497 (Baker 2002, 438; *Anon* (1497) YB Trin 12 Hen VII, fo 22, pl 2 (KB); B & M 624–5).

The Limitations of the Ecclesiastical Jurisdiction over Defamation Claims

There were limitations to the ecclesiastical courts' jurisdiction over defamation claims. Firstly, the requirement of a *crimen* immediately excluded certain classes of imputations. For example, even on an expansive interpretation of 'crime', the imputation of professional incompetence contained no spiritual element which could attract the jurisdiction of the Church courts. Secondly, the inability of the ecclesiastical courts to award damages left litigants without an effective remedy. A claimant may have suffered a pecuniary loss, such as the loss of credit, the loss of sales or the loss of a chance of marriage, as a result of false words being spoken about him or her, depending upon the allegations made (Kiralfy 1951, 118). The ecclesiastical courts could not always provide such litigants with commensurate relief.

In the late fifteenth century, the royal courts themselves imposed further limitations on the ecclesiastical courts and their ability to provide an effective remedy for defamation in a wide range of cases. The extant evidence suggests that the ecclesiastical courts exercised jurisdiction over defamation claims during the thirteenth and fourteenth centuries without interference from the royal courts (Milsom 1981, 381). Yet this was the period in which the royal courts were developing and consolidating their own jurisdiction. The royal courts had at their disposal the effective means by which to curtail the ecclesiastical courts' jurisdiction over defamation claims, had they desired to do so. Using the writ of prohibition, the royal courts could have prevented ecclesiastical courts from hearing and determining cases over which they had no authority (Milsom 1981, 381; see also Adams 1936; Flahiff 1941; Flahiff 1944; Flahiff 1945; Helmholz 1976; Helmholz 1981; Millon 1984). Yet throughout the thirteenth and fourteenth centuries, the ecclesiastical and royal courts co-existed amicably and ignored each other in respect of the treatment of defamation claims (Milsom 1981, 381). It was not until the 1470s that the royal courts began using the writ of prohibition to curtail the ecclesiastical courts' jurisdiction over defamation claims (Milsom 1981, 381; Baker 2002, 438). Notably, the royal courts issued the writ of prohibition against the ecclesiastical courts in cases involving imputations of theft – the first category of defamatory imputations eventually recognised by the royal courts (Baker 2002, 438; *Tanner v Cornyssh* (1472) CP 40/844, m 574; CP 40/845, m 340; *Anon* (1482) YB Trin 22 Edw IV fo 20 pl 47; 94 SS 67 n 2).

The reasons for the royal courts' use of the writ of prohibition in this way are unknown but the effect is clear – a further gap was left in the English law of defamation (Donnelly 1949, 110; Milsom 1981, 381; Baker 2002, 438). As late as 1497, the royal courts still maintained that defamation was a purely spiritual matter (*Anon* (1497) B & M 625). However, by the early 1500s, their attitude had changed. According to Baker's research, the first plea appeared in the rolls of the royal courts in 1507 and the first judgment of the royal courts in a defamation case was delivered in 1517 (Baker 2002, 438). The transfer of jurisdiction – and the development of the modern tort of defamation – had begun.

The Royal Courts

The royal courts adopted the ecclesiastical jurisdiction over defamation, locating it within the crystallised form of action, the action on the case (Kiralfy 1951, 117–18; Baker 2002, 438). The action on the case required pleading and proof of damage, in contrast to its complement, trespass, which was actionable *per se*, that is, without proof of damage (Holdsworth 1924a, 304; Baker 2002, 438). Indeed, Pollock (1929, 249) observed, '[t]he law went wrong from the beginning in making the damage and not the insult the cause of action' but, as the High Court of Australia recently noted, it is too late to reverse this entrenched position at common law (*Dow Jones & Co Inc v Gutnick* (2002) 210 CLR 575 at 600 per Gleeson CJ, McHugh, Gummow and Hayne JJ; (2002) 194 ALR 433; (2002) 77 ALJR 255). A claimant before the royal courts needed to demonstrate that he or she had suffered an ascertainable, actual harm as a result of the injurious words uttered by his or her defamer.

The royal courts' adoption and development of the tort of defamation allowed claimants to recover damages. Obviously, this was responding to a real or perceived need for damages, predicated upon an acceptance that words could cause economic harm. This recognition implicitly allowed for an acknowledgement of a novel aspect of reputation: reputation as property. This is most clearly demonstrated by the early recognition, in the 1530s, of claims of professional incompetence (Baker 2002, 439; *Barfote v Smyth* (1533) KB 27/1089, m 79d; *Wanton v Maydewell* (1536) KB 27/1099, m 68; *Yaxley v Watson* (1538) KB 27/1109, m 46d; *Woode v Frogge* (1517) KB 27/1022, m 67; *Haukyn v Lincoln* (1525) KB 27/1055, m 25d; *Elyot v Tofte* (1513) KB 27/1006, m 62; *Southworth v Bady* (1515) KB 27/1017, m 103; *Danby v Thwyng* (1532) KB 27/1083, m 32; *Anon* (1575) and *Anon* (1580) B & M 638–9; *Palmer v Boyer* (1594) Cro Eliz 342; Owen 17; Goulds 26; *Bankes v Allen* (1615) Rolle Abr vol I p 54). An allegation of professional incompetence was an accusation which could cause pecuniary loss to a claimant who had, through his or her exertions in the marketplace for services, acquired a reputation for professional competence. The claimant's reputation for professional competence is the property of the plaintiff; it is a form of personal goodwill, as Post observes (Post 1986, 693). A false accusation of professional incompetence is primarily an economic injury to that personal goodwill – people 'shun and avoid' the services rendered by an incompetent professional person. Likewise, imputations reflecting on the honesty and integrity of professional persons were also considered to be the proper subject of an action in the royal courts (*Barfote v Smyth* (1533) KB27/1089, m 79d; *Moore v Foster* (1605) Cro Jac 65; 79 ER 55;

Stuckley v Bulhead (1602) 4 Co Rep 16a; 76 ER 895; *Kemp v Housgoe* (1605) Cro Jac 90; 79 ER 77). In addition to the proprietary aspects of such claims, there are moral connotations to allegations of professional incompetence and dishonesty – there are expectations that professional persons will act competently and honestly in the discharge of their duties, and a failure to fulfil such standards is a failure to fulfil those expectations.

The development of the principles governing defamation in the royal courts was influenced by judicial attitudes towards the appropriateness of allowing recovery of damages for injurious words. There were frequent expressions of the need to curb the explosion in defamation suits (see, for example, *Anon* (1558) B & M 637 per Dyer J (approved in *Anon* (1557) B & M 638 n 20 per Staunford J); see also *Anon* (1579) B & M 639 n 2; *Gray's Case* (1582) B & M 539; *Crofts v Brown* (1616) 3 Bulst 167 at 167; 81 ER 141 at 141 per Lord Coke CJ; *Lake v King* (1668) 2 Keb 664; 85 ER 137 per Vaughan CJ, CP). The recognition by the royal courts of claims for defamation created a significant increase in litigation, as Kiralfy's statistical analysis of the plea rolls demonstrates (Kiralfy 1951, Appendix A). To curb the periodic explosion in defamation litigation, judges developed a number of doctrines (Baker 2002, 440–42). For instance, in the late sixteenth century, the judges of the royal courts attempted to impose a requirement that words spoken in anger or in sport were not actionable as defamation (*Anon* (1565) B & M 637; *Anon* (1579) B & M 639 n 2). The most important doctrine which the judges of the royal courts developed in order to attempt to curtail the expansion of defamation was the introduction of the *mitior sensus* rule (Donnelly 1949, 113–14; Plucknett 1956, 495; Baker 2002, 441; see also Spencer Bower 1990, 302–5). The *mitior sensus* rule required the determination of cases on the mildest possible interpretation of the words in issue. To demonstrate the absurdities which the *mitior sensus* rule could be deployed to justify, Baker refers to the case of *Holt v Astgrigg* (1607) B & M 643. In this case, the defendant was alleged to have claimed that the plaintiff had 'struck his cook on the head with a cleaver, and cleaved his head; the one part lay on the one shoulder, and another part on the other.'

Whilst this utterance clearly appears to convey an imputation of a crime – and a serious one too – the presiding judge found it ambiguous, suggesting that the cook may have survived, in which case the plaintiff had only committed a trespass to the person – but surely one that would pique the interest of the criminal justice system (Baker 2002, 442; Donnelly 1949, 114). Thus the *mitior sensus* rule acted as a severe limitation on the right to recover damages for defamation.

The Star Chamber

Introduction

In part due to the deficiencies of the remedies at common law and in part to dissuade aggrieved or insulted parties from resorting to violent, extra-curial self-help in the form of duelling, the Star Chamber began to exercise jurisdiction over defamation actions (Veeder 1903, 555; Holdsworth 1924b, 404; Donnelly 1949, 113, 116; Plucknett 1956, 490; Lovell 1962, 1059). The precise origin of the Star Chamber is unclear and remains the subject of academic controversy (Stuckey 1993, 117; Stuckey 1998, 2–3). If not established by Henry VII, then legislation passed in his reign, what has been styled 'the Star Chamber Act' of 1487 (3 Hen VII c 1), certainly cemented its composition, powers and procedures. It was a conciliar court, thus being integrated into the executive government. The first documented case of defamation it entertained appears to be the case of *Vale v Broke* (1493) 16 SS 39, occurring in the final decade of the fifteenth century (Kiralfy 1957, 320–21). In this case, Symon Vale claimed that John and Alice Broke had 'dislandered' him and his family as 'strong thieves and common robbers' in the neighbourhood where they resided. Vale asserted that he was unable to obtain a remedy against Broke at common law and thus petitioned the Star Chamber for punishment of Broke. What *Vale v Broke* makes clear is that the jurisdiction exercised by the Star Chamber, in contrast to that of the royal courts, was a criminal one. Additionally, it indicates that the Star Chamber was more prepared than the royal courts to provide a remedy for defamation. Finally, it demonstrates that the Star Chamber in its defamation jurisdiction was not limited to cases of libel but was willing to entertain cases of slander (Baker 2002, 446). However, cases involving libel did preponderate.

Its overwhelming concern with libel, as opposed to slander, emanated from the fact that the Star Chamber was also the mechanism by which the Crown controlled the printing press. During the Tudor and Stuart period, printing was tightly regulated by the state (Veeder 1903, 561–2; Donnelly 1949, 116–17; Lovell 1962, 1062–3). The combination of these three factors – deficiencies at common law, discouragement of duelling, and fear of the power of the printed word – led to the Star Chamber developing its distinctive defamation jurisprudence. Importantly, the Star Chamber, by attempting to eradicate duelling, aimed to prevent breaches of the peace. Consequently, the jurisdiction that the Star Chamber developed over defamation was criminal (Baker 2002, 436). Furthermore, as Stuckey argues, because Henry VII's victory over Richard III at the Battle of Bosworth Field in 1485 established relative peace and stability in England, the criminal law generally, and the Star Chamber specifically, became centrally concerned with 'covert crimes', such as defamation, perjury, forgery, fraud and sedition (Stuckey 1998, 48).

The greatest impetus for the development of the Star Chamber's jurisdiction over defamation matters occurred in the early seventeenth century. Until 1605, the Star Chamber appears to have dealt with defamation cases by analogy to *scandalum magnatum* (Donnelly 1949, 117; Plucknett 1956, 490). In that year, however, a significant development occurred with the judgment in *De Libellis Famosis* (1605) 5 Co Rep 125; 77 ER 250, a case concerning 'an infamous libel in verse', allegedly defaming the former and the incumbent Archbishop of Canterbury. Drawing heavily upon Roman law, the case created the offence of criminal libel in the following terms:

> Every libel which is called Famosus Libellus is made either against a private man or against a magistrate or public person. If it be against a private man it deserves a severe punishment, for although the libel be against one, yet it incites all those of the same family, kindred or society to revenge, and so tends to quarrel, and Breach of the Peace, and may be the cause of shedding of blood and of great offense, for it concerns not only the Breach of the Peace, but also the scandal of government …
>
> It is not material whether the Libel be true, or whether the Party against whom it is made, be of a good or ill Fame, for in a settled State of Government the party grieved ought to complain for every Injury done to him in an ordinary course of law, and not by any means to revenge himself, either by the odious Course of Libelling, or otherwise.' (See Veeder 1903, 563; *De Libellis Famosis* (1605) 5 Co Rep 125; 77 ER 250 at 125a–b, 251).

Although the stated purpose of the offence of criminal libel was the prevention of breaches of the peace and thereby the maintenance of public order and stable government, it incidentally provided a strong measure of protection for the reputations of litigants. Those litigants tended to be the 'magnates' within English society – great men and occasionally great women. The defamation jurisdiction of the Star Chamber therefore principally protected reputation in the sense of rank, which is understandable, given its initial reliance on the statutory cause of action for *scandalum magnatum*.

The case of *Viscount Falkland v Lord Mountnorris* illustrates this. In this case, one of the defendants, Philip Bushell, was accused of presenting a false petition to the Lower House of Parliament, wherein he accused Viscount Falkland, the then Lord Deputy of Ireland, of conspiring with the Chief Justice of Common Pleas, Sir Dominick Sarsfield, to secure the conviction of Philip Bushell's father for his mother's murder (Gardiner 1886, 1, 2). He alleged that Viscount Falkland did this in order to secure Bushell's father's estate, worth almost £4,000, for himself (Gardiner 1886, 4). Another of the defendants, Sir Arthur Savage, a Privy Councillor, advised Bushell to present the petition to the Duke of Buckingham, endorsing the letter for Bushell. The Duke of Buckingham wrote to Viscount Falkland on behalf of Bushell but, before his reply could be sent, he died. Savage opened the Duke of Buckingham's reply, intending to attach it to a fresh petition to be presented to the parliament (Gardiner 1886, 3). Another of the defendants, Lord Mountnorris, accused Viscount Falkland of operating a tyrannical government in Ireland (Gardiner 1886, 3–4). Although Bushell suspected Viscount Falkland of attempting to obtain his father's estate, in fact Sir Arthur Savage posed a greater threat, embezzling the overwhelming majority of the estate (Gardiner 1886, 4).

Viscount Falkland brought proceedings in the Star Chamber, claiming that the defendants had conspired to bring the King and his government in Ireland into dishonour. One of the members of the Star Chamber, Sir John Cooke, agreed that the instant case was 'a great cause trenching upon the honor of a noble gentleman, and upon the honor of the King and State' (Gardiner 1886, 20). In dealing with the issue of Sir Arthur Savage's guilt, another member, Lord Richardson, referred to the prohibition of such conduct pursuant to the Statute of Westminster, the legislation creating the offence of *scandalum magnatum* (Gardiner 1886, 16). The Star Chamber found overwhelmingly in favour of Viscount Falkland, imposing a £500 fine on Bushell and a heftier penalty on Sir Arthur Savage, a £2,000 fine and an award of £3,000 damages in favour of Viscount Falkland (Gardiner 1886, 12, 22–34, 37, 56–8). Lord Mountnorris evaded punishment (Gardiner 1886, 13–14, 18, 23–34).

Another example of this reference to *scandalum magnatum* in the development of the law of criminal libel occurs in *Earl of Suffolk v Grenville*, decided in 1632 (Gardiner 1886, 108). In this case, the Earl of Suffolk was seeking to compel Sir Richard Grenville to pay alimony in the ecclesiastical court (Gardiner 1886, 108–9). He sent a notice to Grenville through a messenger. Grenville told the messenger, in the presence of Lady Grenville, that the Earl of Suffolk was 'a base lord' who had 'dealt basely' with him (Gardiner 1886, 109).

Clearly the messenger reported Grenville's feelings back to the Earl of Suffolk because the Earl of Suffolk brought proceedings for slander in the Star Chamber. Lord Richardson roundly rejected the aspersion made against the Earl of Suffolk, stating that he was 'a noble Lord and a man of great office and trust and honorable in his birth and actions and not base' (Gardiner 1886, 109). As in *Viscount Falkland v Lord Mountnorris*, Lord Richardson also noted that the slander amounted to an offence of *scandalum magnatum* in contravention of the Statute of Westminster. In this case, the Star Chamber voted to impose a £4,000 fine on Sir Richard Grenville and to order him to pay the Earl of Suffolk £4,000 damages as well as being detained at His Majesty's pleasure (Gardiner 1886, 109–10).

The Star Chamber did, however, entertain suits brought by less exalted litigants. For example, in *Dalton v Heydon*, decided in 1632, the Vicar of Shap, John Dalton, brought proceedings against a pedlar, Robert Jackson, and his wife, who had accused him of committing adultery with Mrs Jackson and of impregnating another woman, Elizabeth Beck (Gardiner 1886, 70–71). The Star Chamber accepted that a 'libellous scandal' against a minister was an allegation made against 'noe common person' (Gardiner 1886, 71). It imposed a hefty sentence of three months' imprisonment on Jackson and his wife, as well as being compelled to pay a £40 fine to the Crown and to pay Dalton a 100 marks 'fine' and £50 damages (Gardiner 1886, 71–2). The Star Chamber also ordered that a sentence clearing Dalton of the charge be read at the Assizes, in his parish and to the clergy in Carlisle and that Jackson and his wife make a public acknowledgement of their offence (Gardiner 1886, 72). As Plucknett (1956, 495) observes, '[t]he Star Chamber seems to have felt that severity was the proper remedy'.

As Plucknett (1956, 497) notes, the offence of criminal libel, as it developed in the Star Chamber, did not distinguish between its tortious and its criminal aspects. There were certain dissimilarities between the common law of defamation developing in the royal courts and the defamation jurisprudence of the Star Chamber. For example, unlike in civil proceedings before the royal courts, where damage was the gist of the action on the case for defamation, in criminal proceedings in the Star Chamber for the offence of defamation, there was no requirement of publication, as the purpose was the prevention of breaches of the peace (see, for example, *Edwardes v Wootton* (1607) B & M 648; Donnelly 1949, 119; Baker 2002, 444).

However, there were similarities which were more accidental than intentional. For example, as its jurisdiction developed, the Star Chamber not only imposed fines and punishments on guilty defendants but also began to award damages, payable by defendants, to plaintiffs. Unlike the common law of defamation, these damages were not premised on the plaintiffs establishing provable loss flowing from the defamatory publication because, in part, publication was not an essential requirement of liability for defamation before the Star Chamber. Thus, following the abolition of the Star Chamber by the Long Parliament in 1641 and the eventual integration of its jurisdiction over criminal libel into the common law of defamation before the royal courts, the common law's heavy emphasis on damages as a remedy for defamation and the anomalous presumption of damages in cases involving libel became entrenched (16 Charles I c 10; Donnelly 1949, 120).

Defamation in the Royal Courts after the Abolition of the Star Chamber

As Plucknett observed, the two decades that elapsed between the abolition of the Star Chamber and the Restoration was a period of turmoil. The implications of the abolition of the Star Chamber for the development of the law of defamation were thus only fully explored by the royal courts after 1660 (Holdsworth 1924b, 412; Holdsworth 1925, 19–30). The common law of defamation adopted certain aspects of the law of libel, as it had developed in the Star Chamber, such as a rejection of the *mitior sensus* rule and the acceptance of the presumption of damage, but did not incorporate other aspects, such as the rejection of the defence of truth and the questionable status of the defence of privilege (Plucknett 1956, 497). Importantly, the abolition of the Star Chamber allowed for the full development of the civil law of defamation, not motivated by the need to regulate the press. Increasingly, legislation was viewed as the appropriate vehicle to achieve that end (Plucknett 1956, 499).

By the late seventeenth century, the common law of defamation had crystallised so that it required proof of damage in all cases, except for four notable exceptions. Three involve forms of slander conveying imputations of criminal conduct, imputations of certain types of communicable disease (leprosy, syphilis and 'the plague') and imputations affecting the plaintiff's business, trade, profession or office (Donnelly 1949, 111; Veeder 1903, 558; Holdsworth 1924b, 398; Plucknett 1956, 494; Ibbetson 1999, 120–21; Baker 2002, 438–40). The fourth category, however, has become incredibly important. The view that developed in the seventeenth century was that greater injury to a person's reputation could be done through the printed word, as opposed to the spoken word (*Lake v King* (1668) 2 Keb 664; 85 ER 137). The printed word was permanent; the spoken word was evanescent. The printed word could be circulated; the spoken word was limited to the immediate audience. This view of libel was formed at a time when the printed word was only emerging, was highly regulated by the state and had not become as pervasive as it has in the centuries since then. The consequence of this view was that actual damage did not need to be pleaded and proven in order for a plaintiff to argue successfully that he or she had been libelled. Libel became actionable *per se*, whereas most forms of slander still required proof of actual damage. Given that none of the cases before the ecclesiastical and local courts recorded by Helmholz dealt with libel and that the overwhelming majority of cases before the royal courts involved slander, rather than libel, it is unsurprising that the view prevailed in the seventeenth century that the printed word was special and it ought to be ascribed a special power (Veeder 1903, 561). Yet now, slander is rarely pleaded (for recent examples of slander, see *Strasberg v Westfield Ltd* [2002] NSWSC 340 at [3]–[8] per Levine J; *McManus v Beckham* [2002] 4 All ER 497 at 499–502; [2002] 1 WLR 2982 per Waller LJ; *Hambly v Joseph Charles Learmonth Duffy Pty Ltd* [2004] WASC 142 at [4] per Newnes M; *Clover Bond Pty Ltd v Carroll* [2004] WASC 216 at [4] per Commissioner Zilko SC). Indeed, in certain jurisdictions, for instance, throughout Australia, the distinction between libel and slander has been abolished, with all defamations being treated as libels, thus actionable without proof of special damage.[4] The printed word has overtaken the spoken word as the basis for liability in defamation but the basic principles developed in the seventeenth century have not changed to reflect this technological reality. The implications of this altered reality will need to be explored.

Scandalum Magnatum

The protection of reputation, or at least a particular kind of reputation, in English law also had an independent, statutory basis, which developed alongside the ecclesiastical and common law jurisdictions over defamation. In 1378, the Statute of Westminster was passed, creating the offence of *scandalum magnatum* (literally, the 'scandalising of magnates') (Baker 2002, 437). Under this legislation, it was an offence to derogate the reputation of 'magnates': dignitaries, lords and judges. Thus, through the vehicle of *scandalum magnatum*, English law developed a specific protection for reputation based on rank or social status. *Scandalum magnatum* presumed that peers and judges had and deserved a high reputation simply by virtue of their social position. Equally, it was assumed that a verbal attack on a peer or a judge necessarily diminished that peer or judge's standing. A peer or a judge's rank in the community was a reputational interest intrinsically worthy of specific legislative protection.

---

4 *Civil Law (Wrongs) Act* 2002 (ACT) s 119; *Defamation Act* 2006 (NT) s 6; *Defamation Act* 2005 (NSW) s 7; *Defamation Act* 2005 (Qld) s 7; *Defamation Act* 2005 (SA) s 7; *Defamation Act* 2005 (Tas) s 7; *Defamation Act* 2005 (Vic) s 7; *Defamation Act* 2005 (WA) s 7.

Baker notes that the legislation was passed three years before the Peasants' Revolt in 1381 – a time of considerable political, social and economic turmoil (Baker 2002, 437). He identifies the legislative policy as being the facilitation of harmony between the classes and the legislative purpose as being the provision of a civil remedy to magnates for attacks on their reputation (Baker 2002, 437). Importantly, however, there is scant evidence for the use of this legislation before the end of the fifteenth century. (This tends to confirm the view, expressed in *Lord Townsend v Hughes* (1677) 1 Mod 232, that there were no medieval actions for *scandalum magnatum* (Kiralfy 1951, 116).) The earliest reported case identified by legal historians occurred in 1497: *Lord Beauchamp v Sir Richard Croft* (1497) 72 ER 182 (see also *Duke of Gloucester v Clere* (1442) CP 40/727, m. 586d and *Duke of Exeter v Smyth* (1456) CP 40/781, m. 450d; Baker 2002, 437). Notably, the claim in this case was unsuccessful. Croft, the Treasurer of the King's Household, accused Lord Beauchamp in court of forging false deeds. Lord Beauchamp's claim failed because the action for *scandalum magnatum* was held to apply only to 'extrajudicial slanders' (Lassiter 1978, 218–19).

Lassiter posits several possible reasons for the lack of litigation on the statute. There were other cognate remedies available to a peer or particularly a judge, which did not require the litigant to rely specifically upon the statute. At this time, the law of civil contempt was developing, affording judges particularly with a means of redressing any insulting words uttered against them in court (Baker 2002, 437). Yet even when peers began bringing actions for *scandalum magnatum*, judges still did not, even though the statute clearly conferred protection on such persons (Kiralfy 1951, 117). Indeed, Kiralfy notes that many of the cases found in the plea rolls, originally thought to be cases of *scandalum magnatum*, are properly explained on some other juridical basis (Kiralfy 1951, 115–16).

Another explanation could be that, aside from short periods of political instability, the feudal system did not begin to come under sustained attack until the Tudor period. According to Lassiter, the increase in claims for *scandalum magnatum* occurred when the peerage felt its prestige most under attack (Kiralfy 1951, 220). Whilst it remained confident of its social position, there was no need to defend it. The challenges mounted to the nobility during the seventeenth century – the Civil War, the resistance to Stuart absolutism and the rise of factional politics – demanded a resort to litigation. Lassiter, reconstructing from the admittedly fragmentary evidence, suggests that the plaintiffs in *scandalum magnatum* cases before the Restoration tended to be members of established noble families, whilst the defendants tended to be members of the gentry (Lassiter 1978, 220–21).

As Lassiter notes, *scandalum magnatum* perpetuated the distinction between peers and commoners. With the breakdown of feudal society and the closing of the gap between the peerage and the landed gentry in the Tudor and early Stuart period, this rigid demarcation of status became less defined and less defensible. Lassiter argues that these social changes led peers to resort more frequently to reliance on *scandalum magnatum* to reaffirm their standing in society, usually suing those persons whom they perceived as posing the greatest threat (Lassiter 1978, 219).

Lassiter notes that the reason for the increase in suits for *scandalum magnatum* was twofold: firstly, individual peers reacted to the loss of respect by instituting suits; and secondly, the legal system, comprised of judges who undoubtedly had sympathy with noble plaintiffs and were themselves potential beneficiaries of the legislation, as an institution provided a remedy (Lassiter 1978, 220).

The incidence of suits for *scandalum magnatum* increased rapidly from the late sixteenth century onwards. The jurisdiction of the Star Chamber facilitated this increase, concerned as it was with politicised proceedings between prominent litigants (Plucknett 1956, 489). Common insults levelled against peers included baseness and treachery (Lassiter 1978, 220). For example, in 1629, the Viscount Saye and Sele received £2,000 in damages against the defendant, Stephens, for being denounced as a traitor and, in 1632, the Earl of Suffolk was awarded £4,000 in damages against Sir Richard Grenville for being called 'a base lord' (*William, Viscount Saye and Sele v Stephens* (1629) Cro Car 135; 79 ER 719; (1629) Ley 82; 80 ER 646; *Earl of Suffolk v Grenville* in Gardiner 1886, 108). The action for *scandalum magnatum*, as one of the privileges of the peers, persisted through the Interregnum and after the Restoration. During Cromwell's protectorate, the Earl of Leicester successfully sued a parson, Mandy, for calling him wicked, cruel and 'an enemy of the Reformation in England' (*Lord of Leicester v Mandy* (1657) 2 Sid 21; 82 ER 1234).

Following the Restoration, the number of actions for *scandalum magnatum* increased significantly as this jurisdiction was integrated into the royal courts' jurisdiction (Lassiter 1978, 225). Even judges commented adversely on the proliferation of suits based on *scandalum magnatum* being brought in the late seventeenth century (*Lord Townshend v Hughes* (1677) 2 Mod 154; 86 ER 997 per Atkyns J). After the Restoration, the action for *scandalum magnatum* was transformed into a political tool, deployed by both Whigs and Tories to pursue their respective political agendas. Litigation, rather than war, became the continuation of politics by other means. For example, the leader of the Whigs, the first Earl of Shaftesbury, successfully sued Lord Digby, the son of a prominent Tory, for claiming that he was 'against the King and for seditions and factions, and for a commonwealth', recovering an award of £1,000 damages (*Earl of Shaftesbury v Lord Digby* (1676) 3 Keble 631; 84 ER 920). The Tory Earl of Peterborough recovered an award of £6,700 damages against the Whig Speaker of the House of Commons, Sir William Williams (*Earl of Peterborough v Williams* (1687) Comb 42; 90 ER 332).

Lassiter suggests that there were several related reasons why actions for *scandalum magnatum* declined in the late seventeenth century. The extensive litigation by James II, when he was the Duke of York, effectively discredited the action for *scandalum magnatum* as a partisan, political tool, deployed vigorously in the defence of the cause of Stuart absolutism (Lassiter 1978, 230; for example *Duke of York v Pilkington* (1682) Skinner 71; 90 ER 34; *Duke of York v Oates* (1684) 10 State Trials 125). (During the period between 1682 and 1684, the Duke of York brought at least ten claims for *scandalum magnatum* against various plaintiffs (Lassiter 1978, 229).) Following the Glorious Revolution in 1688, there was no need for nobles to have recourse to such litigation (Lassiter 1978, 230). The judiciary, after the Glorious Revolution, was also less willing to provide remedies to nobles for insulting words (Lassiter 1978, 231–2; see also *Duke of Schomberg v Murrey* (1700) Holt KB 640; 90 ER 1254; (1700) 12 Mod 420; 88 ER 1423). Even before 1688, the courts were attempting to discourage claims for *scandalum magnatum* by declining to award costs to successful plaintiffs (*Earl of Peterborough v Williams* (1687) 2 Show 505; 89 ER 1068). In addition, after the Glorious Revolution, the House of Commons, if not the House of Lords, was willing to pass bills of reversal in relation to decisions which were too favourable to litigating peers (Lassiter 1978, 231). Even though the decisions were not overturned, the intervention of Parliament at least placed pressure on nobles not to sue. Perhaps most important, the developments in the common law of defamation had effectively overtaken and subsumed the substance of the statutory cause of action, rendering reliance on *scandalum magnatum* redundant. Thus, there were few decided cases of *scandalum magnatum* in the eighteenth century, ending in 1773 with the decision in *Earl of Sandwich v Miller* (1773) Lofft 210; 98 ER 614. Notwithstanding that actions for *scandalum magnatum* had fallen into abeyance by the end of the eighteenth century, the statute itself was not repealed until the *Statute Law Revision Act* 1887 (UK) (Lassiter 1978, 233).

Despite the decline of *scandalum magnatum* as an independent, statutory cause of action for defamatory words, the implicit view about the connection between social status, inherent virtue and the right to reputation did not disappear immediately. Rather, it lingered, informing the development of the common law. For example, Blackstone, in his *Commentaries on the Laws of England*, writing in the 1760s, discusses *scandalum magnatum* in his treatment of the law of slander and libel, describing the legislative policy underpinning *scandalum magnatum* thus:

> Words spoken in derogation of a peer, a judge, or other great officer of the realm, which are called *scandalum magnatum*, are held to be still more heinous; and, though they be such as would not be actionable in the case of a common person, yet when spoken in disgrace of such high and respectable characters, they amount to an atrocious injury.... (Blackstone 1768, 123; see also Sheppard 1662, 5; Hudson *c.*1620, 102; Brydall 1704)

It is clear that *scandalum magnatum* reflected a society in which there was a clear nexus between social rank and prominence and good reputation. By suing for *scandalum magnatum*, peers were both affirming a social hierarchy and exposing the challenges being made to that same hierarchy. That social hierarchy changed, and the legitimacy of bringing actions to vindicate reputations based solely on that hierarchy became less tenable. The rise of capitalism and the consequent commodification of reputation severed the nexus between rank and the right to reputation.

The Local Courts

The local courts in England, comprised of the borough courts and the manorial courts, provided an early remedy for defamation (Kiralfy 1951, 117; Milsom 1981, 379; Baker 2002, 22, 436). There were obvious advantages for litigants approaching local courts for a remedy for defamation. Such courts provided quick, cheap justice. Also, a litigant's reputation was located in his or her community, thus a local court would be able to vindicate that litigant's reputation in that same locality. Given the nature of the jurisdiction and the passage of time, it is unsurprising that there is scant evidence for the local courts' jurisdiction over defamation claims. Such evidence as exists for the defamation practice of local courts indicates that there was a tension between the approach adopted by ecclesiastical and royal courts played out in the local courts.

In certain respects, the local courts' disposition of defamation proceedings imitated the ecclesiastical courts (Milsom 1981, 381; Ibbetson 1999, 113). There are cases recorded in which a litigant claimed that the alleged defamer had accused him or her of a *crimen*, echoing the requirement of the Constitution *Auctoritate Dei Patris* (*Wyke v Ywon* (1245) 101 SS 31; *Butcher v Smalegrave* (1291) 101 SS 39; *Bychemore v Sanguyner* (1332) 101 SS 53). Likewise, there are cases recorded in which a litigant claims that the alleged defamer had made the accusation false and maliciously (*Ode v Wolston* (1289) 101 SS 37; *Chaplain v Shepherd* (1315) 101 SS 46; *Boghelegh v Edward* (1320) 101 SS 49; *Bychemore v Sanguyner* (1332) 101 SS 53). There are also cases recorded in which a litigant claims that his or her reputation has been traduced amongst good and substantial persons (*apud bonos et graves*) (*Otewy v Dallynge* (1309) 101 SS 44; *Porter v Davy* (1332) 101 SS 52). Importantly, there are cases recorded in which a litigant seeks the excommunication of the alleged defamer (*Boghelegh v Edward* (1320) 101 SS 49). However, these cases all depart from the ecclesiastical courts' treatment of defamation in a significant respect, namely the local courts were willing to award damages as a remedy to a successful litigant – a deficiency the royal courts were later to overcome.

However, the local jurisdiction seems to have disappeared in the fourteenth century, presumably out of deference for the common law position that mere words were not actionable (Baker 2002, 436; Ibbetson 1999, 113). The clearest example is provided by the case of *Chaplain v Shepherd* (1315) 101 SS 46. In this case, Richard, the chaplain of the chapel of Palgrave, claimed that Geoffrey Shepherd had lied before the sheriff's tourn, telling it that the chaplain had wounded a man. The manor court of Redgrave, Suffolk, denied the chaplain's claim, stating that 'for wind no action should accrue'. A further example is provided by *Lumyner v Wylde* (1285) 101 SS 33, in which the injured party, Nicholas de Lumyner, complained that Richard de Wylde, insulted him with 'opprobrious' words, thereby causing him unspecified damage. The borough court of Ipswich dismissed the claim because Lumyner complained of being attacked 'with words and with nothing else'. Again, in *Snel v Aylse* (1325) 101 SS 51, the manor court of Hatfield Chase, Yorkshire, found that Peter of Aylse had defamed Jordan Snel by claiming that Snel had disturbed the King's agistment but that, as Snel had suffered no pecuniary loss, he should recover no damages from Peter of Aylse.

Significantly, however, the local courts' jurisdiction over defamation claims prefigured the way in which the royal courts eventually began to deal with defamation, namely by making damage the gist of the action. There are several examples of cases decided by local courts in which a defamatory statement which caused a claimant pecuniary loss sounded in damages (*Engham v Burton* (1287) 101 SS 35; *Curteys v Poyfoy* (1289) 101 SS 38; *Geyst v Dunwich* (1292) 101 SS 40; *Angle v Sweyn* (1300) 101 SS 41; *Wakefield v Brownsmith* (1306–08) 101 SS 43; *Otewy v Dallynge* (1309) 101 SS 44; *Clerk v Ode* (1315) 101 SS 45; *Smith v Norman* (1318) 101 SS 48; *Porter v Davy* (1332) 101 SS 52; *Wetwang v Isabelle* (1339) 101 SS 54).

Given the nature of the local jurisdiction, it is unsurprising that no clear, consistent principles of defamation law emerged from it and consequently no clear identification of reputational interests. However, such case law as does exist from the local courts in the thirteenth and fourteenth centuries indicates that there was a tension between the divergent approaches adopted by the ecclesiastical and the royal courts of the time, which the local courts attempted to mediate and complement. This tension sought to balance the need to discourage the spreading of lies, to provide a forum and a remedy for aggrieved persons whilst retaining a suspicion about the real damage that 'mere words' could have, in the absence of actual, pecuniary loss.

Conclusion

The English law of defamation had a variegated history. The ecclesiastical courts, the Star Chamber, the local courts, statute and ultimately the royal courts all contributed to the development of the law of defamation. Given these diverse origins, it is unsurprising that a variety of distinct reputational interests were afforded protection.

The ecclesiastical courts provided protection not only for the honour of litigants – the public, moral *opinio* – but also provided protection explicitly based on rank. The statutory cause of action for *scandalum magnatum* also facilitated the preservation of rank as a reputational interest. The common law's refusal to recognise defamation until around 1500 is telling. When the common law began to recognise claims for defamation in the sixteenth century, the royal courts required proof of actual harm as a consequence of insulting or injurious words. The royal courts conceived of reputation as a form of goodwill, a piece of personal property, which could be harmed and healed in economic terms. Assimilating the former ecclesiastical jurisdiction and later the peculiar jurisdiction of the Star Chamber, the common law also attempted to continue to provide relief for reputational interests based on honour and rank.

Because of the diverse origins of defamation law and consequently the variety of reputational interests protected, it is understandable that there is no unitary concept of reputation in contemporary Australian defamation law. Yet, judges and academics still refer to the concept of 'reputation' as being the central interest protected by defamation.

This tends to understate the importance of social changes on the meaning and content of reputation historically. Reputation should not be viewed as an immutable concept. The law of defamation originated in a feudal society; its basic principles crystallised at a time when capitalism and liberal democracy were in their infancy. Reputation as rank had declined in importance during this period, whilst reputation as property has emerged as an important, new dynamic in the development of the law of defamation. Historically, the concept of reputation had already adapted somewhat to accommodate these social changes.

The concept of reputation also responded to changes in modes of communication. At its inception, the law of defamation provided a remedy for oral slanders uttered within local communities. Reputations and the damage done to them by injurious words could be closely circumscribed. The development of the printing press and the exponential increase in its use created further opportunities for individuals to create their reputation and for defamers to denigrate them. Beyond the printing press, the nineteenth and especially the twentieth centuries saw the development of electronic means of communication – radio, film, television and the Internet, to name but a few. These, in turn, generated even greater opportunities for the creation of, and damage to, reputations. This historical analysis, indicating the confluence of social and media changes and their impact on the concept of reputation, provides the background for the future development of the tort of defamation, which will be discussed in a later chapter – the emergence of reputation as celebrity. It remains to be seen how adequately defamation law, particularly the central concept of reputation, has developed to accommodate these profound social and technological changes, which are characteristic of the contemporary world.

Chapter 3

The Basic Principles of Liability for Defamation: Meaning, Publication, Identification and Damages

Introduction

Historically, then, there have been different reputational interests afforded protection by defamation law. Accordingly, it is unsurprising that the basic principles of liability for defamation law also embody different concepts of reputation. In subsequent chapters, the ways in which these concepts of reputation manifest themselves in practice will be analysed through a series of case studies. However, as the essential background to these case studies, it is necessary to examine the principles underpinning liability for defamation – namely, defamatory capacity and meaning; identification; and publication. This chapter will examine those principles and will also explore the purposes for which defamation damages are awarded. The focus of this chapter will not be solely on the elucidation of the relevant principles but more particularly on how these principles themselves manifest and reinforce competing concepts of reputation.

Defamatory Capacity and Meaning[1]

In order for a defendant to be held liable for the publication of a matter, a judge must find that the matter is capable of conveying a defamatory meaning of and concerning the plaintiff and a jury must find that the matter does in fact convey a defamatory meaning.[2] The questions of defamatory capacity and meaning are

1 As to the issue of defamatory capacity and meaning generally, see Tobin and Sexton 1991, [3001]ff; Carter-Ruck and Starte 1997, Ch. 4; Gillooly 1998, Ch. 3; Milmo and Rogers (eds) 2004, Chs 2 and 3; Price and Duodu 2004, 2-13-2-23; George 2006, Ch. 9.

2 As to the respective roles of judge and jury in a defamation action, see *Nevill v Fine Art and General Insurance Co* [1897] AC 68 at 72 per Lord Halsbury LC; *Jones v Skelton* [1964] NSWR 485 at 491 per Lord Morris of Borth-y-Gest; *Farquhar v Bottom* [1980] 2 NSWLR 380 at 385 per Hunt J; *Lloyd v David Syme & Co Ltd* (1985) 3 NSWLR 728 at 729 *per curiam*; *Safeway Stores plc v Tate* [2001] QB 1120 at 1130; [2001] 4 All ER 193 per Otton LJ.

therefore the first threshold of liability for defamation. As Walker has emphasised, it is important to distinguish between the tests for defamatory meaning and the concept of reputation (Walker 2000, [3.8.4]). The tests for defamatory meaning are not themselves definitions of reputation but they may, however, illuminate the underlying concepts of reputation.

The tests for defamatory meaning are well-known. The starting-point for this issue is generally considered to be Parke B's judgment in *Parmiter v Coupland* (1840) 6 M & W 104; 151 ER 340. According to Parke B, a publication is defamatory if it is 'calculated to injure the reputation of another, by exposing him to hatred, contempt, or ridicule' ((1840) 6 M & W 104 at 108; 151 ER 340 at 342). It is important to note at the outset that the test is not whether the defamatory matter actually exposed the plaintiff to hatred, contempt or ridicule but rather whether it had the tendency to do so ((1840) 6 M & W 104 at 108; 151 ER 340 at 342 per Parke B; *Capital and Counties Bank v Henty* (1882) 7 App Cas 741 at 768 per Lord Penzance, at 775 per Lord Blackburn).

The exposure of a plaintiff then to hatred or contempt appears to fit most closely with the concept of reputation as honour, in the sense of publicly mediated morality (as to the concept of reputation as honour, see Chapter 1). It entails a social assessment of the plaintiff's conduct or personal characteristics as hateful or contemptible. By contrast, to expose a plaintiff to ridicule appears to be most consistent with the concept of reputation as dignity (as to the concept of reputation as dignity, see Chapter 1). Rather than exposing the plaintiff as the proper object of hatred or contempt, unjustifiably portraying the plaintiff as a figure of ridicule seems designed to attack the plaintiff's subjective sense of self. The defamatory quality of ridicule has proven to be a particularly fertile, and problematic, area of contemporary Australian defamation law. It is important to note, therefore, that even within the *locus classicus* of defamatory meaning, there are manifest at least two distinct concepts of reputation.

However, Parke B's formulation has been criticised for being couched in overly strong, emotive terms (Cottrell 1998, 151) and, more importantly, for being too narrow, failing to encapsulate adequately the range of publications that have been found defamatory (see generally *John Fairfax & Sons Ltd v Punch* (1980) 31 ALR 624; (1980) 47 FLR 458 at 467 per Brennan J). In *Youssoupoff v Metro-Goldwyn-Mayer Pictures Ltd* (1934) 50 TLR 581 at 584, Scrutton LJ claimed that Parke B's formulation in *Parmiter v Coupland* was too narrow, instead expressing his own preference for Cave J's general test in *Scott v Sampson* (1882) 8 QBD 491 at 503 of 'a false statement about a man to his discredit' (see also *Tournier v National Provincial Union Bank of England Ltd* [1924] 1 KB 461 at 477). More influentially, as an alternative, in *Sim v Stretch* [1936] 2 All ER 1237 at 1240, Atkin LJ suggested a broader test for defamatory meaning, encompassing the publication of defamatory matter that tended to lower the plaintiff in the estimation of right-thinking people generally (see also *Tournier v National Provincial Union Bank of England Ltd* [1924] 1 KB 461 at 486–7). This test for defamatory meaning is also clearly premised on the concept of reputation as honour. It seeks to assess the plaintiff's reputation by reference to the 'normative standards of personal conduct' (Post 1986, 701).

According to Prosser and Keeton, the unifying element of the tests for defamatory meaning is 'the idea of disgrace', clearly suggesting that reputation is a form of honour (Keeton et al. 1984, 773). Yet the extent to which the notion of disgrace informs the tests for defamatory meaning should not be overstated. Whilst it may be stated that there is generally a requirement of disparagement as an essential element of defamatory meaning (*Sungravure Pty Ltd v Middle East Airlines Airliban SAL* (1975) 134 CLR 1 at 9–11 per Gibbs J, at 23–4 per Mason J; *Boyd v Mirror Newspapers Ltd* [1980] 2 NSWLR 449 at 452–3 per Hunt J. See also Watterson 1993, 812 (defamation directed at plaintiff's personal, not physical, characteristics); Bar-Am 2000, 307 (traditional tests for defamatory meaning moralistic)), there are also recognised categories of defamatory imputations that have no such requirement. For instance, the publication of matter that tends to make others shun and avoid the plaintiff even though it does not suggest any 'moral discredit' on the plaintiff's part, nonetheless satisfies the test for defamatory meaning (*Boyd v Mirror Newspapers Ltd* [1980] 2 NSWLR 449 at 452–3 per Hunt J; *Berkoff v Burchill* [1996] 4 All ER 1008 at 1013 per Neill LJ, at 1020 per Phillips LJ). Thus, in *Youssoupoff v Metro-Goldwyn-Mayer Pictures Ltd* (see generally Bar-Am, 2000), the English Court of Appeal found that an imputation of rape or seduction was capable of being defamatory because, notwithstanding the fact that it did not disparage the plaintiff's character, it would tend to lead to others shunning and avoiding her. Giving the leading judgment on the test of shunning and avoiding, Slesser LJ reasoned that this notion of defamatory character necessarily underpinned imputations of insanity and certain types of infectious disease that the common law had long held to be defamatory. In relation to allegations of rape or seduction made against a woman, his Lordship asserted that, as a matter of judicial notice, he could consider the fact that such a woman would be injured 'in social reputation and in opportunities of receiving respectful consideration from the world' ((1934) 50 TLR 581 at 587). Whether this case would be decided in the same way in contemporary Australia, and would be justified in the same way, is, somewhat surprisingly, the subject of divided authority (compare *Krahe v T.C.N. Channel Nine Pty Ltd* (1986) 4 NSWLR 536 at 546 per Hunt J; *Galea v Amalgamated Television Services Pty Ltd* (unreported, SC(NSW), No. 20747/97, Levine J, 20 February 1998) at 12–13. See also Faulks Committee 1975, Appendix V, [7]–[8] (recommendation for abolition of 'shun and avoid' standard)).

The use of shunning and avoiding as a test for defamatory meaning clearly proceeds on the basis of a concept of reputation as honour. Accepting that a plaintiff's reputation is constructed and experienced socially, the criterion of shunning and avoiding focuses upon the adverse impact of the publication of a defamatory matter on an individual's relationship to his or her society. Yet it does not entail an assessment of the plaintiff's failure to satisfy the 'normative standards of personal conduct' (Post 1986, 701). It is not ultimately a judgment of publicly or socially mediated morality. Rather, it is more a recognition of the real possibility that the plaintiff's social exclusion or ostracism, following the publication of defamatory matter with the tendency to make others shun and avoid him or her, necessarily has an adverse impact on the plaintiff's sense of self. In this way, then, the test of shunning and avoiding also partly reflects reputation as dignity.

In Parke B's formulation of defamatory meaning in *Parmiter v Coupland*, ridicule is expressly mentioned. Ridicule as a basis for defamatory meaning is well-established in the common law, dating back to at least the seventeenth century (see, for example, *Cropp v Tilney* (1693) 3 Salk 225 at 226; 90 ER 1132 at 1132 per Holt CJ). Whilst the tests for defamatory meaning generally are problematic, Phillips LJ has suggested that the test of ridicule itself is 'too elusive to encapsulate in any definition' (*Berkoff v Burchill* [1996] 4 All ER 1008 at 1021). Whatever the difficulty in defining ridicule, the defamatory character of ridicule is recognisably different to other tests for defamatory meaning. To expose a plaintiff to ridicule does not necessarily suggest that the plaintiff is morally blameworthy or discreditable. Thus, the publication of a matter that exposes the plaintiff to more than a trivial degree of ridicule has been held to be defamatory, notwithstanding the fact that it does not disparage the plaintiff's character.[3] Unlike hatred and contempt, ridicule is more directed towards the plaintiff's subjective reaction to the publication. As Hand J observed in *Burton v Crowell Publishing Co* 82 F (2d) 154 (1936) at 156 in relation to the defamatory quality of ridicule, '[t]he gravamen of the wrong in defamation is not so much the injury to reputation, measured by the opinion of others, as the feelings, that is, the repulsion or the light esteem, which those opinions engender.' By exposing a plaintiff to ridicule, a defendant diminishes the plaintiff's sense of self. As such, it principally attacks the plaintiff's reputation as a part of his or her dignity (see, for example, *Cook v Ward* (1830) 6 Bing 409 at 415–16; 130 ER 1138 at 1341 per Tindal CJ; *Dolby v Newnes* (1887) 3 TLR 393 at 394 per Stephen J).

There are a number of recent Australian cases dealing with exposure to ridicule that provide evidence for an understanding of reputation as dignity in Australian law, including a disproportionate amount of litigation equating exposure of the plaintiff's body with exposure to ridicule. In *Ettingshausen v Australian Consolidated Press Ltd* (1991) 23 NSWLR 443 (for a discussion of the *Ettingshausen* litigation, see Chapter 7), a national magazine published a photograph of a prominent rugby

3 *Dunlop Rubber Co v Dunlop* [1921] 1 AC 367 at 370 per Lord Birkenhead LC; *Burton v Crowell Publishing Co* (1936) 82 F (2d) 154 at 156 per Hand J; *Zbyszko v New York American Inc* 239 NYS 411 (1930) at 413 per McAvoy J; *Boyd v Mirror Newspapers Ltd* [1980] 2 NSWLR 449 at 453 per Hunt J; *Berkoff v Burchill* [1996] 4 All ER 1008 at 1013 per Neill LJ, at 1021 per Phillips LJ; *Brander v Ryan* (2000) 78 SASR 234; (2001) Aust Torts Reports ¶81-593 at 66,547–8 per Lander J. As to the requirement of more than a trivial degree of ridicule, see *Charleston v News Group Newspapers Ltd* [1995] 2 AC 65 at 69 per Lord Bridge of Harwich; *Norman v Future Publishing Ltd* [1999] EMLR 325 at 332 per Hirst LJ, at 332, 334 per Peter Gibson LJ.

league player naked under the showers after a match. The prominence of the plaintiff and the trials' attendant publicity undoubtedly inspired or encouraged subsequent plaintiffs to bring their actions. In *Shepherd v Walsh* [2001] QSC 358 (for a discussion of the *Shepherd v Walsh* litigation, see Chapter 7), the *Picture* magazine, best described as 'soft-core pornography' (*Obermann v ACP Publishing Pty Ltd* [2001] NSWSC 1022 at [4] per Simpson J) reproduced a nude photograph of the female plaintiff sent to it by the plaintiff's disgruntled ex-boyfriend and accompanied it with a spurious, suggestive interview. In *Haines v Australian Broadcasting Corporation* (unreported, SC(NSW), No. 19417/93, Levine J, 9 May 1995), the plaintiff accountant complained of a documentary screened twice by the defendant network in which he was shown, from the back only, posing nude for prominent Australian artist, Donald Friend. In *McDonald v The North Queensland Newspaper Co. Ltd* [1997] 1 Qd R 62, a local newspaper published two photographs, including one on the front page, of the plaintiff rugby league player, in which his penis was partially exposed during a tackle. In *Obermann v A.C.P. Publishing Pty Ltd*, the *Picture* magazine published a photograph of the plaintiff water polo player, in which her breasts were accidentally exposed during the course of a match. In all of these cases, relying on the precedent set by the pleading in *Ettingshausen*, the plaintiffs submitted that they had been defamed because the defendants' photographic exposure of their bodies, in varying states of undress, had exposed them to more than a trivial degree of ridicule. It is not imperative for a plaintiff's body to be exposed in order for a plaintiff to be able to claim that he or she has been portrayed in a ridiculous light. For example, in *Wild v John Fairfax Publications Pty Ltd* (unreported, SC(NSW), No. 20395/97, Levine J, 8 August 1997), the male plaintiff complained that a photograph of him standing in front of and looking at a billboard bearing an advertisement for women's lingerie exposed him to ridicule as a sexist and a voyeur. Again, in *Darbyshir v Daily Examiner Pty Ltd* (unreported, SC(NSW), No. 21467.96, Levine J, 29 August 1997), the plaintiff solicitor claimed that she had been defamed by a cartoon in the local newspaper which depicted her as a vulture. Over the last decade, Australian defamation law has been willing to provide redress for plaintiffs who claim that they have been portrayed in a ridiculous light (Watterson 1993, 818). As such, it has allowed them to attempt to assuage their wounded dignity.

Given that defamation law protects professional, as well as personal, reputations, it is unsurprising that there are tests for defamatory meaning which encode a notion of reputation as property (as to the concept of reputation as property, see Chapter 1). The common law, however, draws a distinction between imputations that reflect adversely upon the plaintiff's reputation in his or her conduct of the business, profession or trade and imputations that merely tend to injure the plaintiff's business, profession or trade. Only the former category of imputations is capable of being defamatory. Such imputations must suggest that the plaintiff possesses a detrimental quality or lacks an essential quality for the conduct of his or her business, profession or trade (Milmo and Rogers (eds) 2004, [2.26]). For instance, if a matter alleges that a person is incompetent or incapable of performing his or her office or vocation, it may be considered defamatory. There is no additional requirement of disparagement in respect of such imputations.[4] In this way, defamation law recognises that a plaintiff's professional reputation is an asset that can be damaged and therefore deserves protection. However, in order for other allegations against professional reputation to be defamatory, it is insufficient that their publication merely injure the plaintiff's profession or trade (*Sungravure Pty Ltd v Middle East Airlines SAL* (1975) 134 CLR 1 at 23 per Mason J; *Dawson Bloodstock Agency v Mirror Newspapers Ltd* [1979] 1 NSWLR 16 at 18 per Begg J). Therefore, at common law, whilst the tests for defamatory meaning accept that there is a concept of reputation as property, such a concept does not wholly explain it. There is necessarily involved an element of reputation as honour. The notion of a profession itself conveys something more than simply a job; it conveys moral and ethical duties and obligations imposed on and undertaken by the plaintiff in his or her capacity as a professional person in addition to the performance of the tasks that form the substance of the role. Consequently, a professional reputation cannot be understood in purely proprietary terms; there is an additional element of honour (for a discussion of professional reputation, see Chapter 4).

Whichever of these tests for defamatory meaning is applied, the application requires reference to the hypothetical referee of defamation law, the 'ordinary, reasonable reader'. The 'ordinary, reasonable reader' is an integral part of the test for defamatory meaning. Whether a publication is likely to expose a plaintiff to hatred, contempt or ridicule, is likely to lead to a plaintiff being shunned or avoided, is likely to lower the plaintiff in the estimation of others, is determined by reference to the objective standard of 'the ordinary, reasonable reader'. As with the tests for determining defamatory meaning, the identification of the hypothetical referee has been variously articulated. He or she is usefully characterised by Hunt J in *Farquhar v Bottom* [1980] 2 NSWLR 380:

> [T]he ordinary reasonable reader is a person of fair, average intelligence … who is neither perverse … nor morbid or suspicious of mind … nor avid for scandal … This ordinary reasonable reader does not, we are told, live in an ivory tower. He can, and does, read between the lines, in the light of his general knowledge and experience of worldly affairs … It is important to bear in mind that the ordinary reasonable reader is a

4 *Capital and Counties Bank Ltd v George Henty & Sons* (1882) 7 App Cas 741 at 762 per Lord Penzance, at 771 per Lord Blackburn; *Alexander v Jenkins* [1892] 1 QB 797 at 800 per Lord Herschell; *South Hetton Coal Co v North-Eastern News Association Ltd* [1894] 1 QB 133 at 139 per Lord Esher MR; *Tournier v National Provincial and Union Bank of England* [1924] 1 KB 461 at 477 per Scrutton LJ; *Pratten v Labour Daily Mail Ltd* [1926] VLR 115 at 118 per Cussen J; *Drummond-Jackson v British Medical Association* [1970] 1 All ER 1094 at 1104; [1970] 1 WLR 688 per Lord Pearson; *Potts v Moran* (1976) 16 SASR 284 at 302 per Bray CJ; *John Fairfax & Sons Ltd v Punch* (1980) 31 ALR 624; (1980) 47 FLR 458 at 464 per Blackburn and Northrop JJ, at 467–9 per Brennan J; *John Fairfax Publications Pty Ltd v Gacic* (2007) 235 ALR 402 at 404 per Gleeson CJ and Crennan J, at 451 per Callinan and Heydon JJ; cf. at 422–4 per Kirby J.

> layman, not a lawyer, and that his capacity for implication is much greater than that of a lawyer. (At 385–6 (footnotes omitted). See also *Lewis v Daily Telegraph Ltd* [1964] AC 234 at 259–60 per Lord Reid)

The judge, when assessing the defamatory capacity of an imputation, and the jury, when assessing whether the imputation is in fact conveyed and is in fact defamatory, apply the test of the 'ordinary, reasonable reader'. In doing so, as Brennan J makes clear in his influential judgment in *Reader's Digest Services Pty Ltd v Lamb* (1982) 150 CLR 500 at 506, both the judge and jury proceed on the basis that there is embodied in the 'ordinary, reasonable reader' not only a uniform view on the meaning of the language of the defamatory meaning but also a shared moral and social standard that is common to society generally. Moreover, the shared moral and social standard is not a matter about which evidence may be adduced. It is considered to be a matter for the jury to determine in its representative capacity.

The 'ordinary, reasonable reader' therefore embodies and reflects what Lord Atkin describes as 'right-thinking members of society generally' (*Sim v Stretch* [1936] 2 All ER 1237 at 1240), what Jordan CJ describes as 'ordinary decent folk in the community, taken in general' (*Gardiner v John Fairfax & Sons Pty Ltd* (1942) 42 SR(NSW) 171 at 172; *Consolidated Trust Co Ltd v Browne* (1948) 49 SR(NSW) 86 at 88; see also *Boyd v Mirror Newspapers Ltd* [1980] 2 NSWLR 449 at 452 per Hunt J), what Griffith CJ describes as 'a man of fair average intelligence' (*Slatyer v Daily Telegraph Newspaper Co Ltd* (1908) 6 CLR 1 at 7), what Lord Reid describes as 'an ordinary man, not avid for scandal' (*Lewis v Daily Telegraph Ltd* [1964] AC 234 at 260) and what Lord Selborne calls fundamentally 'reasonable men' (*Capital and Counties Bank v Henty* (1882) LR 7 App Cas 741 at 745. See also *Nevill v Fine Art & General Insurance Co Ltd* [1897] AC 68 at 72–3 per Lord Halsbury LC. See further *Byrne v Deane* [1937] 1 KB 818 at 833 per Slesser LJ: '*arbitrium boni*' or 'the ordinary good and worthy subject of the king'). Notwithstanding the various articulations of the shared moral and social standard, it is clear that the tests of defamatory meaning reaffirm the fundamentally social nature of the tort of defamation. Moreover, they encode a notion of reputation as honour, engaging the judge and later the jury in an assessment of the plaintiff by reference to 'normative standards of personal conduct' (Post 1986, 701).

The concept of the 'ordinary, reasonable reader' reflecting 'right-thinking members of society generally' or 'ordinary decent folk' proceeds on the basis that there is a uniform moral and social standard, a claim that seems difficult to defend in modern, pluralistic societies. The contentious nature of imputations of adultery, pre-marital sex, 'unchastity' (as to imputations of 'unchastity', see Chapter 5), homosexuality (as to imputations of homosexuality, see Chapter 6) and public nudity (as to imputations involving the defamatory character of displays of public nudity, see Chapter 7) gesture towards this difficulty.

However, there have been circumstances in which defamation law has been willing to acknowledge these limitations and protect sectional standards within the community. Thus, in *Hepburn v T.C.N. Channel Nine Pty Ltd* [1983] 2 NSWLR 682, Glass JA acknowledged that, in a pluralist society, there are a range of issues over which citizens may differ widely, citing abortion (at 693), uranium mining and state funding of private schools (at 694) as three examples. his Honour accepted that it may be defamatory to ascribe to the plaintiff a view that 'an appreciable and reputable section of the community' would agree was defamatory, even though the same view might 'exalt him to the level of a hero in other quarters' (at 694). In *Hepburn*, the New South Wales Court of Appeal found that, even though social views were shifting on abortion, an imputation that the plaintiff was an abortionist was capable of being defamatory because at least 'an appreciable and reputable section of the community' would consider it thus (at 694). It should be noted that the 'sectional standard' test articulated in *Hepburn* has not been widely applied in Australia.

Exploring how courts construct a notion of community in order to determine the standard to be applied by the 'ordinary, reasonable reader', Lidsky suggests that the US counterpart of the sectional standard test, the 'substantial and respectable minority' test, 'has a curiously modern ring to it' (Lidsky 1996, 7). It does, as Lidsky observes, at least ostensibly reflect the pluralistic nature of contemporary Western societies (Lidsky 1996, 7). However, in its application, the 'sectional standard' test for defamatory capacity and meaning has arguably led to conservative outcomes. *Hepburn* is itself an example of this. There is therefore a difference between an acknowledgement of the pluralistic nature of society in the test for defamatory capacity and meaning and the promotion or enforcement of the values underpinning a pluralistic society by the same means.

Whether applying a uniform social or moral standard or a sectional one, there is nevertheless a live issue as to whether judges, in determining issues of defamatory capacity, should, and juries, in determining issues of defamatory meaning, do adopt an idealistic or a realistic view of the community to which they belong – with real consequences for defamation plaintiffs (see, for example, *Hepburn v T.C.N. Channel Nine Pty Ltd* [1983] 2 NSWLR 682 at 694 per Glass JA. See also Lidsky 1996, 9).

It is clear that there is no single, satisfactory test for determining defamatory meaning (see, for example, *Berkoff v Burchill* [1996] 4 All ER 1008 at 1011 per Neill LJ. See further Carter-Ruck and Starte 1997, 37; Milmo and Rogers (eds) 2004, [2.1]). As Cottrell observes, the reason that there is no single test for defamatory meaning is because the common law has never clarified what defamation law actually protects and why (Cottrell 1998, 150–51) – that is, it has never clarified what it means by 'reputation'. As a result, the various tests for defamatory meaning encode different notions of reputation. In light of the historical development of defamation law, it becomes more understandable why there is no single test for defamation meaning, namely because defamation law, as it developed, provided protection for different reputational interests in different jurisdictions, never settling upon a unitary conception of reputation (as to the historical development of the concept of reputation, see generally Chapter 2).

The Requirement of Publication[5]

It is well-established that, for the purposes of the common law of defamation, publication is an essential requirement of liability (*Toomey v Mirror Newspapers Ltd* (1985) 1 NSWLR 73 at 77 per Hunt J; *Dow Jones & Co Inc v Gutnick* (2002) 210 CLR 575 at 639; 194 ALR 433; 77 ALJR 255; Aust Torts Reports ¶81-682 per Kirby J). However, for the purposes of defamation law, the term, 'publication', is used in a specialised sense. In lay terms, a publication might refer to a physical object, such as a newspaper or a book. In defamation law, these are not so much publications themselves as 'vehicles' for publication (*Webb v Bloch* (1928) 41 CLR 331 at 363 per Isaacs J. See also *Toomey v Mirror Newspapers Ltd* (1985) 1 NSWLR 73 at 77 per Hunt J).

For the purposes of defamation law, publication is properly understood as a process. However, it is not merely the process of composing defamatory matter (*Lee v Wilson and Mackinnon* (1934) 51 CLR 276 at 287 per Dixon J; *Dow Jones & Co Inc v Gutnick* (2002) 210 CLR 575 at 639; 194 ALR 433; 77 ALJR 255; Aust Torts Reports ¶81-682 per Kirby J). Rather, in defamation law, the publication of a defamatory matter entails its communication, rather than simply its composition (*Pullman v Walter Hill & Co Ltd* [1891] 1 QB 524 at 527 per Lord Esher MR; *Webb v Bloch* (1928) 41 CLR 331 at 363 per Isaacs J; *Toomey v Mirror Newspapers Ltd* (1985) 1 NSWLR 73 at 77 per Hunt J; *Jones v Amalgamated Television Services Pty Ltd* (1991) 23 NSWLR 365 at 367 per Hunt J). The publication of the defamatory matter to the plaintiff only is insufficient; the defendant must communicate the defamatory matter to a third party (*Pullman v Walter Hill & Co Ltd* [1891] 1 QB 524 at 527 per Lord Esher MR, at 529 per Lopes LJ; *Toomey v Mirror Newspapers Ltd* (1985) 1 NSWLR 73 at 77 per Hunt J; *Jones v Amalgamated Television Services Pty Ltd* (1991) 23 NSWLR 365 at 367 per Hunt J). Given that reputation is comprehended as a social phenomenon, not a purely personal or private interest, no damage to the plaintiff's reputation, so defined, would result from a publication only to the plaintiff. No one would think less of the plaintiff or shun or avoid the plaintiff as a result of a publication made only to the plaintiff (*Lee v Wilson and Mackinnon* (1934) 51 CLR 276 at 287 per Dixon J). However, the requirement of publication in defamation law does not demand that a defamatory matter be widely disseminated. It is sufficient that the defamatory matter is published to only one person other than the plaintiff (*Capital and Counties Bank v Henty* (1882) 7 App Cas 741 at 765 per Lord Penzance; *Consolidated Trust Co Ltd v Browne* (1948) 49 SR(NSW) 86 at 89 per Jordan CJ). Once the fact of publication has been established, the extent of publication is relevant not to liability but to the assessment of damages (*John v Mirror Group Newspapers* [1997] QB 586 at 607 *per curiam*; Gillooly 1998, 74).

---

5 As to the requirement of publication generally, see Tobin and Sexton, 1991, [5001]ff; Carter-Ruck and Starte 1997, Ch. 6; Gillooly 1998, Ch. 5; Milmo and Rogers (eds) 2004, Ch. 6; Price and Duodu 2004, Ch. 3; George 2006, Ch. 7.

The common law of defamation has further refined the requirements of reputation. Publication entails communication of a defamatory matter. This means that the defamatory matter must be conveyed to a third party in a comprehensible form. The third party needs to be able to understand the defamatory impact of the matter, otherwise no harm is done to the plaintiff's reputation (*Dow Jones & Co Inc v Gutnick* (2002) 210 CLR 575 at 600; 194 ALR 433; 77 ALJR 255; Aust Torts Reports ¶81-682 per Gleeson CJ, McHugh, Gummow and Hayne JJ).

This element of comprehension by a third party, as part of the requirement of publication, underpins the principles relating to the publication of innuendoes. If a matter is not self-evidently defamatory but would be defamatory to persons with knowledge of extrinsic facts, the matter is only published if the plaintiff can prove its communication to one or more such persons (*Consolidated Trust Co Ltd v Browne* (1948) 49 SR(NSW) 86 at 89 per Jordan CJ). Likewise, if a matter does not identify the plaintiff, the matter is only published if the plaintiff can prove its communication to one or more persons who would have identified him or her from the matter.

The element of comprehension as part of publication also informs the principles relating to the publication of defamatory matter in a foreign language. If a defamatory matter is conveyed to a recipient in a language with which that recipient is not familiar, there has been no effective publication because the defamatory matter is not comprehensible to the recipient (*Jones v Davers* (1597) Cro Eliz 496; 78 ER 747; *Price v Jenkings* (1601) Cro Eliz 865; 78 ER 1091; *Amann v Damm* (1860) 8 CB (NS) 595; 141 ER 1300; *Fullam v Newcastle Chronicle & Journal* [1977] 3 All ER 32; [1977] 1 WLR 651 at 657–8 per Scarman LJ).

It also underscores the principles relating to interspousal and internal corporate communications. If husband and wife are considered a single entity, then it may be that a communication from husband to wife (or *vice versa*) of defamatory matter may not satisfy the requirement of publication for defamation law (as to the issue of publication in the context of interspousal communications, see *Wennhak v Morgan* (1888) 20 QBD 637 at 637 per Huddleston B, at 639 per Manisty J. Cf. *Tanner v Miles* [1912] QWN 7; [1912] QLR 7. See also *Consolidated Trust Co Ltd v Browne* (1948) 49 SR(NSW) 86 at 88 per Jordan CJ. See further Milmo and Rogers (eds) 2004, [6.6]). Equally, it may be that the conveying of defamatory matter to an employee or an agent of a corporate entity is not a publication for the purposes of defamation law.[6]

6 As to the issue of publication in the context of internal corporate communications, see *Pullman v Walter Hill & Co Ltd* [1891] 1 QB 524 at 527 per Lord Esher MR, at 529 per Lopes LJ; *Riddick v Thames Board Mills Ltd* [1977] QB 881 at 895 per Lord Denning MR, at 901 per Stephenson LJ, at 907 per Waller LJ; *Traztand Pty Ltd v Government Insurance Office of New South Wales* [1984] 2 NSWLR 598 at 599–600; (1985) Aust Torts Reports ¶80-743 per Hunt J; *Jones v Amalgamated Television Services Pty Ltd* (1991) 23 NSWLR 364 at 366; Aust Torts Reports ¶81-107 per Hunt J; *State Bank of New South Wales Ltd v*

Once the defamatory matter is communicated to a third party in a comprehensible form, the requirement of publication is satisfied. There is no additional requirement that the third party actually understand the defamatory impact of the matter in the way contended for by the plaintiff (*Hough v London Express Newspaper Ltd* [1940] 2 KB 507 at 514 per Slesser LJ, at 515 per Goddard LJ; *Van Riet v A C P Publishing Pty Ltd* [2004] 1 Qd R 194 at 200–201 per McMurdo P and Jerrard JA). Indeed, the third party may know that the imputation is false (*Hough v London Express Newspaper Ltd* [1940] 2 KB 507 at 515 per Goddard LJ; *Morgan v Odhams Press Ltd* [1971] 1 WLR 1239; [1971] 2 All ER 1156 at 1163 per Lord Reid, at 1168 per Lord Morris of Borth-y-gest; *Barbaro v Amalgamated Television Services Pty Ltd* (1985) 1 NSWLR 30 at 37 per Hunt J). This is consistent with the principle that defamation law proscribes matters with a tendency to cause harm to reputation, rather than matters that actually cause harm (*Parmiter v Coupland* (1840) 6 M & W 104 at 108; 151 ER 340 at 342 per Parke B; *Capital and Counties Bank v Henty* (1882) 7 App Cas 741 at 768 per Lord Penzance, at 775 per Lord Blackburn).

Thus, the requirement of publication, at a very basic level, affirms the fundamentally social nature of reputation and the tort of defamation more generally (See, for example, Spencer Bower 1990, 258; Pound 1915, 448; Gillooly 1998, 74; Milmo and Rogers (eds) 2004, [6.1]).

Publication can be effected through an infinite variety of media or, to adopt Isaacs J's terminology, vehicles (*Webb v Bloch* (1928) 41 CLR 331 at 363 per Isaacs J. See also *Toomey v Mirror Newspapers Ltd* (1985) 1 NSWLR 73 at 77 per Hunt J). The national, uniform defamation laws in Australia do not define the term, 'publication' itself but do define the 'matter' that can be published and do so broadly and inclusively.[7] The case law also recognises the multifarious ways in which defamatory matter may be published. Publication may be achieved through spoken word,[8] gesture (*Cook v Cox* (1814) 3 M & S 110 at 114; 105 ER 552 per Lord Ellenborough CJ; *Gutsole v Mathers* (1836) 1 M & W 495 at 501), conduct (*Gregory v Duke of Brunswick* (1843) 6 M & Gr 953 (hissing in theatre); *Jefferies v Duncombe* (1809) 2 Camp 3; 103 ER 991 (placing a lamp outside plaintiff's house during night to designate place as brothel)), newspaper, book, magazine, periodical

---

Currabubula Holdings Pty Ltd (2001) 51 NSWLR 399 at 414–15; Aust Torts Reports ¶81-618 per Giles JA. See also Milmo and Rogers (eds) 2004, [6.7]–[6.8].

7 *Civil Law (Wrongs) Act* 2002 (ACT) s 116; *Defamation Act* 2006 (NT) s 3; *Defamation Act* 2005 (NSW) s 4; *Defamation Act* 2005 (Qld) s 4; *Defamation Act* 2005 (SA) s 4; *Defamation Act* 2005 (Tas) s 4; *Defamation Act* 2005 (Vic) s 4; *Defamation Act* 2005 (WA) s 4.

8 As argued in Chapter 2, the dominant form of defamation in the early history of the law. For some recent examples of slander, see *Strasberg v Westfield Ltd* [2002] NSWSC 340 at [3]–[8] per Levine J; *McManus v Beckham* [2002] 4 All ER 497 at 499–502; [2002] 1 WLR 2982 per Waller LJ; *Hambly v Joseph Charles Learmonth Duffy Pty Ltd* [2004] WASC 142 at [4] per Newnes M; *Clover Bond Pty Ltd v Carroll* [2004] WASC 216 at [4] per Commissioner Zilko SC.

(see, for example, *Bashford v Information Australia (Newsletters) Pty Ltd* (2004) 218 CLR 366; 204 ALR 193 at 204–5 per McHugh J, at 250–51 per Callinan J; 78 ALJR 346; Aust Torts Reports ¶81-727), letter (see, for example, *Pullman v Walter Hill & Co Ltd* [1891] 1 QB 524; *Crampton v Nugawela* (1996) 41 NSWLR 176 at 180–81 per Mahoney ACJ; *Cinevest Ltd v Yirandi Productions Ltd* (2001) Aust Torts Reports ¶81-610 at 67,032–3 per Spigelman CJ; *Burden v Ainsworth* (2004) 59 NSWLR 506 at 507 per Ipp JA), postcard (*Sadgrove v Hole* [1901] 2 KB 1 at 4–5 per A L Smith MR; *Roberts v Bass* (2002) 212 CLR 1 at 22 per Gaudron, McHugh and Gummow JJ, at 82 per Callinan J; 194 ALR 161; 77 ALJR 292; (2003) Aust Torts Reports ¶81-683), pamphlet (*Roberts v Bass* (2002) 212 CLR 1 at 22–3 per Gaudron, McHugh and Gummow JJ, at 81–2, 83–8 per Callinan J; 194 ALR 161; 77 ALJR 292; (2003) Aust Torts Reports ¶81-683), picture (see, for example, *Cropp v Tilney* (1693) 3 Salk 225 at 226; 90 ER 1132 at 1132 per Holt CJ; *Austin v Culpepper* (1684) 2 Show 313; 89 ER 960; *Du Bost v Beresford* (1810) 2 Camp 511; 170 ER 1235), cartoon (see, for example, *Darbyshir v Daily Examiner Pty Ltd* (unreported, SC(NSW), No. 21467.96, Levine J, 29 August 1997); *Falkenberg v Nationwide News Pty Ltd* (unreported, SC(NSW), 20832/94, Levine J, 16 December 1994; BC9403516)), caricature (see, for example, *Roberts v Bass* (2002) 212 CLR 1 at 83–4 per Callinan J; *Smith v Wood* (1813) 3 Camp 323; 170 ER 1397; *Dunlop Rubber Co Ltd v Dunlop* [1921] 1 AC 367; *Tolley & J S Fry & Sons Ltd* [1931] AC 333 at 336–7 per Viscount Hailsham), photograph (*Cassidy v Daily Mirror Newspapers Ltd* [1929] 2 KB 331 at 337 per Scrutton LJ, at 342 per Greer LJ; *Nixon v Slater & Gordon* (2000) 175 ALR 15 at 18–19; Aust Torts Reports ¶81-565 per Merkel J), sign (*Gulf Oil (Great Britain) Ltd v Page* [1987] 1 Ch 327 at 330–32; [1987] 3 All ER 14; [1987] 3 WLR 166 per Eady J; *Howlett v Holding* [2002] EWHC 286 (QB) at [7]–[8] per Eady J), poster (*West v Mirror Newspapers Ltd* (1973) A Def R [50-001]; *Urbanchich v Drummoyne Municipal Council* (1988) A Def R [50-035]; (1991) Aust Torts Reports ¶81-127 at 69,191 per Hunt J), notice board (*Byrne v Deane* [1937] 1 KB 818 at 838 per Greene LJ), radio, television, film (*Youssoupoff v Metro-Goldwyn-Mayer Pictures Ltd* (1934) 50 TLR 581 at 582 per Scrutton LJ), public exhibition (*Monson v Tussauds Ltd* [1894] 1 QB 671 at 685 per Lord Halsbury LC, at 691–2 per Lopes LJ; *Corelli v Ward* (1906) 22 TLR 532 at 532 per Swinfen Eady J), theatrical performance (*Bishop v State of New South Wales* [2000] NSWSC 1042 at [1]–[4] per Dunford J), telephone (*Uniflex (Australia) Pty Ltd v Hanneybel* [2001] WASC 138 at [36]–[57] per Hasluck J; *Crothers v Adkins* [2003] WASC 179 at [2] per Newnes M), facsimile (*Timms v Clift* [1998] 2 Qd R 100 at 102 *per curiam*; *State Bank of New South Wales Ltd v Currabubula Holdings Pty Ltd* (2001) 51 NSWLR 399 at 402 per Giles JA), e-mail (see, for example, *Markovic v White* [2004] NSWSC 37 at [3]–[4], Schs 4 per Levine J; *Edith Cowan University Student Guild v Edith Cowan University* [2004] WASC 83 at [1] per McKechnie J), internet website (*Macquarie Bank Ltd v Berg* (1999) A Def R 53-035 at 44,791 per Simpson J; *Buddhist Society of Western Australia Inc v Bristile Ltd* [2000] WASCA 210 at [2]–[5] per Anderson and Owen JJ; *Loutchansky v Times Newspapers Ltd (No 2)*

[2002] QB 783 at 798–800; [2002] 1 All ER 652; [2002] 2 WLR 640 *per curiam*; above n 79 at 643–6 per Callinan J; *Cullen v White* [2003] WASC 153 at [7] per Newnes M), internet bulletin board (*Godfrey v Demon Internet Ltd* [2001] QB 201 at 204–5; [1999] 4 All ER 342; [2000] 3 WLR 1020 per Morland J; *Totalise plc v Motley Fool Ltd* [2001] EMLR 29 at 752–3 per Owen J, QBD) and webcast (*Mickelberg v 6PR Southern Cross Radio Pty Ltd* [2002] WASCA 270 at [10] per Steytler J). As Lopes LJ in *Monson v Tussauds Ltd* [1894] 1 QB 671 at 692 makes clear, although defamatory matter is usually written or printed, it is not necessary for it to be in that form. According to his Lordship, 'a statue, a caricature, an effigy, chalk marks on a wall, signs, or pictures may constitute a libel.' (See also *Toomey v Mirror Newspapers Ltd* (1985) 1 NSWLR 73 at 77 per Hunt J). In *Monson*, the somewhat irregular defamatory matter in question was a waxwork dummy of the plaintiff, an acquitted murder suspect, on display in the 'Chamber of Horrors' in the famous London waxworks museum, Madame Tussauds (*Monson v Tussauds Ltd* [1894] 1 QB 671 at 685 per Lord Halsbury LC, at 691–2 per Lopes LJ). The means of publishing defamatory matter are indeed many and varied.

The High Court of Australia has given recent consideration to the issue of publication for the purposes of defamation law in its decision in *Dow Jones & Co. Inc. v Gutnick* (2002) 210 CLR 575 at 600; 194 ALR 433; 77 ALJR 255; Aust Torts Reports ¶81-682. It used the opportunity to reaffirm the basic principles of the requirement of publication and their applicability regardless of the medium of communication (*Dow Jones & Co. Inc. v Gutnick* (2002) 210 CLR 575 at 600, 605, 607 per Gleeson CJ, McHugh, Gummow and Hayne JJ, at 649, 652 per Callinan J. See also *Bata v Bata* [1948] WN 366 at 366 per Scott LJ; Tobin and Sexton 1991, [5125]; Milmo and Rogers (eds) 2004, [6.1]).

In their joint judgment, Gleeson CJ, McHugh, Gummow and Hayne JJ were not convinced of the need to reform common law principles to deal with the challenges posed by internet technologies. They acknowledged that the Internet represented a significant technological advance but also noted that the problems of multistate defamation preceded its advent. Mass communications, such as newspapers, magazines and, more significantly, radio and television, already presented difficulties (*Dow Jones & Co. Inc. v Gutnick* (2002) 210 CLR 575 at 605 per Gleeson CJ, McHugh, Gummow and Hayne JJ. Compare at 649 per Callinan J). The majority judgment also rejected attempts to overstate the ubiquity of the Internet, observing that, arguably, satellite television was equally ubiquitous in its coverage (*Dow Jones & Co. Inc. v Gutnick* (2002) 210 CLR 575 at 605 per Gleeson CJ, McHugh, Gummow and Hayne JJ. Compare at 649 per Callinan J). Callinan J went further, reasoning that the ubiquity of the Internet was one of its chief commercial attractions and that publishers who chose to publish defamatory matter online did so in the full knowledge that the greater the coverage, the greater the potential profit and thus the greater the risk of defamation that such publishers ought to consider or bear (*Dow Jones & Co. Inc. v Gutnick* (2002) 210 CLR 575 at 648–9 per Callinan J). Kirby J was the most sympathetic to submissions based on the uniqueness of the Internet (*Dow Jones & Co. Inc. v Gutnick* (2002) 210 CLR

575 at 619, 625–9, 642–3. Compare at 647 per Callinan J). However, ultimately, his Honour concluded that it would 'exceed the judicial function' to reformulate the common law principles relating to publication in defamation law specifically for internet publications (*Dow Jones & Co. Inc. v Gutnick* (2002) 210 CLR 575 at 635). Kirby J styled this outcome as 'a result contrary to intuition' (*Dow Jones & Co. Inc. v Gutnick* (2002) 210 CLR 575 at 642–3).

What emerges clearly from the High Court's decision in *Dow Jones v Gutnick* is that the principles relating to publication in defamation law are medium-neutral. However, whilst it may be accepted that publication is medium-neutral, this book contends that reputations are not. The ways in which reputations are created and cultivated or are damaged are intimately related to the media in which they are represented.

The Requirement of Identification[9]

The final element a plaintiff must prove in order to establish the defendant's liability for defamation is the requirement of identification. The defamatory matter must be published of and concerning the plaintiff (*Lee v Wilson and Mackinnon* (1934) 51 CLR 276 at 288 per Dixon J; *Knupffer v London Express Newspaper Ltd* [1944] AC 117; [1944] 1 All ER 495 at 496 per Viscount Simon LC, at 497 per Lord Atkin, at 498 per Lord Rusell of Killowen). As Gillooly has identified, the underlying principle of identification is 'would ordinary, reasonable people understand the matter complained of and the imputations thereby conveyed to be directed at the plaintiff?' (Gillooly 1998, 59).

The requirement of identification underlines the social aspect of reputation. Defamation law does not provide a remedy to a plaintiff merely for the insult to his or her dignity but because there has been an adverse impact on other people's perception of the plaintiff. No such impact is possible if the plaintiff is not identifiable from the defamatory matter.

In a large number of cases, the identification of the plaintiff will present no difficulty – the plaintiff will be explicitly identified by the matter (*Consolidated Trust Co Ltd v Browne* (1948) 49 SR(NSW) 86 at 90–91 per Jordan CJ; *Cross v Denley* (1952) 52 SR(NSW) 112 at 116 per Owen J). However, in cases where the plaintiff is not expressly named, the identification of the plaintiff may be more problematic. In such circumstances, the plaintiff may be required to plead extrinsic facts and to adduce evidence of recipients of the publication who knew of those extrinsic facts. The issue then becomes whether the ordinary, reasonable reader, in possession of the knowledge of those facts, could reasonably have identified the plaintiff from the defamatory matter (*David Syme & Co v Canavan* (1918) 25 CLR

9 As to the requirement of identification generally, see Tobin and Sexton 1991, [6001]ff; Carter-Ruck and Starte 1997, Ch. 5; Gillooly 1998, Ch. 4; Milmo and Rogers (eds) 2004, Ch. 7; Price and Duodu 2004, Ch. 4; George 2006, Ch. 8.

234 at 238 per Isaacs J; *Morgan v Odhams Press Ltd* [1971] 1 WLR 1239; [1971] 2 All ER 1156 at 1160–62 per Lord Reid; *Healy v Askin* [1974] 1 NSWLR 436 at 439 per Lee J; *Steele v Mirror Newspapers Ltd* [1974] 2 NSWLR 348 at 362–4 per Hutley JA, at 371 per Samuels JA).

It is irrelevant that the defendant intended to identify the plaintiff.[10] The gist of the action is the tendency of the publication to cause harm to the plaintiff's reputation, not the defendant's intentional conduct to harm the plaintiff's reputation. For example, in circumstances where a defendant intends to refer to a particular person and the plaintiff shares the same name as the intended target (*Lee v Wilson and Mackinnon* (1934) 51 CLR 276 at 282–3 per Starke J, at 286–7 per Dixon J; *Newstead v London Express Newspaper Ltd* [1940] 1 KB 377 at 395; [1939] 4 All ER 319 per du Parcq) or where a defendant creates a name for a fictional character which is shared by an actual person (*E Hulton & Co v Jones* [1910] AC 20), the plaintiff may still have been identified by the matter for the purposes of defamation law because the subjective intention of the defendant is irrelevant to the question of whether the ordinary, reasonable reader could have identified the plaintiff from the matter.

The principles of identification also encode notions about who is well-known and who is not, who is identifiable and recognisable by the wider community and who is not. Where a plaintiff is not directly identified by a defamatory matter, he or she may be alleviated of the need to provide proof of extrinsic facts supporting his or her identification. For example, it may be that a person is identifiable from his or her stated office or position. The classic example is given by Jordan CJ in *Consolidated Trust Co v Browne*, wherein his Honour suggests that, if a defamatory matter refers to, but does not name, 'the Prime Minister of Australia', the holder of that office is a matter of general knowledge such that he or she does not need to provide particulars of identification ((1948) 49 SR(NSW) 86 at 91. See also *Cross v Denley* (1952) 52 SR(NSW) 112 at 116; 69 WN(NSW) 137 per Owen J). There is also support in the decided cases for the broader proposition that a plaintiff need not provide particulars of extrinsic facts if the plaintiff or such facts are sufficiently notorious (*Fullam v Newcastle Chronicle & Journal Ltd* [1977] 1 WLR 651 at 659 per Scarman LJ; *Grappelli v Derek Block (Holdings) Ltd* [1981] 2 All ER 272 at 278; [1981] 1 WLR 822 per Dunn LJ). At the other end of the scale, it may be that a person is only known to a limited group (see, for example, *Shepherd v Walsh* [2000] QSC 177 at [11]–[12] per Jones J. As to the *Shepherd v*

10 *E Hulton & Co v Jones* [1910] AC 20 at 23 per Lord Loreburn LC; *Morgan v Odhams Press Ltd* [1971] 1 WLR 1239; [1971] 2 All ER 1156 at 1160 per Lord Reid; *Baltinos v Foreign Language Publications Pty Ltd* (1986) 6 NSWLR 85 at 90 per Hunt J. There is, however, divided authority on whether an actual intention by the defendant to identify the plaintiff is determinative of the issue of identification. For a range of views, see *Lee v Wilson and Mackinnon* (1934) 51 CLR 276 at 288–9 per Dixon J; *Lloyd v David Syme & Co Ltd* (1985) 3 NSWLR 728 at 734; [1986] AC 350 at 364 *per curiam*; *Baltinos v Foreign Language Publications Pty Ltd* (1986) 6 NSWLR 85 at 89–96 per Hunt J.

Walsh litigation specifically, see Chapter 7). In such a case, the plaintiff will need to provide sufficient particulars of identification.

However, there is an intermediate group, reflecting the fact that the criterion of notoriety is vague. Thus, in *Irvine v John Fairfax & Sons Ltd* (unreported, SC(Qld), No. 3652/84, Lee M, 21 May 1985), the plaintiff, who described himself as 'the sole News Executive in the State of Queensland' for the Australian Broadcasting Corporation (at 2), sued Fairfax over an article published in *The Sydney Morning Herald* in early November 1984. The article dealt with a police raid on the premises of an unnamed Queensland ABC executive suspected of being involved in child molestation (at 2–3). In his pleading, Irvine claimed that the article was published of and concerning him without providing satisfactory particulars of the persons who identified him as such (at 3). Fairfax sought an order for particulars supporting identification (at 1) and Lee M granted it (at 30). Giving reasons for making the order, the Master observed that '[t]he office of Australian Broadcasting Corp news executive is not a notoriously well known office, nor can it be said that it is a matter of general notoriety who the holder of that office is' (at 24). This suggests that some plaintiffs are immediately recognised by the law of defamation, whilst others have to prove themselves.

Although the requirement of identification underscores the social aspect of reputation, the principles relating to it demonstrate that reputation cannot be understood as wholly social. Given that reputation inheres in the individual and that each individual's reputation is unique, there is equally an indelibly personal aspect to reputation. Indeed, it is precisely this tension between the social and personal aspects of reputation that makes reputation such a difficult legal interest with which to grapple. The individualistic nature of reputation is clearly demonstrated through the common law's treatment of 'group defamation'. If an aspersion is cast upon a group of persons, a member of that group cannot sue for defamation merely by virtue of his or her membership. Rather, such a person would need to demonstrate that the allegation made against the group was reasonably capable of reflecting adversely upon him or her as an individual (*Mann v The Medicine Group* (1992) 38 FCR 400 at 402–3 per Wilcox J; *Christchurch Press Co v McGaveston* [1986] 1 NZLR 610 at 614 per Cooke J; *Hyams v Peterson* [1991] 3 NZLR 648 at 654–5 per Cooke P). A number of factors needs to be considered when addressing this question, such as 'the size of the class, the generality of the charge and the extravagance of the accusation' (*Knupffer v London Express Newspaper Ltd* [1944] AC 117; [1944] 1 All ER 495 at 499 per Lord Porter). Generally, the larger the group, the less likely it is that members of the groups will be able to establish that the imputation redounds upon them individually[11] and the smaller the group, the more likely (*Le Fanu v Malcolmson* (1848) 1 HL Cas 637;

11 *Eastwood v Holmes* (1858) 1 F & F 347 at 349; 175 ER 758 at 759 per Willes J; *David Syme & Co v Canavan* (1918) 25 CLR 234 at 237 per Barton J, at 239 per Isaacs J; above n 151 at 496 per Viscount Simon LC, at 498 per Lord Russell of Killowen, at 499 per Lord Porter; *Dowding v Ockerby* [1962] WAR 110; *Healy v Askin* [1974] 1 NSWLR 436 at

9 ER 910; *Pryke v Advertiser Newspapers* (1984) 37 SASR 175; *Bjelke-Petersen v Warburton* [1987] 2 Qd R 465). As Lord Atkin counsels in *Knupffer v London Express Newspaper Ltd*, the focus ultimately should be on whether the plaintiff was identified, not whether the plaintiff was the member of a group ([1944] AC 117; [1944] 1 All ER 495 at 498). Thus, although reputation has a significant social aspect, the common law of defamation is directed towards protecting individual, not collective, reputations.

The Purposes of Defamation Damages[12]

Introduction

Due to the constraints of space, it is not possible to undertake an exhaustive review of the complex principles and pleading rules which attend the assessment of defamation damages. However, given that damages are the primary remedy for defamation, it is necessary to discuss the types of damages available for defamation and the purposes for which they are awarded as part of the background to the case studies in the succeeding chapters. Importantly, the focus will again be on what concepts of reputation are encoded in the basic principles relating to defamation damages.

In defamation cases, there are three principal heads of damages awarded to a successful plaintiff: compensatory damages; aggravated damages; and exemplary damages. Each of these types of damages will be examined in turn.

Compensatory Damages

Like other torts, the principal type of damages awarded for defamation is compensatory damages. Once the plaintiff has established the defendant's liability and the defendant has failed to establish any defence, compensatory damages are awarded to the plaintiff as of right, even if they are nominal in amount – the 'one shilling' or 'one farthing' damages or now, thanks to inflation, the 'one dollar' or 'one pound' damages (see, for example, *Wisdom v Brown* (1885) 1 TLR 412 at 412 per Lord Coleridge CJ. For further examples of nominal or derisory damages for defamation, see *Newstead v London Express Newspaper Ltd* [1940] 1 KB 377; [1939] 4 All ER 319 (one farthing); *Grobbelaar v News Group Newspapers Ltd* [2002] 4 All ER 732; [2002] 1 WLR 3024 (one pound)). The guiding principle in tort law is *restitutio in integrum* – to place the successful plaintiff in the position he

---

439–40 per Lee J; *McCormick v John Fairfax & Sons Ltd* (1989) 16 NSWLR 484 at 488–91 per Hunt J. See Milmo and Rogers (eds) 2004, [7.9].

12 As to the issue of damages for defamation generally, see Tobin and Sexton 1991, [20,001]ff; Gillooly 1998, Ch. 15; McGregor 2003, Ch. 39; Milmo and Rogers (eds) 2004, Ch. 9; Price and Duodu 2004, Ch. 20; George 2006, Chs 31–8.

or she would have been in, had the tort not been committed (*McCarey v Associated Newspapers Ltd (No 2)* [1965] 2 QB 86 at 106 per Diplock LJ; *Uren v John Fairfax & Sons Pty Ltd* (1966) 117 CLR 118 at 149 per Windeyer J). At this level of principle, compensatory damages appear to encode a notion of reputation as property – that reputation is a valuable right owned and controlled by the plaintiff which has been infringed and thereby diminished in value by the defendant's conduct. The award of damages 'restores' the plaintiff's reputation to the value it previously had. This seems consistent with the view occasionally expressed that the jury's assessment of damages reflects the amount of money necessary to restore the plaintiff's reputation (*Youssoupoff v Metro-Goldwyn-Mayer Pictures Ltd* (1934) 50 TLR 581 at 584 per Scrutton LJ; *Dingle v Associated Newspapers Ltd* [1964] AC 371 at 393 per Lord Radcliffe; *Sutcliffe v Pressdram Ltd* [1991] 1 QB 153 at 182 per Nourse LJ; *Kiam II v MGN Ltd* [2002] 2 All ER 219 at 235; [2002] 1 WLR 2810 per Simon Brown LJ).

The concept of reputation as property also manifests itself in any component of compensatory damages awarded for actual economic loss. If a plaintiff can identify and establish pecuniary losses caused by the publication of defamatory matter, he or she can recover them as compensatory damages. In this regard, reputation may be viewed as a form of property that has been damaged in an economically quantifiable way. However, it should be noted that compensatory damages for actual economic loss are comparatively rare (for a recent example of compensatory damages for actual economic loss, see *Crampton v Nugawela* (1996) 41 NSWLR 176 at 189–90 per Mahoney ACJ).

Another way in which reputation as property manifests itself in the award of compensatory damages is in the assessment of damages for defamation of a corporate entity (as to corporate reputation, see Chapter 4). As Lord Reid emphasised in *Lewis v Daily Telegraph Ltd* [1964] AC 234 at 262 '[a] company cannot be injured in its feelings, it can only be injured in its pockets. Its reputation can be injured by a libel but that injury must sound in money. The injury need not necessarily be confined to loss of income. Its goodwill may be injured.'

Thus, the award of compensatory damages for a corporate entity is economic in character (*Australian Broadcasting Corporation v Comalco Ltd* (1986) 12 FCR 510 at 599–602 per Pincus J. Cf. *Andrews v John Fairfax & Sons Ltd* [1980] 2 NSWLR 225 at 254–6 per Mahoney JA (damages for injury to trading corporation's 'reputation as such')). It suggests that the value attributed to a corporate entity's reputation is economic – thus a form of property – and that the damage done to a corporate entity's reputation is an economic injury – and a defamatory publication amounts to an invasion of a property interest.

The difficulty with viewing compensatory damages as encoding a purely proprietary conception of reputation is twofold. Firstly, it does not accurately reflect the historical processes by which damages as the principal remedy came to be awarded in defamation cases. The award of damages as a remedy derived, in part, from the royal courts, where defamation was eventually adopted and recognised as an action on the case. In order to bring a claim for defamation, a plaintiff had to prove that he or she had suffered injury as a result of the defendant's words, except in certain categories of cases. In the royal courts, the damage to the plaintiff's reputation, not the insult experienced by the plaintiff, was the gist of the action (as to the development of the cause of action in defamation in the royal courts, see Chapter 2). This aspect of the history of defamation damages seems consistent with the concept of reputation as property.

However, the common law of defamation also derived from the jurisprudence of the Star Chamber. Notwithstanding the fact that the jurisdiction of the Star Chamber was criminal, defendants could be exposed to an award of damages payable to the plaintiff as well as punishments, such as fines or imprisonment, imposed by the Crown (as to the development of the cause of action in defamation in the Star Chamber, see Chapter 2). There was no necessary relationship with provable damage to reputation and the damages awarded. Rather, it seems to have developed as a pragmatic remedy. As an historical approach to defamation demonstrates, damages for defamation not only entered the common law because the royal courts located the tort of defamation, received from the ecclesiastical courts, within the action on the case but also because the other significant contributor to the tort of defamation, the Star Chamber, also awarded damages, albeit for a reason unrelated to actual or provable damage suffered by the plaintiff. Historically, therefore, the award of compensatory damages at best reflects a concept of reputation as property only in part.

More importantly, compensatory damages do not necessarily reflect a concept of reputation as property because compensation, for the purposes of defamation law, operates in a unique way. This becomes evident from an examination of the consistent line of authority in the High Court of Australia on the purposes of defamation damages. The starting-point is Windeyer J's influential judgment in *Uren v John Fairfax & Sons Pty Ltd* (1966) 117 CLR 118 at 150, wherein his Honour observed:

> A man's reputation, his good name, the estimation in which he is held in the opinion of others, is not a possession of his as a chattel is. Damage to it cannot be measured as harm to a tangible thing is measured. Apart from special damages strictly so called and damages for a loss of clients or customers, money and reputation are not commensurables. It seems to me that, properly speaking, a man defamed does not get compensation for his damaged reputation. He gets damages because he was injured in his reputation, that is simply because he was publicly defamed. For this reason, compensation by damages operates in two ways – as a vindication of the plaintiff to the public and as consolation to him for a wrong done. Compensation is here a solatium rather than a monetary recompense for harm measurable in money.

To similar effect was the joint judgment of Mason CJ, Deane, Dawson and Toohey JJ in *Carson v John Fairfax & Sons Ltd* (1993) 178 CLR 44 at 60–61 (footnotes omitted); 113 ALR 577; 67 ALJR 634; Aust Torts Reports ¶81-227, wherein their Honours stated:

> [s]pecific economic loss and exemplary or punitive damages aside, there are three purposes to be served by damages awarded for defamation. The three purposes no doubt overlap considerably in reality and ensure that 'the amount of a verdict is the product of a mixture of inextricable considerations'. The three purposes are consolation for the personal distress and hurt caused to the appellant by the publication, reparation for the harm done to the appellant's personal and (if relevant) business reputation and vindication of the appellant's reputation. The first two purposes are frequently considered together and constitute consolation for the wrong done to the appellant. Vindication looks to the attitude of others to the appellant: the sum awarded must be at least the minimum necessary to signal to the public the vindication of the appellant's reputation.

Most recently, in *Rogers v Nationwide News Pty Ltd* (2003) 216 CLR 327; 201 ALR 184 at 198; 77 ALJR 1739; Aust Tort Reports ¶81-713, Hayne J restated the purposes of defamation damages, relying upon the joint judgment in *Carson* (see also *Crampton v Nugawela* (1996) 41 NSWLR 176 at 191 per Mahoney ACJ).

A number of important points about the concept of reputation and its manifestation in the principles of compensatory damages emerge from these three judgments. Firstly, it is clear that Australian defamation law rejects the concept of reputation as property, at least in relation to natural persons. Windeyer J is tolerably clear on this issue – for his Honour, the reputation of a natural person is not a possession, a chattel or an asset. Hayne J is even more emphatic, stating that not only is reputation not an item of property, there is no real marketplace for reputations:

> [D]amage to reputation is not a commodity having a market value. Reputation and money are in that sense incommensurable …
>
> The measure of what is reasonable compensation, if not supplied by the collective wisdom of a jury, must be distilled from within the transactions of the law. That is, the standard against which an allegation that damages for defamation are manifestly excessive must be judged is a standard which is to be found within the administration of the law. It is not some external standard supplied, for example, by transactions within a market. Because reputation is not bought and sold, it is only in the courts that money values are assigned to the consequences of infliction of harm to reputation. (*Rogers v Nationwide News Pty Ltd* (2003) 201 ALR 184 at 199–200)

Secondly, these judgments indicate that the compensatory impulse of tort law – *restitutio in integrum* – serves decidedly non-proprietary ends in the context of defamation law (see also *Broome v Cassell & Co Ltd* [1972] AC 1027 at 1071 per Lord Hailsham LC). It is clear that compensation, for the purposes of defamation law, is principally directed towards the vindication and the consolation of the plaintiff. The notion of vindication, looking as it does to the attitudes of others towards the plaintiff, seems consistent with the concept of reputation as honour. The plaintiff seeks to be vindicated within his or her society (as to the concept of reputation as honour, see Chapter 1). Moreover, the vindication of the plaintiff is not solely achieved through the mere fact of a favourable defamation verdict. The common law adopts the view that the size of the damages awarded matters. Damages are 'at large' (*McCarey v Associated Newspapers Ltd (No 2)* [1965] 2 QB 86 at 104 per Pearson LJ). The quantum of damages awarded must be 'sufficient to convince a bystander of the baselessness of the charge' (*Broome v Cassell & Co Ltd* [1972] AC 1027 at 1071 per Lord Hailsham LC. See also *Ley v Hamilton* (1935) 153 LT 384 at 386 per Lord Atkin). By contrast, the notion of consolation, looking as it does to the subjective experience of the plaintiff, seems consistent with the concept of reputation as dignity (as to the concept of reputation as dignity, see Chapter 1). It acknowledges that the publication of defamatory matter will not only injure the plaintiff's 'reputation' but necessarily injures the plaintiff's feelings, to the extent that these injuries are distinguishable.

Indeed, these twin purposes of compensatory damages, vindication and consolation, align with the two principal heads of compensatory damages usually awarded in a defamation case. An award of compensatory damages for defamation largely consists of damages for injury to reputation and injury to feelings. Because of the difficulty of ascertaining the precise extent of injury to reputation, damage is presumed in most defamation cases (*Ratcliffe v Evans* [1892] 2 QB 524 at 528). In relation to injury to feelings (see also *Broome v Cassell & Co Ltd* [1972] AC 1027 at 1125 per Lord Diplock; McGregor 2003, [39-027]), an award of compensatory damages may encompass the grief and distress following the publication of defamatory matter, as well as any pain and suffering or loss of pride or self-confidence (*McCarey v Associated Newspapers Ltd (No 2)* [1965] 2 QB 86 at 104 per Pearson LJ). Damages awarded in vindication and in consolation may therefore traverse a wide area of human experience (*Broome v Cassell & Co Ltd* [1972] AC 1027 at 1071 per Lord Hailsham LC).

As Windeyer J noted in *Uren*, echoed by the joint judgment in *Carson*, the assessment of compensatory damages is 'a mixture of inextricable considerations' (*Uren v John Fairfax & Sons Pty Ltd* (1966) 117 CLR 118 at 150; *Carson v John Fairfax & Sons Ltd* (1993) 178 CLR 44 at 60 per Mason CJ, Deane, Dawson and Toohey JJ). This may be viewed as a recognition that the honourable aspect is inextricable from the dignitary aspect of a person's reputation (as to the relationship between reputation as honour and reputation as dignity, see Chapter 1). It suggests that there is a necessary interdependence between what others think of the plaintiff and what the plaintiff thinks of himself or herself. It further suggests that it is impossible and undesirable to attempt to demarcate between the injury to the plaintiff's honour and the injury to the plaintiff's dignity. There are understandably few instances where judges and juries have assessed injury to reputation and injury to feelings as separate components of compensatory damages (for a comparatively rare example, see *Costello v Random House Australia Pty Ltd* (1999) 137 ACTR 1 at 52; 149 FLR 367; Aust Tort Reports ¶81-503 per Higgins J).

It is clear, therefore, that, given the stated purposes for which compensatory damages are awarded, more than one concept of reputation manifests itself in the relevant principles by which such damages are assessed.

Aggravated Damages

The second type of damages that may be awarded for defamation is aggravated damages. Aggravated damages are a form of compensatory damages (*Carson v John Fairfax & Sons Ltd* (1993) 178 CLR 44 at 79 per McHugh J) that may be awarded in circumstances where the defendant's conduct has increased the injury to the plaintiff's reputation and feelings. In order for a defendant to be held liable to pay aggravated damages as a component of compensatory damages, his or her conduct must be able to be characterised as improper, unjustifiable or lacking in *bona fides* (*Triggell v Pheeney* (1951) 82 CLR 497 at 514 per Dixon, Williams, Webb and Kitto JJ; *Clark v Ainsworth* (1996) 40 NSWLR 463 at 466 per Sheller JA, at 473 per Abadee AJA). In determining whether to award aggravated damages, the focus of the inquiry is on the plaintiff's reaction, not the defendant's conduct, in contrast to exemplary damages (*Gray v Motor Accident Commission* (1998) 196 CLR 1 at 7 per Gleeson CJ, McHugh, Gummow and Hayne JJ). The types of conduct that may give rise to an award of aggravated damages include the falsity of the defamatory matter (*Carson v John Fairfax & Sons Ltd* (1993) 178 CLR 44 at 76 per Brennan J; *Rigby v Associated Newspapers Ltd (No 2)* [1969] 1 NSWR 729 at 738 per Walsh JA; *Aldridge v John Fairfax & Sons Ltd* [1984] 2 NSWLR 544 at 551 per Hunt J; *Anderson v Mirror Newspapers Ltd (No 2)* (1986) 5 NSWLR 735 at 737 per Hunt J), the failure to make inquiries (*Andrews v John Fairfax & Sons Ltd* [1980] 2 NSWLR 225 at 250 per Glass JA; *Waterhouse v Broadcasting Station 2GB Pty Ltd* (1985) 1 NSWLR 58 at 76 per Hunt J), the refusal to make an apology in certain circumstances[13] or the making of an inadequate apology in certain circumstances (*Rigby v Associated Newspapers Ltd* [1969] 1 NSWR 729 at 739–40 per Walsh JA; *David Syme & Co Ltd v Mather* [1977] VR 516 at 525 per Lush J; *Jools v Mirror Newspapers Ltd* (1984) 56 ACTR 1 at 11 per Kelly J; *Packer v Australian Broadcasting Corporation* (1993) 116 FLR 306 at 312 per Higgins J) and the conduct of the defamation litigation itself (*Carson v John Fairfax & Sons Ltd* (1993) 178 CLR 44 at 120 per McHugh J; *Humphries v TWT* (1993) 120 ALR 693 at 702–3; (1993) Aust Torts Reports ¶81-219 *per curiam*). With its focus on the plaintiff's subjective response to the publication of defamatory matter and those circumstances which exacerbate the injury to his or her reputation and feelings particularly, the principles relating to aggravated damages clearly manifest the concept of reputation as dignity (as to the concept of reputation as dignity, see Chapter 1).

13 *Carson v John Fairfax & Sons Ltd* (1993) 178 CLR 44 at 119 per McHugh J; *Praed v Graham* (1889) 24 QBD 53 at 55 per Lord Esher MR; *Fielding v Variety Inc* [1967] 2 QB 841; *Andrews v John Fairfax & Sons Ltd* [1980] 2 NSWLR 225 at 243 per Hutley JA; *Mirror Newspapers Ltd v Fitzpatrick* [1984] 1 NSWLR 643 at 660 per Samuels JA; *Clark v Ainsworth* (1996) 40 NSWLR 463 at 469 per Sheller JA, at 473 per Abadee AJA. See also *Herald & Weekly Times Ltd v McGregor* (1928) 41 CLR 254 at 263 per Knox CJ, Gavan Duffy and Starke JJ.

Exemplary Damages

The third type of damages that may be awarded for defamation is exemplary damages. Following the introduction of national, uniform defamation laws in early 2006, these are no longer available in Australia.[14] When they were available, they were rarely awarded.[15] Exemplary damages serve to punish the defendant and to deter the defendant specifically and the community generally from engaging in the impugned conduct (*Gray v Motor Accident Commission* (1998) 196 CLR 1 at 28 per Kirby J; *XL Petroleum (NSW) Pty Ltd v Caltex Oil (Australia) Pty Ltd* (1985) 155 CLR 448 at 470 per Brennan J; *Lamb v Cotogno* (1987) 164 CLR 1 at 10 *per curiam*). In determining whether to award exemplary damages, the focus of the inquiry is on the defendant's conduct, not on the plaintiff's reaction, in contrast to aggravated damages (*Gray v Motor Accident Commission* (1998) 196 CLR 1 at 7 per Gleeson CJ, McHugh, Gummow and Hayne JJ). In Australia, they were generally awarded only in cases where the defendant's conduct could be characterised as being 'conscious wrongdoing in contumelious disregard of the plaintiff's rights' (*Gray v Motor Accident Commission* (1998) 196 CLR 1 at 9 per Gleeson CJ, McHugh, Gummow and Hayne JJ, at 28 per Kirby J; *Whitfield v De Lauret & Co Ltd* (1920) 29 CLR 71 at 77 per Knox CJ). Given the purposes for the award of these damages and the focus of the inquiry of the court before imposing them, it is unsurprising that they did not really encode or reflect a concept of reputation. As Windeyer J observed in *Uren*, they instead reflected the original intermingling of tort and crime in the common law (*Uren v John Fairfax & Sons Ltd* (1966) 117 CLR 118 at 149. For the divergence of Australian and English law on the issue of exemplary damages in tort, compare *Uren v John Fairfax & Sons Ltd* with *Rookes v Barnard* [1964] AC 1129 and *Broome v Cassell & Co Ltd* [1972] AC 1027).

Overview

The principles relating to defamatory meaning, the requirements of publication and identification and the purposes for which defamation damages are awarded

14 *Civil Law (Wrongs) Act* 2002 (ACT) s 139H; *Defamation Act* 2006 (NT) s 34; *Defamation Act* 2005 (NSW) s 37; *Defamation Act* 2005 (Qld) s 37; *Defamation Act* 2005 (SA) s 35; *Defamation Act* 2005 (Tas) s 37; *Defamation Act* 2005 (Vic) s 37; *Defamation Act* 2005 (WA) s 37.

15 For recent examples, see *Shepherd v Walsh* [2001] QSC 358 ($50,000 compensatory damages and $20,000 exemplary damages); *Martin v Trustrum* [2003] TASSC 22 ($35,000 compensatory damages and $5,000 exemplary damages); *Cullen v White* [2003] WASC 173 ($70,000 compensatory damages and $25,000 exemplary damages). See also *Gray v Motor Accident Commission* (1998) 196 CLR 1 at 6 per Gleeson CJ, McHugh, Gummow and Hayne JJ.

all encode assumptions about the nature of reputation. Consistent with its diverse historical origins, contemporary Australian defamation law provides protection for a range of reputational interests – reputation as honour, reputation as dignity, reputation as property. Defamation law itself implicitly serves the function of creating and enforcing uniform societal norms, thereby producing ‘good reputations’ and ‘bad reputations’. Importantly, reputation reveals itself as at once indelibly social yet highly individual. With this background, it is now possible to turn to a series of case studies which examine reputation in Australian defamation law in closer context.

PART II

Chapter 4
Reputation as Property

Fame is the spur that the clear spirit doth raise
(That last infirmity of noble mind)
To scorn delights, and live laborious days …

(John Milton, 'Lycidas', ll 70–72 in Orgel and Goldberg (eds) 1991, 41)

Stolen property may be replaced or recovered, but where does one go to restore one's reputation?

(*Bernson v Browning-Ferris Industries of California Inc* 873 P 2d 613; 30 Cal Rptr 2d 440 (1994) at 447 per Arabian J)

Introduction

Given that notions of reputation inhere in and inform the principles relating to the publication of defamatory matter, it is instructive to examine how those principles in practice manifest competing concepts of reputation. In the next four chapters, a series of case studies will be used to examine the concepts of reputation and their place in Australian defamation law.

This chapter takes as its starting-point and focus the concept of reputation as property in Australian defamation law. According to Post, this conception of reputation is the most readily understood and applicable (Post 1986, 693), yet *dicta* in Anglo-Australian cases suggest that judges are not so willing to acknowledge its primacy.[1] This chapter seeks to explore the concept of reputation as property through a case study involving injury to professional reputation by means of allegations of professional dishonesty, incompetence and negligence. In doing so, it also raises the somewhat difficult reputational issues surrounding corporate entities.

1 See, for example, *Uren v John Fairfax & Sons Ltd* (1966) 117 CLR 118 at 150 per Windeyer J; *Carson v John Fairfax & Sons Ltd* (1993) 178 CLR 44 at 70; 113 ALR 577; 67 ALJR 634; Aust Torts Reports ¶81-227 per Brennan J; *Rogers v Nationwide News Pty Ltd* (2003) 216 CLR 327; 201 ALR 184 at 199; 77 ALJR 1739; Aust Torts Reports ¶81-713 per Hayne J.

Case Study 1: Professional Reputation

Introduction

The recognition of the importance of reputation to a business or a professional person has a long history. When the royal courts began to recognise a cause of action in defamation, imputations of professional dishonesty and incompetence were amongst the first categories of cases to receive protection (for the historical origins of actions for defamation in relation to allegations of professional dishonesty and incompetence, see Chapter 2). In the mid-nineteenth century, Sir Richard Malins V.-C. asserted that a merchant's good reputation is 'property of a most valuable description' and indeed 'more valuable than other property' (*Dixon v Holden* (1869) 7 LR Eq 488 at 492). Moreover, the Vice-Chancellor stated that '[p]rofessional reputation is the means of acquiring wealth, and is the same as wealth itself' (at 494), an asset in itself. In contemporary Australian defamation law, there has been an equally vigorous protection of professional reputations by recourse to the courts in relation to imputations of professional dishonesty and incompetence.[2]

The reputation of a professional person is an example of a reputation which is in large measure proprietary. Through training, accreditation and eventual practice in a chosen profession, the professional person invests directly and indirectly in his

2 See, for example, in relation to imputations of professional dishonesty, *Kay v Chesser* [1999] 3 VR 55 at 56 per Ormiston JA (motor repairers); *Waterhouse v Nationwide News Pty Ltd* [2001] NSWSC 723 at [10]–[11] per Simpson J (racehorse trainer); *Mularczyk v John Fairfax Publications Pty Ltd* [2001] NSWCA 467 at [32] per Beazley JA (schoolteachers); *Markovic v White* [2004] NSWSC 37 at [3]–[4] per Levine J (solicitor); *John Fairfax Publications Pty Ltd v Jones* [2004] NSWCA 205 at 28 per Hodgson JA, at [106] per Ipp JA (radio broadcaster); *Australian Broadcasting Corporation v Reading* [2004] NSWCA 411 at [28] per Santow JA, at [127] per Ipp JA (company director); *Nationwide News Pty Ltd v Sleeman* [2005] NSWCA 349 at [4] per Brownie AJA (journalist); *Mahommed v Channel Seven Pty Ltd* [2006] NSWCA 213 at [9] per McColl JA (mortgage broker and financial advisor). See, for example, in relation to imputations of professional incompetence or negligence. *O'Neill v Jones* [1999] NSWSC 270 at [5] per Levine J (banker); *Haertsch v Andrews* [1999] NSWSC 359 at [4] per Levine J (sexual reconstruction surgeon); *Roberman v Australian Broadcasting Corporation* [2002] WASC 56 at [21] per Steytler J (obstetrician and gynaecologist); *Oakley v 3AW Southern Cross Pty Ltd* [1999] VSCA 96 at [5] per Charles JA (sports commentator); *Warren v Tweed Shire Council* [2002] NSWSC 211 at [16] per Levine J (environmental consultant); *Saint v John Fairfax Publications Pty Ltd* [2002] NSWSC 312 at [3] per Kirby J (public servant); *Moloney v Bales* [2002] NSWSC 381 at [2] per Levine J (business manager); *Coleman v John Fairfax Publications Pty Ltd* [2003] NSWSC 564 at [2] per Levine J (rugby league coach); *Phelps v Nationwide News Pty Ltd* [2003] NSWSC 614 at [2] per Levine J (general practitioner); *Stokes v John Fairfax Publications Pty Ltd* [2003] NSWSC 678 at [3] per Simpson J (chairman of public company); *Craftsman Homes Australia Pty Ltd v T.C.N. Channel Nine Pty Ltd* [2006] NSWSC 519 at [13] per Smart AJ (builder).

or her reputation – directly, through the payment for education and membership of professional bodies; indirectly, through time and labour. The professional person enters the marketplace for his or her services and attempts to earn a reward for those services, thereby creating and enhancing his or her reputation. The reputation of a professional person is valuable in an economic sense and is therefore vulnerable, again in an economic sense, to defamatory allegations. However, as will be demonstrated in the following case studies, aspersions on professional reputation should not be conceptualised purely as an injury to a proprietary interest. The defamatory allegations of dishonesty, incompetence and negligence still connote some degree of moral failure on the part of the professional person in question, confirming the complex nature of reputation. This is illustrated clearly by the case of *Crampton v Nugawela* (1996) 41 NSWLR 176.

Case Study 1(a): Professional Dishonesty – Crampton v Nugawela

In *Crampton v Nugawela* (1996) 41 NSWLR 176, the plaintiff, Dr Patrick Nugawela, was attempting to establish a body, the Australian Medical Informatics Association (AMIA). The AMIA was interested in the use and development of computer technology in medicine. Nugawela intended that the AMIA would be established nationwide and would become affiliated with the Royal Australian College of General Practitioners (RACGP) ((1996) 41 NSWLR 176 at 179).

The defendant, Dr Reginald Crampton, sought to prevent the AMIA establishing itself in New South Wales by creating an alternative organisation ((1996) 41 NSWLR 176 at 178–9). (Crampton was himself a 'computer fellow' and chairman of the RACGP's national computing committee ((1996) 41 NSWLR 176 at 181). At a meeting at Royal North Shore Hospital in mid-July 1990, Crampton presented a letter to a meeting of 22 doctors interested in medical computing. Although not present at the meeting, Nugawela became aware of the existence and the contents of the letter ((1996) 41 NSWLR 176 at 180) and instituted defamation proceedings against Crampton and the RACGP in respect of it ((1996) 41 NSWLR 176 at 178)).

Crampton's letter concerned Nugawela's presentation of a report to the International Medical Informatics Associations (IMIA) (the contents of the letter are set out in full in the judgment of Mahoney ACJ: (1996) 41 NSWLR 176 at 180–81). Both sides acknowledged that the RACGP and the Australian Computer Society (ACS) had initially provided a measure of support for Nugawela's initiatives ((1996) 41 NSWLR 176 at 179–80). However, such support as had been given was withdrawn when the RACGP concluded that its reputation had been 'used and abused' by Nugawela. According to Crampton, Nugawela compromised the RACGP's reputation by directly and falsely representing to the IMIA that the RACGP knew of and supported the AMIA's proposed activities. By making this independent representation, Nugawela also bypassed the Australian representative to the IMIA, Dr David Bennett of the ACS ((1996) 41 NSWLR 176 at 180). In Crampton's opinion, the making of separate representations, with the clear implication of a lack of a unified front, embarrassed the RACGP and the ACS ((1996) 41 NSWLR 176 at 180–81). As Mahoney ACJ stated, the essence of Nugawela's complaint about the letter was its suggestion that he had lied to the world professional body, the IMIA ((1996) 41 NSWLR 176 at 182).

Nugawela claimed that the letter conveyed the following four imputations:

a. That the Plaintiff had represented to the International Medical Informatics Association that the AMIA had the support of the Australian Computing Society and the Royal College of Australian General Practitioners, knowing that representation to be untrue.
b. That the Plaintiff had caused embarrassment to the Australian Computer Society and the Royal Australian College of General Practitioners and harm to their reputation by falsely claiming to the International Medical Informatics Association that they supported his organisation, the AMIA.
c. That the Plaintiff was prepared to make false claims in order to secure support for the AMIA and thereby enhance his standing amongst professional colleagues.
d. That the Plaintiff by the making of false statements had damaged and impeded the advancement of medical informatics in Australia. ((1996) 41 NSWLR 176 at 181)

At the trial before Levine J, which lasted 37 days, the jury found in favour of Nugawela and awarded him $600,000 damages ((1996) 41 NSWLR 176 at 178).

On appeal, Crampton and the RACGP unsuccessfully challenged the jury's verdict on the basis that the four imputations were not reasonably capable of being conveyed by the letter ((1996) 41 NSWLR 176 at 182–5 per Mahoney ACJ) and that the trial judge had erred in providing the jury with guidance as to the factors relevant to the assessment of aggravated damages ((1996) 41 NSWLR 176 at 186–7 per Mahoney ACJ). The principal challenge to the jury's verdict mounted by Crampton and the RACGP on appeal was, however, that the award of damages was manifestly excessive ((1996) 41 NSWLR 176 at 187ff. per Mahoney ACJ).

Crampton v Nugawela is an unusual case because a component of the award of damages was compensation for actual economic loss ((1996) 41 NSWLR 176 at 187 per Mahoney ACJ). The actual economic loss Nugawela claimed was the amounts he could have earned from consultancy fees, conference speaking fees and other benefits that would have accrued from his reputation as the Australian expert on medical informatics. On appeal, it was suggested that the component of the compensatory damages relating to actual economic loss should not be interpreted as applying to identifiable sums which Nugawela lost but rather was the assessment of a loss of chance to earn income. Ultimately, Mahoney ACJ rejected this. His Honour did note that the evidence before the trial judge was deficient in a number of respects relating to the quantification of Nugawela's pecuniary losses ((1996) 41 NSWLR 176 at 189). However, Mahoney ACJ found that there was no appealable error in the jury's assessment of damages in relation to this aspect of the case ((1996) 41 NSWLR 176 at 190. Handley JA agreed with Mahoney ACJ's analysis. See at 196. See also at 202 per Giles AJA).

The New South Wales Court of Appeal expressed the view that the defamatory sting was a serious one ((1996) 41 NSWLR 176 at 187 per Mahoney ACJ). Drawing inferences from the jury's verdict, Mahoney ACJ concluded that Crampton had publicly accused Nugawela of 'lying in a professional context' ((1996) 41 NSWLR 176 at 187 per Mahoney ACJ). Crampton's allegation was not made purely in a personal capacity but was made with the backing of the RACGP, thereby giving it greater effect. The allegation was made by Crampton without a reasonable basis and indeed without a belief in its veracity. It was knowingly made behind Nugawela's back, depriving him of an opportunity to respond. It was made primarily to advance Crampton's interests. The injury caused by the allegation was exacerbated by Crampton's failure to apologise, his persistence with the allegation up until the time of the trial and Crampton's gratuitous reference to Nugawela as 'the black fella' ((1996) 41 NSWLR 176 at 187 per Mahoney ACJ) in front of mutual professional colleagues, albeit in Nugawela's absence, in circumstances where Crampton would have foreseen Nugawela becoming aware of this derogatory reference ((1996) 41 NSWLR 176 at 191). Considering the injury to Nugawela's reputation and feelings and comparing it, somewhat perfunctorily, to the level of damages in personal injury cases, Mahoney ACJ concluded that the jury verdict was not manifestly excessive.

In reaching this conclusion, his Honour noted that the defamatory matter published by Crampton cast serious aspersions on Nugawela's reputation:

> They involved, in general, lying to professional colleagues, lying in a matter affecting the Royal College and its members, doing so for the purpose of securing an advantage to himself, and using and abusing his relationship with the Royal College. Charges of this kind, if true, would have a particular effect in the case of a professional man, a member of the medical profession. Such conduct would be likely to destroy his reputation not merely among College members and his professional associates but among the medical profession generally. A fellow professional would be likely to refuse to have significant dealings with a person who acted in that way; he could, he might think, not be trusted …. ((1996) 41 NSWLR 176 at 192)

Mahoney ACJ accepted that it was not merely a matter of gossip amongst the medical community. Such allegations would receive 'significant coverage' because, according to his Honour, the trustworthiness of a colleague in such a profession is 'a matter of legitimate and ongoing interest' ((1996) 41 NSWLR 176 at 193).

In light of this, Mahoney ACJ then addressed the worth of a professional reputation. His Honour ventured to suggest that, in the absence of any aggravating or extenuating circumstances, an amount of $500,000 would not be manifestly excessive. However, in the present case, Mahoney ACJ noted that there were additional factors to be considered. His Honour identified the importance of vindication for Nugawela, noting that it would need to be substantial to convince his medical colleagues, well-remunerated as they were, that the allegations were baseless ((1996) 41 NSWLR 176 at 194). Additionally, Mahoney ACJ considered the current case one in which the 'grapevine effect' operated ((1996) 41 NSWLR

176 at 194–5) – that is, the damage would be 'driven underground', only to resurface and cause injury anew at a later time and in an unspecified place (see *Broome v Cassell & Co Ltd* [1972] AC 1027 at 1071 per Lord Hailsham LC. See also *Ley v Hamilton* (1935) 153 LT 384 at 386 per Lord Atkin).

Mahoney ACJ observed that '[i]n some cases, a person's reputation is, in a relevant sense, his whole life' ((1996) 41 NSWLR 176 at 193). Nugawela's reputation demonstrated this. The allegations of dishonesty made against Nugawela by Crampton impugned not only his professional reputation but also reflected on his personal integrity ((1996) 41 NSWLR 176 at 194).

Mahoney ACJ concluded:

> … the law should place a high value upon reputation and in particular upon the reputation of those whose work and life depend upon their honesty, integrity and judgment. This Court should record that its view is such. And it should record that, where hurt and reputation are involved, the vindication of the plaintiff should not be left to speculation: the damage to be awarded will be so large as to make what the Court has done plain and clear. ((1996) 41 NSWLR 176 at 195)

In the course of his separate reasons for judgment, Handley JA also made a telling observation about the nature of a professional reputation, suggesting that the cultivation and exploitation of such a reputation as an asset was not the only motivating factor: '[m]en and women pursue careers, and activities associated with their careers, for reasons other than money, such as job satisfaction, prestige, honour, and recognition by one's professional peers, locally, nationally and internationally' ((1996) 41 NSWLR 176 at 198).

The New South Wales Court of Appeal unanimously upheld Nugawela's award of $600,000 damages.

Case Study 1(b): Professional Incompetence and Negligence – Andrews v John Fairfax & Sons Ltd

In *Andrews v John Fairfax & Sons Ltd* [1980] 2 NSWLR 225, the plaintiffs were the Australian architect, John Andrews, and his private company through which he conducted his business, John Andrews International Pty Ltd. Andrews and John Andrews International sued three media outlets, John Fairfax & Sons Ltd, Herald & Weekly Times Ltd and Queensland Newspapers Ltd, for defamation. On 15 and 16 June 1978, all three media outlets published substantially similar reports in their respective newspapers, detailing problems with a Commonwealth building designed by Andrews, the Cameron Centre in Belconnen, Canberra. The articles alleged that the Cameron Centre, which housed the Australian Bureau of Statistics and the Survey Office, had become 'an administrative nightmare'. The construction costs of the building were stated approximately 75 per cent higher than those of other Commonwealth buildings. Moreover, the operating costs of the building were claimed to be 27 per cent higher. This was due in part to the fact that the inclusion of 240 doors in the design of the building required a large number of security guards to lock and unlock all these entries on a daily basis; and it was due in part to the fact that there was significant water leakage within the Cameron Centre, causing substantial damage to carpets (the full text of *The Sydney Morning Herald* article, printed under the headline, 'One Government Leak Is Caught In Buckets', is reproduced in [1980] 2 NSWLR 225 at 232–3).

Both Andrews and John Andrews International pleaded the following imputations against all three media outlets arising out of their respective articles:

> a. That the Plaintiff was professionally negligent and incompetent in and about the design of the building complex known as the Cameron Offices, Belconnen, Canberra.
> b. That the Plaintiff was professionally negligent and incompetent in and about the supervision of the construction of the building complex known as the Cameron Offices, Belconnen, Canberra. ([1980] 2 NSWLR 225 at 233)

The articles mentioned neither Andrews nor John Andrews International directly.

In a trial before Maxwell J and a jury in the Supreme Court of New South Wales lasting over thirteen days in August 1979, both Andrews personally and his private company succeeded in their claims. The jury awarded Andrews $150,000 against Fairfax, $90,000 against Herald & Weekly Times and $60,000 against Queensland Newspapers. It awarded John Andrews International $90,000 against Fairfax, $50,000 against Herald & Weekly Times and $40,000 against Queensland Newspapers ([1980] 2 NSWLR 225 at 231 per Hutley JA).

The fact that neither Andrews nor John Andrews International was identified directly by the articles was important. On behalf of the plaintiffs, four witnesses, including the then Professor of Architecture at the University of Sydney, Professor Johnson, gave evidence that, not only had they identified Andrews and his private company as being the subject of the articles, but also that Andrews and John Andrews International were 'spontaneously identified' by other persons with whom the witnesses had spoken. Andrews himself gave evidence that he had been identified by others from the articles ([1980] 2 NSWLR 225 at 234 per Hutley JA). The media outlets objected to the admission of this evidence on the basis that it was hearsay but Hutley JA ruled that it was clearly admissible on the issue of identification and the range of publication. Indeed, Hutley JA stated that it was open to the jury to infer that 'a very large number of persons, including virtually the whole of the architects, engineers and quantity surveyors concerned with building construction, officers of governments and of statutory corporations in Australia concerned with the commissioning of architects to design and supervise major buildings' would form a class of persons who would have readily identified Andrews and John Andrews International as being responsible for the design of the building in question ([1980] 2 NSWLR 225 at 232. See also at 248 per Glass JA).

Unlike in *Crampton v Nugawela*, Andrews and his private company made no claim for actual economic loss, instead relying on general loss of business as a consequence of the publications ([1980] 2 NSWLR 225 at 235–9 per Hutley JA, at 251–2 per Glass JA). They also relied upon several factors to support the award of aggravated damages, including the conduct of the litigation ([1980] 2 NSWLR 225 at 242–3 per Hutley JA), the unjustifiable failure to retract and apologise ([1980] 2 NSWLR 225 at 243 per Hutley JA), the recklessness in publication ([1980] 2 NSWLR 225 at 243–4 per Hutley JA) and the failure to make inquiries of Andrews ([1980] 2 NSWLR 225 at 244 per Hutley JA).

On appeal, the newspaper appellants submitted that the jury verdicts were manifestly excessive. In relation to Andrews's private company, the New South Wales Court of Appeal disagreed ([1980] 2 NSWLR 225 at 244–5 per Hutley JA, at 248 per Glass JA. See also at 254 per Mahoney JA (dissenting)). However, in relation to the amounts awarded to Andrews personally, it agreed ([1980] 2 NSWLR 225 at 245 per Hutley JA, at 248 per Glass JA, at 264 per Mahoney JA). Hutley JA referred to the quantum of damages awarded to Andrews as 'a most spectacular solatium' ([1980] 2 NSWLR 225 at 245). Through the amount of damages awarded to his private company, Andrews's reputation as an architect had already been substantially vindicated, such that an equally generous amount of damages to Andrews personally was unnecessary and manifestly excessive ([1980] 2 NSWLR 225 at 246 per Hutley JA). As Glass JA observed:

> The libel cast no aspersions upon Andrews except as an architect. It did not otherwise derogate from his personal reputation .... The sum of $300,000 as a measure of solatium where there is no loss of personal reputation, no financial loss from damage to professional reputation, but only wounded feelings cannot it seems to me be accepted as a reasonable assessment of damages. ([1980] 2 NSWLR 225 at 253)

A new trial as the assessment of Andrews's damages was ordered ([1980] 2 NSWLR 225 at 247 per Hutley JA, at 248 per Glass JA).

Reputation as Property – Analysis

The Application of the Concepts of Reputation to Imputations of Professional Dishonesty and Incompetence

It is useful to attempt to apply the concepts of reputation identified by Post to *Crampton v Nugawela* and *Andrews* to see what insights this might yield about the reputational interests of the respective plaintiffs and the nature of reputation generally. It is clear that both cases centrally involve the professional reputations of the natural plaintiffs – Nugawela as a doctor and as an emerging expert on medical informatics; Andrews as an architect. Like all forms of professional reputation, the plaintiffs' respective reputations are thus significant assets that have been assiduously created and cultivated – through education, training, accreditation and ultimately through excellence in the marketplace for their professional services. Both suffered a loss that was economic in character – Nugawela managed to establish actual economic loss flowing from the publication of defamatory matter, whereas Andrews only managed to demonstrate a general loss of business for his private company. The economic impact of the defamatory publications on Nugawela particularly suggests the proprietary nature of the reputations at issue.

However, it needs to be considered whether the concept of reputation as property provides a complete explanation for the plaintiffs' reputations. In the context of discussing professional reputation in *Crampton v Nugawela*, Mahoney ACJ suggested that there are circumstances in which a person's reputation represents his or her whole life ((1996) 41 NSWLR 176 at 193). This close identification of the professional reputation with the personal character of the plaintiff reflects the concept of reputation as honour (Post 1986, 701. See also Chapter 1). Thus, the notion of a professional reputation – where a person does not merely perform certain tasks or fulfil certain functions but seeks to fulfil higher ethical or moral obligations in the discharge of those tasks or functions – necessarily conveys not simply the concept of reputation as property but also reputation as honour.

The extent to which a professional reputation is damaged by a defamatory publication will vary according to the nature of the allegation contained therein. Consequently, the extent to which the plaintiff's honour is assailed will vary. *Crampton v Nugawela* and *Andrews* illustrate such a contrast. In *Crampton v Nugawela*, the allegation of dishonesty not only affected Nugawela's professional reputation, it fundamentally touched his personal character. In *Andrews*, however, the allegation of incompetence necessarily affected his professional reputation but did not reflect adversely upon his personal character to the same extent. It was much less serious than the imputation made against Nugawela. As the English Court of Appeal recognised in *John v MGN Ltd* [1997] QB 587 at 607, there is a continuum of imputations, varying in gradations of seriousness from the minor to the major: '[i]n assessing the appropriate damages for injury to reputation the most important factor is the gravity of the libel; the more closely it touches the plaintiff's personal integrity, professional reputation, honour, courage, loyalty and the core attributes of his personality, the more serious it is likely to be.'

However, as natural persons, both Nugawela and Andrews received damages for injury to feelings and aggravated damages (as to compensatory and aggravated damages, see Chapter 3). In both cases, these heads of damages focus upon the subjective experience of the plaintiff in response to the defamatory publication. In this sense, they are both directed towards providing protection for the plaintiff's reputation as dignity. Indeed, Andrews's damages were principally to assuage his wounded dignity, the vindication of his professional reputation being largely achieved through the award of substantial damages to his private company ([1980] 2 NSWLR 225 at 245 per Hutley JA, at 253 per Glass JA). Nugawela also received substantial damages for injury to feelings and aggravated damages ((1996) 41 NSWLR 176 at 187, 191 per Mahoney ACJ). Damages for injury to feelings and aggravated damages are both components of damages that reflect the concept of reputation as dignity and are thus present in defamation claims brought by natural persons to protect and vindicate their professional reputations.

The concepts of reputation as property, honour and dignity appear to be able to be deployed to produce an adequate account of the reputations at issue in *Crampton v Nugawela* and *Andrews*. It remains to be tested whether they can provide a complete explanation of all plaintiffs' reputations.

The Application of the Concepts of Reputation to Instances of Corporate Reputation

Andrews not only provides a useful illustration of the potential application of the concepts of reputation to professional reputations. Because Andrews and his private company both sued for defamation, their case provides a convenient starting-point for an examination of the differential treatment of natural and artificial persons for the purposes of defamation law. In this way, it further highlights the operation of the concept of reputation as property in defamation law. Indeed, Post himself suggests that corporate reputation is perhaps the clearest manifestation of this concept in defamation law (Post 1986, 696).

Given that the partnership preceded the corporation as the dominant form of business organisation, the right of a partnership to sue for defamation self-evidently preceded the right of a corporation to sue for defamation. As Patfield has convincingly argued, the development of the right for corporations to sue for defamation involves the gradual extension of the right to sue from individuals to unincorporated associations, then ultimately to incorporated associations (Patfield 1994, 233). The common law of defamation may have developed to protect the reputations of natural persons but, with the development and legal recognition of artificial persons as juridical entities, it had to decide whether the right to reputation should be extended to them and, if it did, what aspects should and should not apply to them.

The right of a partnership to sue for defamation was well-established at common law.[3] The common law recognised that 'a partnership has a personality which is capable of being defamed and in respect of which it can bring an action for libel' (*Electrical, Electronic, Telecommunication and Plumbing Union v Times Newspapers Ltd* [1980] QB 585 at 595 per O'Connor J; *Todd v Swan Television and Radio Broadcasters Pty Ltd* (2001) 25 WAR 284 at 298 per Steytler J). The personality of a partnership was not co-extensive with the personalities of the constituent partners. Consequently, the partnership could only sue in respect

3 See, for example, *Cook v Batchellor* (1802) 3 Bos & Pul 150; 127 ER 83 (imputation of dishonesty made against partnership of wool-staplers); *Forster v Lawson* (1826) 3 Bing 452; 130 ER 587 (imputation of business failure against partnership of bankers); *Le Fanu v Malcolmson* (1848) 1 HL Cas 637 at 669; 9 ER 910 at 924 per Lord Campbell (imputation of cruelty against factory owners).

of defamatory statements against its trading or business reputation (*Haythorn v Lawson* (1827) 3 Car & P 195 at 197; 172 ER 384 per Gaselee J; *Smith v McQuiggan* (1863) 2 SCR(NSW) (L) 268 at 270 per Stephen CJ). Allegations which would be defamatory of a natural person, such as murder, incest or forgery, are not allegations which could be defamatory of a partnership, because a partnership, as distinct from the constituent partners, cannot commit these acts (*Todd v Swan Television and Radio Broadcasters Pty Ltd* (2001) 25 WAR 284 at 299–300 per Steytler J). However, the constituent partners retained the right to sue for defamation if the imputations reflected personally upon them (*Harrison v Bevington* (1838) 8 Car & P 711 at 713; 173 ER 683 per Lord Abinger CB; *Smith v McQuiggan* (1863) 2 SCR(NSW) (L) 268 at 270 per Stephen CJ). Thus, in *Todd v Swan Television and Radio Broadcasters Pty Ltd* (2001) 25 WAR 284 at 301, Steytler J held that a partnership was not defamed by a television broadcast that falsely suggested that the business was owned by a man who had murdered his wife and had attempted suicide during a domestic dispute, even though the evidence established that customers did in fact shun and avoid the business. His Honour found that the imputation was not defamatory because it did not reflect upon the 'character' of the partnership business ((2001) 25 WAR 284 at 302). Steytler J had no difficulty, however, finding that the imputations that one of the partners, Mr Todd, had murdered his wife and had attempted suicide were defamatory of him personally ((2001) 25 WAR 284 at 297–8). Whilst refusing the claim of the partnership business, his Honour awarded Todd personally $70,000 ((2001) 25 WAR 284 at 308–9).

It is equally clear that, at common law, corporations are entitled to sue for defamation (*South Hetton Coal Co v North-Eastern News Association* [1894] 1 QB 133 at 142 per Lopes LJ). Even more clearly than partnerships, corporations have a separate legal personality which can be defamed and therefore can be protected and vindicated by defamation law (*Salomon v A Salomon & Co Ltd* [1897] AC 22). Like partnerships, a corporation can only sue for aspersions cast upon its business or trading reputation (*South Hetton Coal Co v North-Eastern News Association* [1894] 1 QB 133 at 138–9 per Lord Esher MR, at 141 per Lopes LJ; *Metropolitan Saloon Omnibus Co v Hawkins* 4 H & N 87 at 90; 157 ER 769 per Pollock CB; *Barnes & Co Ltd v Sharpe* (1910) 11 CLR 462 at 485 per Higgins J; *D & L Caterers Ltd v D'Ajou* [1945] KB 364 at 366 per Lord Goddard). It is no more capable than a partnership of committing murder or incest or forgery.[4] Again, like partnerships,

4 *South Hetton Coal Co v North-Eastern News Association* [1894] 1 QB 133 at 141 per Lopes LJ; *Metropolitan Saloon Omnibus Co v Hawkins* 4 H & N 87 at 90; 157 ER 769 per Pollock CB; *Barnes & Co Ltd v Sharpe* (1910) 11 CLR 462 at 474 per Griffith CJ; *D & L Caterers Ltd v D'Ajou* [1945] KB 364 at 366 per Lord Goddard. However, see further *Todd v Swan Television and Radio Broadcasters Pty Ltd* (2001) 25 WAR 284 at 300; Spencer Bower 1990, 244; *Australian Liquor, Hospitality and Miscellaneous Workers Union (Miscellaneous Workers Division) WA Branch v Mulligan* (1996) 15 WAR 385 at 387 per Anderson J.

the directors of a company may be entitled to sue for imputations made against the company, so long as those imputations reflect personally upon those directors (*South Hetton Coal Co v North-Eastern News Association* [1894] 1 QB 133 at 141 per Lopes LJ; *Randwick Labor Club Ltd v Amalgamated Television Services Pty Ltd* [1999] NSWSC 880. This is also, of course, subject to the plaintiffs satisfying the requirements of identification. As to the requirements of identification, see Chapter 3).

If a corporation succeeds in an action for defamation, it is entitled to damages as of a right, just like a natural person. However, the heads of available damages for defamation vary for natural persons and corporations. As Lord Thurlow LC famously said, a corporation has 'no body to be kicked and no soul to be damned' and, by extension, no feelings to injure. Whilst an award of compensatory damages for defamation to a natural person comprises injury to reputation and injury to feelings, and moreover, these components are inextricably linked (as to the relationship of injury to reputation and injury to feelings in the award of compensatory damages, see Chapter 3), such an award for a corporation comprises only injury to reputation. A component for injury to feelings is not awarded because corporations do not have feelings. As Lord Reid makes clear in *Lewis v Daily Telegraph Ltd* [1964] AC 234 at 262, the only compensable damage to it is necessarily economic. The suggestion by Mahoney JA in *Andrews* that a corporation might be entitled to recover damages for injury to its 'reputation as such', seemingly by way of solatium ([1980] 2 NSWLR 225 at 254–6), has been effectively criticised by the Full Federal Court in *Australian Broadcasting Corporation v Comalco Ltd* (1986) 12 FCR 510 (at 599–602 per Pincus J). A corporation is not limited to a claim for special damages, based on proof of actual pecuniary loss; it may also recover general compensatory damages for injury to its reputation, albeit economic in character (*Kay v Chesser* [1999] 3 VR 55 at 58–9 per Ormiston JA; *Feo v Pioneer Concrete (Vic) Pty Ltd* [1999] 3 VR 417 at 433 per Winneke P).

Corporate reputation clearly manifests the concept of reputation as property. Yet even in this regard, it is not the only type of reputational interest involved. The mere publication of matter that injures a corporate plaintiff's business, profession or trade is not defamatory. There needs to be an additional element that reflects adversely upon the corporate reputation (as to the requirements of defamatory character and meaning, see Chapter 3). This engages the notion of reputation as honour, that in order for corporations to be able to sue for defamation, they must be able to establish that they have been wrongly accused of having failed to meet the 'normative standards of personal [or, rather, corporate] conduct' (Post 1986, 701). Thus, corporate reputation is not purely proprietary but, given the requirements of defamation law, necessarily involves reputation as honour. What is unique about corporate reputation is that, whilst it involves reputation as property and as honour, it does not involve reputation as dignity – corporate entities have no subjective selves, thus no subjective reactions to defamation to compensate.

Although the common law recognises that corporations have a (somewhat attenuated) right to reputation which may be vindicated and protected through defamation law, it should not be assumed that it is natural for artificial persons to have such a right. After all, the common law position was merely an extension of the right to reputation of natural persons to artificial persons, without advertence to whether such an extension was a desirable development. The international and national human rights documents which explicitly protect the right to reputation do so for the benefit of natural, not artificial, persons.

Moreover, the right for corporations to sue for defamation can be, and has been, abrogated by statute. In 2002, in New South Wales, a provision was inserted by the *Defamation Amendment Act* 2002 (NSW) in the *Defamation Act* 1974 (NSW) abolishing the right of corporations to sue for defamation (*Defamation Act* 1974 (NSW) s 8A(1). See also *ING Direct (Australia) Ltd v Muscat* [2003] NSWSC 11 at [3]–[5] per Levine J.). An exception was made for corporations with less than ten employees and no subsidiaries (s 8A(3)). The legislation explicitly preserved the right of individual members of the corporation bringing defamation proceedings if the publication of defamatory matter reflected upon them personally (s 8A(2)). This position has now been adopted throughout Australia as part of the introduction of national, uniform defamation laws,[5] although it was not without controversy (cf. the views of Morgan 2005 and Marr 2005. See further Commonwealth Attorney-General, *Revised Outline of a Possible National Defamation Law*, 2004, 38–9). Thus, the ability of corporations to protect their reputations, already attenuated at common law, has been severely restricted by statute in Australia.

One of the justifications the Attorney-General's Taskforce on Defamation Law Reform recommending this change relied upon (Attorney-General's Taskforce on Defamation Law Reform 2002, 13), echoed in the more recent Standing Committee of Attorneys-General Working Group of State and Territory Officers' *Proposal for Uniform Defamation Laws* (at 14–16), was that corporations have available to them other remedies, such as the torts of injurious falsehood and passing off and the statutory cause of action for misleading and deceptive conduct (*Trade Practices Act* 1974 (Cth) s 52). These remedies confer a measure of reputational protection on corporations, to which natural persons generally cannot have recourse. However, as recent examples demonstrate, defamation can be much more favourable to corporate plaintiffs than these other causes of action.

For instance, in *Orion Pet Products Pty Ltd v Royal Society for the Prevention of Cruelty to Animals (Vic.) Inc.* (2002) 120 FCR 191, the applicant, a manufacturer of electronic dog collars which administered an electric shock to the dog when it barked in order to deter it, sued the RSPCA and its Victorian president, Dr Hugh Wirth, over comments made about its products by Wirth on radio, on the Internet

---

5 *Civil Law (Wrongs) Act* 2002 (ACT) s 121; *Defamation Act* 2006 (NT) s 8; *Defamation Act* 2005 (NSW) s 9; *Defamation Act* 2005 (Qld) s 9; *Defamation Act* 2005 (SA) s 9; *Defamation Act* 2005 (Tas) s 9; *Defamation Act* 2005 (Vic) s 9; *Defamation Act* 2005 (WA) s 9.

and in the newspapers ((2002) 120 FCR 191 at 194–8 per Weinberg J). Orion Pet Products claimed that Wirth made allegations that its products were cruel, illegal and ineffective for dog training ((2002) 120 FCR 191 195–8 per Weinberg J). Its claim for misleading and deceptive conduct failed because the representations were genuinely held, reasonably based opinions ((2002) 120 FCR 191 at 213–15 per Weinberg J). Weinberg J also found that Orion Pet Products' claim for injurious falsehood failed because it could not establish that the statements made about its products were made recklessly, maliciously or did not represent the genuinely held opinions of the makers of the statements ((2002) 120 FCR 191 at 227 per Weinberg J). However, its claim for defamation did succeed, the defences of justification ((2002) 120 FCR 191 at 232–3 per Weinberg J), fair comment ((2002) 120 FCR 191 at 233–4 per Weinberg J) and qualified privilege ((2002) 120 FCR 191 at 234–5 per Weinberg J) being readily defeated. Weinberg J awarded Orion Pet Products $85,000 damages ((2002) 120 FCR 191 at 238). This case demonstrates that defamation is more readily established than the other causes of action available to a corporate plaintiff.

A further example is provided by *Kannegieter v Hair Testing Laboratory Pty Ltd* (2004) 63 IPR 232. Although the applicant is a natural person, it illustrates circumstances in which, whilst concurrent causes of action may be available for damage to a business, trading or professional reputation, defamation still has a substantial advantage. It is equally applicable to corporate plaintiffs. In this case, the applicant, a specialist equine veterinary surgeon, sued the publishers of two magazines, *Turf Monthly* and *The Australian Standardbred*, as well as an advertiser, Hair Testing Laboratory, over an advertisement printed in these magazines ((2004) 63 IPR 232 at 233 per Whitlam J). He brought proceedings against the respondents for misleading and deceptive conduct and for defamation ((2004) 63 IPR 232 at 233 per Whitlam J). During his radio programme on radio station, 2KY, Kannegieter made critical comments about Hair Testing Laboratory's products. There were also some positive comments made ((2004) 63 IPR 232 at 235 per Whitlam J). Hair Testing Laboratory used those comments out of context in an advertisement, suggesting that Kannegieter endorsed their products ((2004) 63 IPR 232 at 236 per Whitlam J). Whitlam J found that Kannegieter had established his case for misleading and deceptive conduct ((2004) 63 IPR 232 at 238 per Whitlam J), awarding him $25,000 damages ((2004) 63 IPR 232 at 240 per Whitlam J). His Honour also found that, with knowledge of extrinsic facts about Kannegieter ((2004) 63 IPR 232 at 240–41 per Whitlam J), the advertisement conveyed the imputations that the applicant had acted unethically, has compromised his credibility and was a hypocrite ((2004) 63 IPR 232 at 240–41 per Whitlam J). The defences of qualified privilege, at common law and under the *Defamation Act* 1974 (NSW) s 22, were not established ((2004) 63 IPR 232 at 241–2 per Whitlam J). Whitlam J assessed Kannegieter's damages for the two publications at $100,000 ((2004) 63 IPR 232 at 242 per Whitlam J). Even when a remedy for an alternative cause of action to defamation is available, defamation may still prove to be more lucrative.

Despite having been deprived of their right to sue for defamation in Australia, corporate plaintiffs still have a number of avenues by which to seek redress for their damaged reputations. They can still have access to the courts, admittedly only if they can establish the more onerous requirements of injurious falsehood and misleading and deceptive conduct. (For a recent example, see *David Jones Ltd v The Australia Institute Ltd* [2007] FCA 962 at [2]–[10] per Edmonds J.) Moreover, their continuing operation in the marketplace for their goods and services also offers corporations the opportunity to rebuild their reputations. Indeed, the resources at the disposal of large corporations particularly, which allow such corporations to deal with reputational damage by legal and non-legal means, such as marketing campaigns, was cited as one of the main reasons for abolishing their right to sue for defamation (see Standing Committee of Attorneys-General Working Group of State and Territory Officers' *Proposal for Uniform Defamation Laws*, 15). (The spectre of the McLibel litigation loomed large over this proposal. See *McDonald's Corporation v Steel* (unreported, No. 1990-M-NO 5724, High Court of Justice, Queen's Bench Division, Bell J, 19 June 1997); *Steel v McDonald's Corporation* [1999] EWCA Civ 1144; *Steel v United Kingdom* [2005] EMLR 15; (2005) 41 EHRR 22. See also Vidal 1997; Nicholson 2000.) As Post argues, one of the characteristics of reputation as property is that it is contingent and dynamic, allowing its possessor to create or rebuild it (Post 1986, 695–6).

This suggestion that collective entities may attempt to rebuild their own reputations in *fora* outside the courts is reinforced by the treatment of the right of government bodies to sue in defamation for damage to their 'governing reputations'. In Great Britain and in Australia, the prevailing view is that government bodies are not entitled to sue in defamation (*Derbyshire County Council v Times Newspapers Ltd* [1993] AC 534; *Ballina Shire Council v Ringland* (1994) 33 NSWLR 680; *New South Wales Aboriginal Land Council v Jones* (1998) 43 NSWLR 300. However see further *Robertson v John Fairfax Publications Pty Ltd* (2003) 58 NSWLR 246 at 251 per Simpson J), although they may attempt to bring proceedings for injurious falsehood (*Ballina Shire Council v Ringland* (1994) 33 NSWLR 680 at 694 per Gleeson CJ, at 733 per Mahoney JA. However, see also *Ballina Shire Council v Ringland* [1999] NSWSC 11). Likewise, individual members of those government bodies are not precluded from instituting defamation proceedings, so long as those imputations reflect personally upon those individuals (this is also, of course, subject to the plaintiffs satisfying the requirements of identification. As to the requirements of identification, see Chapter 3. Presumably such plaintiffs would also have to be aware of the implied freedom of political communication. See *Lange v Australian Broadcasting Corporation* (1997) 189 CLR 520). The reasoning for this conclusion relied upon the fact that to allow such claims would impose an impermissible fetter upon freedom of speech in relation to governmental and political matters (*Derbyshire County Council v Times Newspapers Ltd* [1993] AC 534 at 549 per Lord Keith of Kinkel). Moreover, as Lord Keith of Kinkel observes, established political parties tend to dominate governments at all levels, meaning that the reputation is attached to the ruling political party, changing as the ruling political party changes ([1993] AC 534 at 550). Gleeson CJ refines this analysis, precluding government bodies from suing for defamation by recourse to the concept of reputation:

> I regard the matter as turning upon the concept of reputation, and the nature of the reputation which the law of defamation sets out to protect. I understand that concept in its application to individuals (including individual politicians), trading corporations and other bodies, but I have the greatest difficulty with the concept in its application to the governing reputation of an elected governmental institution. The right of an individual, even one in public life, to his or her personal reputation is one thing. Such a right can be recognised and protected by the law without undue interference with the right of free speech. On the other hand, to maintain that an elected governmental institution has a right to reputation as a governing body is to contend for the existence of something that is incompatible with the very process to which the body owes its existence. (*Ballina Shire Council v Ringland* (1994) 33 NSWLR 680 at 691 per Gleeson CJ. See also *Healy v Askin* [1974] 1 NSWLR 436 at 440 per Lee J)

Thus, government bodies were denied access to the courtroom in defamation proceedings as the forum in which to vindicate their reputations because the appropriate forum in which to do so was the ballot box.

Overview

Whilst defamation claims involving professional reputations squarely raise the concept of reputation as property, it is not the only concept so engaged. Indeed, the nature of a profession necessarily conveys certain ethical and moral obligations, which suggest that a professional reputation has proprietary and honourable aspects to it. When a natural person complains of an attack on his or her professional reputation, it involves an attack on a valuable right of the plaintiff as well as the honour of the plaintiff. Given that the plaintiff's subjective reaction to a defamatory publication is intimately connected to the reaction of others, such a publication also affects the plaintiff's dignity. In this way, one defamatory publication can affect the three aspects of a plaintiff's reputation. The concepts of reputation identified by Post may prove effective in providing an adequate explanation of the professional reputations of plaintiffs such as Nugawela and Andrews.

However, not all concepts of reputation identified by Post are necessarily engaged in a given case. The common law's treatment of corporate reputation demonstrates this, with its excision of the right of a corporation to claim damages for injury to feelings and its 'reputation as such'. The fact that corporations do not necessarily have the right to reputation enjoyed by natural persons – that the incidents of a right to reputation vary between natural and artificial persons; that it can fail to be recognised by international and national human rights documents; that it can be abrogated by the legislature – suggests that the presence of reputation as property in Australian defamation law should not be overstated. More importantly, the right of corporate entities to sue for defamation presents the issue of where reputations should be vindicated – and, by extension, where they should be created and rebuilt – suggesting that there are important *fora* outside the courts for the making and finessing of reputations.

Chapter 5
Reputation as Honour: Part I

Introduction

This book has traced the basis of the concept of reputation as honour to notions of publicly or socially mediated and sanctioned morality. The next two chapters seek to contextualise the concept of reputation as honour within Australian defamation law through case studies involving recent instances in which plaintiffs have complained about publications which have portrayed them as deviating from sexual norms.

In the first case study, cases involving engagement in heterosexual sex outside marriage will be the focus. In the *Morosi and Cairns* case study, it will be seen that the plaintiffs sought to assert that they identified with the normative characteristics of the social role of the 'good spouse', notably sexual fidelity to one's husband or wife and that they sued when this was questioned (extensively) by the Australian media. In the *Abbott and Costello* case study, it will be seen that the plaintiffs sought to assert that they identified with the normative characteristics of the social role of the decent person, not engaging in premarital sex, promiscuity or sex for improper motives.

Case Study 2: Imputations of 'Unchastity' – Introduction

Case Study 2(a): Imputations of Adultery – Junie Morosi and Jim Cairns

The background to Morosi's and Cairns's defamation proceedings In early December, 1974, Jim Cairns was appointed Federal Treasurer in the Whitlam Labor Government, replacing Frank Crean. Shortly after his appointment, Cairns appointed Junie Morosi as his private secretary (for the factual background of 'the Morosi affair', see Morosi 1975, 19–40; Ormonde 1981, 189–208; Strangio 2002, 285–344). Thus began the process of what one of Cairns's biographers, Paul Ormonde, styles as 'the great transformation' of Cairns, the catalyst being Morosi (Ormonde 1981, 189). Prior to Morosi's appointment, Cairns had a somewhat puritanical reputation (Ormonde 1981). Following his association, Cairns became more concerned with the attainment of personal freedom (McRae 1976, 7, 13; Ormonde 1981, 191; Morosi 1975, 2, 6).

Thus began also what Morosi herself claimed was 'a press campaign unprecedented in Australian history' (Morosi 1975, 52). Ormonde characterised 'the Morosi affair', as it became known, as 'a saga of sexual innuendo, politics and prejudice that was to provide a titillating diversion for the nation for the next twelve months' (Ormonde 1981, 190). As a consequence of Cairns and particularly Morosi's maintenance of defamation proceedings against a large number of media outlets, they ensured that the 'diversion' continued for some years hence.

From the outset, Morosi was mistrusted by members of Cairns's staff and other Labor parliamentarians and also attracted a hostile response from the Opposition and significant sections of the Australian media. Questions were immediately raised about the propriety of Morosi's appointment. At the time of her appointment, Morosi was being investigated by the New South Wales Corporate Affairs Commission over her involvement in several failed companies, including Tacticair Pty Ltd, Transportation Consultants International (Australia) Pty Ltd and Hotel Express International Pty Ltd. Morosi was well-connected to the Australian Labor Party, being friends with then Attorney-General, Senator Lionel Murphy, and his wife, Ingrid, and having worked as a consultant on community relations for then Minister for Immigration, Al Grassby. The extent of her connections with Murphy and Grassby were used to suggest that she did not obtain her position on merit. Indeed, the attacks emphasised Morosi's alleged lack of qualifications for the position. In the same week as Morosi was appointed, her husband, David Ditchburn, was appointed by the Attorney-General to the Films Board of Review. At the same time, a letter from the Attorney-General to the Minister for the Australian Capital Territory, Gordon Bryant, was leaked to the media. The letter was interpreted as suggesting that the Attorney-General was improperly attempting to procure low-cost housing for Morosi as a matter of priority.

Due to the intensity of the media coverage of her appointment, Morosi resigned from her position on Cairns's staff, less than a week after she was appointed. Following her resignation, Morosi held her first press conference at which she claimed that she had been 'a victim of racial and sexual discrimination' (Holland 1974, 5).

Cairns later re-appointed Morosi as his private secretary. This course of action led to a confrontation with his press secretary, Geoff Cleghorn, particularly concerning the extent of Morosi's media appearances and her public discussion of her (platonic) relationship with Cairns. The leaking of the circumstances surrounding Cleghorn's subsequent sacking led to renewed media interest in the relationship between Cairns and Morosi in February 1975. Cairns further exacerbated the situation by famously telling the Sydney tabloid newspaper, *The Sun*, that he had 'a kind of love' for Junie Morosi (McRae 1975, 1).

Controversy continued to surround Cairns in 1975, in relation to 'the Morosi affair', as well as other matters, in particular 'the Loans Affair', the attempt by certain ministers to raise funds through Pakistani businessman, Tirath Khemlani, so as to bypass the threatened block of supply by the Opposition in the Senate. In July 1975, using Cairns's distraction with Morosi as one of his reasons, the Prime Minister, Gough Whitlam, sacked Cairns as Treasurer, replacing him with Bill Hayden. Cairns thus became the only Federal Treasurer never to hand down a budget.

Morosi and her life, both personal and professional, were subjected to intense media scrutiny throughout late 1974 and well into 1975. Some of the media attention was sympathetic but the majority was hostile (for the flavour of the press coverage of 'the Morosi affair' in late 1974 and early 1975, see, for example, Jost et al., 1974, 1, 3; Jost 1974, 1, 3; *The Australian* (20 February 1975), 1; Grattan 1975, 1; Kelly 1975, 1; Smark 1975, 2; Mitchell 1975, 1; Bowers 1975, 7). Morosi attributed the hostile media attention to the fact that she challenged the prevailing social attitudes about women in the workforce, particularly beautiful women, and that she was not Anglo-Saxon (Ormonde 1981, 189–90; Morosi 1975, 53–5). In an interview with *The Sun* she asked rhetorically: 'Is my face to be my sin?' (McRae 1974a, 1).

Following his expulsion from the ministry in July 1975, Cairns employed Morosi, less controversially, as a research assistant on his personal staff. Cairns and particularly Morosi were, however, intent on holding the media accountable for their publications.

Morosi v Mirror Newspapers Ltd ([1977] 2 NSWLR 749) In response to the press coverage of her appointment to Cairns's staff in late 1974 and early 1975, Morosi instituted eight defamation actions in the Supreme Court of New South Wales and one defamation action in the District Court of New South Wales. The nine claims were brought against *The Daily Mirror*, *The Daily Telegraph* and *The Australian* newspapers. They were ultimately consolidated, pursuant to the *Supreme Court Rules* 1970 (NSW) Pt 31 r 7, in the Supreme Court of New South Wales. Due to the complexity of the matter, the trial judge, Taylor CJ at CL, adopted a peculiar trial procedure, requiring the jury to consider six of Morosi's claims and only return a single verdict in respect of these publications. The trial at first instance occupied 21 sitting days. The appeal occupied nine days and raised over one hundred grounds ([1977] 2 NSWLR 749 at 755 *per curiam*). The task of judge and jury in this case was described as 'unusually formidable' by the New South Wales Court of Appeal ([1977] 2 NSWLR 749 at 756 *per curiam*). In respect of the six defamatory articles, the jury awarded Morosi $17,000 damages.

Given the wide-ranging nature of the allegations levelled against Morosi, it is unsurprising that Morosi's claims raised a variety of imputations. Central to her claims, however, were imputations of sexual impropriety.

For instance, in relation to one of the publications, a cartoon published in *The Sunday Telegraph*, the jury found that it conveyed the imputation that Morosi 'had a romantic attachment with the Treasurer, Dr Cairns', and that this imputation was defamatory ([1977] 2 NSWLR 749 at 769 *per curiam*). The Court dismissed the challenge to the jury verdict on this issue ([1977] 2 NSWLR 749 at 769 *per curiam*).

In relation to a further two newspaper articles, published under the respective headlines, 'No sex with Junie says Clyde' and 'Sexual skeletons in the cupboard: Cameron', detailing a press conference held by then Minister for Labour, Clyde Cameron, to deny that Morosi had made a sexual advance upon him and a move within the Labor Caucus to oust Morosi, the jury found that they conveyed the imputation that Morosi was promiscuous and that it was defamatory ([1977] 2 NSWLR 749 at 770–71 *per curiam*). The articles described Morosi as 'a beautiful three-times married Eurasian grandmother' and detailed Mrs Gwen Cairns's distress at 'the Morosi affair' ([1977] 2 NSWLR 749 at 771 *per curiam*). The New South Wales Court of Appeal found that the appeal against the jury verdict in this regard should be dismissed. According to the Court, '[t]he conduct of a married woman in continuing to live with her husband, and at the same time to have an affair with another man, can properly be described as promiscuous' ([1977] 2 NSWLR 749 at 771).

The Court rejected the argument mounted by the appellant newspapers that the articles in question did not impute promiscuity on the part of Morosi but rather 'sexual immorality of a slightly lesser degree' ([1977] 2 NSWLR 749 at 771). Instead, the Court found that '[t]o say of a woman that she is of loose sexual morals is, in substance, similar to saying that she is promiscuous' ([1977] 2 NSWLR 749 at 771).

The appellant newspapers pleaded defences of common law and statutory qualified privilege, justification, unlikelihood of harm and contextual truth. Whilst at first instance, they enjoyed a degree of success, their appeal in relation to these defences completely failed.[1] Interestingly, in relation to the defence of unlikelihood of harm, the appellant newspapers submitted that the fact that Dr Cairns appeared on television to refute the claims, as they pertained to him, demonstrated that the imputations could not further injure Morosi's reputation. The New South Wales Court of Appeal rejected this consideration, noting that Cairns's television appearances did not relate to 'the circumstances of the publication'. Moreover, Cairns's subsequent television appearances were irrelevant because the statutory provision required an examination of prospective damage, not actual damage assessed after the publication of defamatory matter ([1977] 2 NSWLR 749 at 799).

In relation to the assessment of damages, the jury had found that Morosi had a bad reputation for dishonesty ([1977] 2 NSWLR 749 at 800–801). In light of the adverse finding on Morosi's reputation, the appellant newspapers submitted that she was only entitled to nominal damages. However, the Court noted that the appellant newspapers did not tender evidence of Morosi's bad reputation for promiscuity – a sector of her reputation which the defamatory matters attacked ([1977] 2 NSWLR 749 at 801). Morosi was entitled to substantial damages because she was entitled to consolation for the injury to her feelings occasioned by the publication of the

1 As to the defeat of the defence of common law qualified privilege, see [1977] 2 NSWLR 749 at 790–92; as to the defeat of the defence of statutory qualified privilege pursuant to the *Defamation Act* 1974 (NSW) s 22, see at 797–9; as to the defeat of the defence of unlikelihood of harm pursuant to the *Defamation Act* 1974 (NSW) s 13, see at 801, 803; as to the defeat of the defence of contextual truth pursuant to the *Defamation Act* 1974 (NSW) s 16, see at 803.

defamatory matter, even if there were no need for a significant sum by way of vindication ([1977] 2 NSWLR 749 at 807–8; as to the purposes of an award of compensatory damages, see Chapter 3). Thus, the challenge to Morosi's award of damages also failed ([1977] 2 NSWLR 749 at 803–7). The Court emphasised that Morosi's award of $17,000 consisted of purely compensatory damages. They contained no element of aggravated or exemplary damages ([1977] 2 NSWLR 749 at 804–5).

Morosi v Broadcasting Station 2GB Pty Ltd ([1980] 2 NSWLR 418) Morosi also commenced defamation proceedings against Sydney radio station, 2GB, over a broadcast made by news commentator, Ormsby Wilkins, on 1 August 1975. Wilkins's commentary was motivated by an interview with Morosi conducted by television current affairs host, Mike Willesee, the previous evening.

According to Wilkins, Willesee suggested to Morosi that she was having a sexual relationship with Cairns, that she was bearing Cairns's child and that she might also be a 'Mata Hari', operating undercover for persons, agencies or causes unstated. To the extent that there are winners and losers in such things, Wilkins concluded that Morosi emerged from the interview the clear victor ([1980] 2 NSWLR 418 at 418 per Samuels JA).

Wilkins then explained why he was discussing Morosi again:

> Hers is the most notorious woman's name in the country and now that she's to have a baby there will be a spate of dirty jokes about her, and a variety of speculations as to who is the father, because everybody knows that Junie Morosi is an immoral adventurer … adventuress … who has slept with a variety of notable politicians, and most recently has been sleeping with Jim Cairns. In fact, of course, nobody knows any such thing. ([1980] 2 NSWLR 418 at 419 per Samuels JA)

Wilkins noted that the worst accusation that could be fairly levelled against Morosi was that she had been involved in failed business ventures.

He then observed that Cairns had made many mistakes in his political career but that, from recent events surrounding them, Wilkins thought that Cairns and Morosi 'emerge with more dignity and less soil on them' than those who make 'sniggering jokes' about them ([1980] 2 NSWLR 418 at 419 per Samuels JA).

Morosi then commenced defamation proceedings in the Supreme Court of New South Wales against 2GB in respect of this editorial. The trial was conducted in late February 1978 before Sheppard J and a jury. At the close of the evidence, 2GB sought judgment on the basis that the matter complained of was incapable of being defamatory of Morosi. The trial judge rejected the motion and allowed the jury to retire to consider its verdict. The jury awarded Morosi $10,000 damages ([1980] 2 NSWLR 418 at 419 per Samuels JA).

2GB appealed on the ground that the broadcast was incapable of conveying the pleaded imputations. It submitted that the bane of the broadcast was cured by the presence of the antidote. It contended that it was not an attack on Morosi but rather a defence of her; that it was 'eulogistic', not 'pejorative' ([1980] 2 NSWLR 418 at 419 per Samuels JA).

Giving the leading judgment in the New South Wales Court of Appeal, Samuels JA rejected this argument, finding that whether the antidote negated the bane was a matter of impression. It could not be established that the jury's verdict was manifestly wrong on this issue ([1980] 2 NSWLR 418 at 420).

2GB and particularly Wilkins felt resentful about being sued by Morosi in circumstances where they were attempting to defend her. Samuels JA's response to that was to have recourse to 'a homely phrase': 'With friends like that, who needs enemies?' ([1980] 2 NSWLR 418 at 421).

Cairns v John Fairfax & Sons Ltd ([1983] 2 NSWLR 708) Even in the years after 'the Morosi affair', both Morosi and Cairns were vigilant in protecting their reputations. In late January 1981, the newspaper, *The National Times*, reported a comment made by an American financier, Dudley Schoales, describing Morosi as '[Cairns's] girl friend'. This referred to the period when Cairns was the Federal Treasurer and, as Hutley JA evocatively expresses it, 'both he and Miss Morosi were married and middle aged' ([1983] 2 NSWLR 708 at 709).

Both Cairns and Morosi instituted defamation proceedings in the Supreme Court of New South Wales against the publisher of *The National Times*, John Fairfax & Sons Ltd. On this occasion, unlike Morosi's previous claims, they were unsuccessful.

At first instance, the jury found that the article in question in fact conveyed the imputation that Cairns was 'improperly involved with his assistant, Junie Morosi, in a romantic or sexual association contrary to the obligations of his marriage and to that of Miss Morosi' but that this imputation was not in fact defamatory of Cairns. It reached the same verdict in relation to a similarly structured imputation pleaded by Morosi ([1983] 2 NSWLR 708 at 711 per Samuels JA, at 718 per Mahoney JA).

Cairns and Morosi appealed to the New South Wales Court of Appeal, submitting that the jury verdict was unreasonable or perverse. By majority (Hutley and Mahoney JJA, Samuels JA dissenting) the Court found that it was not ([1983] 2 NSWLR 708 at 710 per Hutley JA).

Hutley JA noted that the term 'girlfriend' admits of an innocent or a sinister meaning, depending on the context. As such, its meaning in the context of the publication in question was pre-eminently one for the jury. His Honour also noted that the concept of an improper romantic relationship covered a broad spectrum of possible meanings, some defamatory, some non-defamatory. Hutley JA went further, suggesting that, rather than the pleaded imputation having a deleterious effect on the reputations of Cairns and Morosi, it may indeed have a positive effect:

> [T]he fact that so intelligent and glamorous a woman as Miss Morosi (Mrs Ditchburn) developed a romantic interest in him may raise his standing in public eyes, and the

> fact that so important a figure as the Treasurer of the Commonwealth reciprocated her interest may raise her standing in public eyes. ([1983] 2 NSWLR 708 at 710)

Dealing then with the imputation of an improper adulterous relationship, his Honour concluded:

> [t]he imputation of an improper relationship would be harder to justify as not being defamatory, but the reputations of Anthony and Cleopatra have not been lowered in the eyes of the public by their romance, and in other days, the title of King's Mistress was one of honour. Despite Rofe QC's confident assertion that the imputation of adultery must lower the two appellants in the public esteem, even in these days in which fault has been officially expelled from the law of domestic relations, passions between the powerful and glamorous may have a quality which transcends middle-class morality. The expulsion of the concept of fault in domestic relations means that as far as the State is concerned anything goes. The official abandonment of standards carries with it the implication that the right thinking person is not easily identified. ([1983] 2 NSWLR 708 at 710)

Reaching the same conclusion, albeit less colourfully, Mahoney JA found that it was open to the jury, applying the standards of the ordinary, reasonable reader as 'reasonable or right-thinking people', to find that the suggestion that a plaintiff acted inconsistently with his or her marriage obligations was not defamatory ([1983] 2 NSWLR 708 at 719; as to the requirements of the 'ordinary, reasonable reader', see Chapter 3). His Honour reasoned that not every act or association contrary to one's marriage obligations is necessarily defamatory. His Honour further noted that the defamatory character of the imputations was not to be assessed by reference to religious or ethical principles, but rather to prevailing community standards. Mahoney JA suggested that general community standards might view religious or ethical principles on sexual matters as 'too high or too rigid' but might themselves be viewed 'if not lower and more flexible, at least different' to those principles ([1983] 2 NSWLR 708 at 720).

His Honour concluded that '[i]t should, in my opinion, be recognized that in this community the attitude to sexual relationships has changed profoundly during the last twenty years.' The consequence of this recognition is that, whilst once it was considered necessarily defamatory to impute that two unmarried persons had a sexual relationship, now, according to Mahoney JA, 'a substantial part of the community' (as to sectional attitudes and defamatory meaning, see Chapter 3) would take the opposite view ([1983] 2 NSWLR 708 at 721). His Honour suggested that community attitudes had not shifted so decisively on the issue of sexual relationships between married persons outside marriage but nonetheless was willing to allow that it was open to the jury to find such an imputation not to be defamatory ([1983] 2 NSWLR 708 at 721).

In his dissenting judgment, Samuels JA found that the imputation was necessarily defamatory, notwithstanding changes to sexual attitudes and the introduction of no-fault divorce ([1983] 2 NSWLR 708 at 717). Importantly, however, as Samuels

JA notes in his judgment, both Cairns and Morosi denied under oath that they had a sexual relationship ([1983] 2 NSWLR 708 at 714, 715–16).

Case Study 2(b): Imputations of 'Unchastity' – Peter and Tanya Costello and Tony and Margaret Abbott

The background to Costello's and Abbott's defamation proceedings In March 1997, Bob Ellis's book, *Goodbye Jerusalem: Night Thoughts of a Labor Outsider*, was published by Random House Australia Pty Ltd. From the outset, it caused controversy. At its book launch, the author was obliged to read out an apology to David Spicer, a political journalist from the national, public broadcaster, the Australian Broadcasting Corporation, because Ellis had misquoted him, wrongly attributing a critical comment about Bob Carr's dealings with Australia's richest man, Kerry Packer, to Spicer (Ellis 2002, 332). This was only the beginning of Ellis's encounters with defamation law. His book also contained a passage that led to one of the highest-profile Australian defamation cases of the late 1990s.

The offending passage occurred in an anecdote about the book launch for *Subhuman Redneck Poems*, a volume of poetry by Australian poet, Les Murray. Ellis recorded that, at the book launch, he was approached by Tony Abbott. Meeting Tony Abbott provided the stimulus for an anecdote about Abbott, allegedly told to Ellis by former Labor politician, Rodney Cavalier:

> 'Abbott and Costello', said Rodney Cavalier, pacing up and down his baronial mansion after serving me for dinner as was his custom bread and water, 'they're both in the right wing of the Labor Party till one woman fucked both of them and married one of them and inducted them into the Young Liberals.' (Ellis 1997a, 472)

Abbott became aware of the anecdote when Christopher Pearson, a journalist and speech-writer for the Liberal Prime Minister, John Howard, alerted him to its existence (*Costello v Random House Australia Pty Ltd* (1999) 137 ACTR 1 at 18 per Higgins J. See also Ellis 2002, 332). Abbott, in turn, alerted Costello.

At the time of publication, Costello was the Federal Treasurer and Abbott was the Parliamentary Secretary to the Minister for Employment, Education, Training and Youth Affairs in the Howard Liberal–National Coalition government. Tanya Costello was the daughter of the former Liberal State Leader of the Opposition, Peter Coleman, and met Costello and Abbott through her involvement in Liberal student politics (*Costello v Random House Australia Pty Ltd* (1999) 137 ACTR 1 at 7 per Higgins J). She married Costello in 1982 ((1999) 137 ACTR 1 at 8 per Higgins J). Margaret Abbott was a New Zealander by birth, emigrating to Australia in 1983 ((1999) 137 ACTR 1 at 8 per Higgins J), and did not have any associations with the Liberal Party prior to her marriage to Tony Abbott in 1988 ((1999) 137 ACTR 1 at 7 per Higgins J).

Costello v Random House Australia Pty Ltd ((1999) 137 ACTR 1; 149 FLR 367; Aust Torts Reports ¶81–503) Both Mr and Mrs Abbott and Mr and Mrs Costello instituted defamation proceedings against the publisher, Random House Australia Pty Ltd, in the Supreme Court of the Australian Capital Territory, described by Ellis as 'a venue famed for its kindliness to slandered politicians' (Ellis 2002, 335).

Mr Abbott and Mr Costello pleaded the following imputations arising from the matter complained of:

> A(i) The … plaintiff … so lacked personal integrity that, in return for sexual favours, he was willing to change his political allegiance.
> A(ii) The … plaintiff's political commitment was so shallow that for sexual favours he was willing to abandon his principles.
> A(iii) The … plaintiff was to be suspected of being a weak and unreliable character who allowed his political decisions to be dictated by his wife. ((1999) 137 ACTR 1 at 7 per Higgins J)

(Mr Abbott and Mr Costello also pleaded one true innuendo but Higgins J found that the case was not one in which a true innuendo arose and accordingly dealt only with the natural and ordinary meanings pleaded: (1999) 137 ACTR 1 at 7–8 per Higgins J.)

Higgins J found that the first and third imputations were not in fact conveyed by the matter complained of because they were founded upon a notion of bargain or ultimatum that was absent from the anecdote itself ((1999) 137 ACTR 1 at 9–10 per Higgins J). However, Higgins J found that the second imputation was in fact conveyed. Indeed, his Honour went further, observing that '[t]his is precisely what the matter complained of means' ((1999) 137 ACTR 1 at 10 per Higgins J). Importantly, Higgins J noted that '[t]here is no complaint by either man that they are defamed by the imputation, not pleaded, that they each engaged in sexual relations before their respective marriages' ((1999) 137 ACTR 1 at 10 per Higgins J. As Baker observes, '[t]here is still no action for imputing unchastity to a man': Baker 2002, 443).

Higgins J then considered whether the one imputation that was in fact conveyed by the matter complained of, that of 'shallow political commitment' ((1999) 137 ACTR 1 at 12 per Higgins J), was defamatory of Mr Abbott and Mr Costello. His Honour acknowledged that Abbott and Costello were not accused of 'unlawful', 'immoral', 'deceitful' or 'reprehensible' conduct. Higgins J observed that political figures sometimes change their political allegiances. Therefore, his Honour concluded that the reputations of Abbott and Costello would not be lowered in the estimation of the ordinary, reasonable reader ((1999) 137 ACTR 1 at 12 per Higgins J). However, his Honour found that the imputation of shallow political commitment was defamatory of Abbott and Costello on the basis that it exposed them to more than a trivial degree of ridicule ((1999) 137 ACTR 1 at 12–13 per Higgins J). Even though the anecdote was intended by Ellis to target

Abbott specifically, Ellis had invited the reader to adopt a suspicious approach to both politicians ((1999) 137 ACTR 1 at 7 per Higgins J, applying *Amalgamated Television Services Pty Ltd v Marsden* (1998) 43 NSWLR 158 at 169 per Hunt CJ at CL). Therefore, it was defamatory of Costello as well as Abbott.

Mrs Abbott and Mrs Costello pleaded the following imputations arising from the matter complained of:

> B(i) The … plaintiff was to be suspected of being sexually promiscuous.
>
> B(ii) The … plaintiff, by virtue of having married the [male] plaintiff, was to be suspected of being a person of such low moral standards that she was even prepared to use sexual relations to get others to change their political allegiance.
>
> B(iii) The … plaintiff, by virtue of having married the [male] plaintiff, was to be suspected of being a political manipulator who used sex in order to recruit Labor Party members into the Liberal Party.
>
> B(iv) The … plaintiff, by virtue of having married the [male] plaintiff, was to be suspected of so lacking respect for her partner that even being married to him did not stop her from trying to subvert his political beliefs. ((1999) 137 ACTR 1 at 7 per Higgins J)

(Mrs Abbott and Mrs Costello also pleaded three true innuendos but Higgins J found that the case was not one in which true innuendos arose and accordingly dealt only with the natural and ordinary meanings pleaded: (1999) 137 ACTR 1 at 7–8 per Higgins J)

Higgins J readily found that the second imputation was conveyed but that the third and fourth imputations were speculative, rather than reasonable, inferences and, as such, were not in fact conveyed by the publication ((1999) 137 ACTR 1 at 11 per Higgins J).

Whether the first imputation was conveyed proved more problematic. Although Mrs Abbott and Mrs Costello pleaded promiscuity, Higgins J found that the matter complained of conveyed the lesser imputation of ‘unchastity’. According to his Honour, promiscuity connotes a serial form of sexual activity. Thus, ‘two episodes of premarital sex’ does not answer the description of promiscuity ((1999) 137 ACTR 1 at 11 per Higgins J). Random House conceded that its publication conveyed the imputation of premarital sex and further that such an imputation was false ((1999) 137 ACTR 1 at 6 per Higgins J). Higgins J held that it was not unfair to hold Random House liable for this imputation because it was relied upon in substance by Mrs Abbott and Mrs Costello ((1999) 137 ACTR 1 at 11 per Higgins J). Thus, his Honour found that the first imputation was conveyed by the publication.

The only defence raised by Random House was that the matter complained of was incapable of being defamatory of any of the four plaintiffs. Higgins J agreed with Random House in relation to the second imputation, finding that ‘[t]he fact that a woman is committed politically and is persuasive, albeit to a weak-willed and sexually driven male, does not, I believe, cause the woman to be regarded less highly' ((1999) 137 ACTR 1 at 13).

The first imputation proved more contentious. Random House submitted that, to say of a woman that she had sex with more than one person prior to marriage is not defamatory according to prevailing community attitudes ((1999) 137 ACTR 1 at 12 per Higgins J). Higgins J noted that Mrs Abbott and Mrs Costello did not attempt to suggest that an imputation of unchastity was defamatory only by reference to a sectional standard within the community (as to sectional standards and the defamatory character of imputations, see Chapter 3). Thus, the defamatory quality of the imputation in question had to be determined by reference to the general moral and social standards of the community ((1999) 137 ACTR 1 at 14 per Higgins J).

In determining those standards, Random House relied upon the majority judgments in *Cairns v John Fairfax & Sons Ltd* [1983] 2 NSWLR 708. However, his Honour distinguished the decision on the basis that it did not find that an imputation of adultery was not capable of being defamatory but rather that a jury verdict that such an imputation was not in fact defamatory was not perverse ((1999) 137 ACTR 1 at 14 per Higgins J). Higgins J endorsed the view, expressed by Hunt J in *Hepburn v T.C.N. Channel Nine Pty Ltd* [1984] 1 NSWLR 386 that the reasoning in *Cairns* was 'an unfortunate muddle' ([1984] 1 NSWLR 386 at 403–4). His Honour agreed that the decision in *Cairns* essentially meant that, even though there was a general, societal condemnation of extra-marital sexual relations, there might be certain exceptional instances where they might be excused ((1999) 137 ACTR 1 at 16). However, Higgins J qualified this somewhat, suggesting that, rather than leading to condemnation, such relations might be viewed 'if not with derision or contempt, then, at least with disappointment' ((1999) 137 ACTR 1 at 16). His Honour emphatically rejected the proposition that *Cairns* conferred a licence on publishers to print allegations of sexual impropriety so long as they did not suggest 'wanton adultery or promiscuity' ((1999) 137 ACTR 1 at 16–17). *Pace* Hutley JA in *Cairns*, Higgins J found that no reasonable interpretation could support the view that the reputations of Mrs Abbott and Mrs Costello were enhanced by Ellis's imputation of unchastity. Ultimately, his Honour found that the ordinary, reasonable reader, even accounting for 'Labor bias' amongst Ellis's readership, would 'predominantly adhere to what Mr Alfred Doolittle in *My Fair Lady* (a film based on the play, *Pygmalion*, by George Bernard Shaw) described as "middle class morality"' ((1999) 137 ACTR 1 at 17).

Higgins J then undertook an extensive review of the evidence given by the witnesses in the case ((1999) 137 ACTR 1 at 17–32) and proceeded to assess damages. His Honour decided that, in the circumstances, an award of aggravated damages was appropriate ((1999) 137 ACTR 1 at 50) due to the delay in withdrawing the book from bookshops and libraries ((1999) 137 ACTR 1 at 36–8, 48–9) and the publisher's failure to apologise adequately ((1999) 137 ACTR 1 at 41, 48–9). His Honour awarded Mrs Costello $40,000 damages for injury to reputation, $30,000 damages for injury to feelings and $15,000 aggravated damages ((1999)

137 ACTR 1 at 45, 50); Mr Costello $40,000 damages for injury to reputation, $20,000 damages for injury to feelings and $10,000 aggravated damages ((1999) 137 ACTR 1 at 45, 50); Mr Abbott (whom he described as the target) $40,000 damages for injury to reputation, $15,000 damages for injury to feelings and $7,500 aggravated damages ((1999) 137 ACTR 1 at 44, 45, 50); and finally, Mrs Abbott (whom he described as 'a case of collateral damage') $30,000 damages for injury to reputation, $10,000 damages for injury to feelings and $5,000 aggravated damages ((1999) 137 ACTR 1 at 44, 45–6, 50).

Random House appealed to the Full Federal Court, arguing that Higgins J erred in finding that the anecdote was defamatory. It particularly objected to his Honour's finding of an imputation of unchastity when Mrs Abbott and Mrs Costello had pleaded an imputation of promiscuity. Random House also argued that the award of damages was manifestly excessive (*Random House Australia Pty Ltd v Abbott* (1999) 94 FCR 296 at 302 per Beaumont J). The Abbotts and the Costellos filed a notice of contention, arguing that Higgins J had erred in his rejection of the balance of their imputations (*Random House Australia Pty Ltd v Abbott* (1999) 94 FCR 296 at 302 per Beaumont J).

The Full Federal Court unanimously found that, in its natural and ordinary meaning, the anecdote defamed the plaintiffs. However, on the imputation of unchastity, there was a division of opinion. As Drummond J suggested, the concepts of unchastity and promiscuity are substantially different. His Honour evocatively contrasted 'the promiscuous Messalina and the unchaste Heloise' to underscore his point ((1999) 94 FCR 296 at 330 per Drummond J). As Drummond J further noted, it was not entirely clear at all points in Higgins J's judgment what was meant by an imputation of 'unchastity' ((1999) 94 FCR 296 at 331 per Drummond J). Dealing with the imputation of unchastity and whether it differed in substance from an imputation of promiscuity, his Honour, with whom Miles J agreed, concluded that Higgins J:

> [I]n finding the imputation of unchastity was doing no kindness to the target of the text: he was only holding that, while the text did not convey the imputation of sexual promiscuity, it did convey a meaning of sexual misconduct close enough to promiscuity as not to alter the substance of the imputation pleaded. ((1999) 94 FCR 296 at 332 per Drummond J; see also at 316 per Miles J)

Drummond J held that the correct reading of Higgins J's judgment was that he did not merely find an imputation of pre-marital sex conveyed, as conceded by Random House, but rather 'a different imputation of much grosser sexual misconduct' ((1999) 94 FCR 296 at 331 per Drummond J).

Dissenting on this issue, Beaumont J found that the imputation was not conveyed because promiscuity connotes indiscriminate sexual conduct, whereas the woman in question was being accused of deliberate, indeed manipulative conduct ((1999) 94 FCR 296 at 309–10 per Beaumont J).

The Full Federal Court also unanimously dismissed the appeal on the quantum of damages ((1999) 94 FCR 296 at 316 per Beaumont J, at 323 per Miles J, at 340 per Drummond J).

Case Study 2: Imputations of Unchastity – Analysis

The Application of the Concepts of Reputation to Imputations of Unchastity

The defamation proceedings brought by Morosi and Cairns and the Abbotts and the Costellos centrally raise the concept of reputation as honour. The substance of the claims deals with issues of 'normative standards of personal [sexual] conduct' (Post 1986, 701). In her consolidated proceedings against Mirror Newspapers and other media outlets, Morosi objected to being portrayed as promiscuous; in her proceedings against 2GB, she objected to being portrayed as 'an immoral … adventuress' engaged in an adulterous relationship with Cairns. In their proceedings against Fairfax, Cairns and Morosi again objected to being portrayed as adulterers. In their proceedings against Random House, Mrs Abbott and Mrs Costello objected to being portrayed as promiscuous or seriously unchaste. All of these plaintiffs complained that the defendants had imputed sexual immorality to them. What they sought in their defamation proceedings was a vindication of their honour. The defamation trials served the purpose of a mediation of public attitudes to sexual morality.

The conclusions they reached are not incontrovertible and not without controversy. The approach of Hutley JA in *Cairns* to shifts in public attitudes towards sexual morality is markedly different to the approach adopted by Higgins J at first instance in *Costello* over fifteen years later. Public attitudes on sexual morality have shifted significantly over the past four decades, rendering the task of identifying the proper standard to apply difficult. Indeed, the outcome in *Costello* was heavily criticised in the media for being fundamentally out of step with contemporary attitudes towards sexual morality. It led *The Canberra Times* to editorialise rhetorically, '[i]s it 1999 or 1899?' (*The Canberra Times* (6 March 1999), 3). As the Fairfax journalist who covered these defamation proceedings extensively, David Marr, observed, '[i]f the law can't protect the reputation of a Christian virgin, it can protect no-one' (Marr 1999a, 1).

Writing in the 1970s, the sociologists, Berger, Berger and Kellner opined that those who assert their chastity are no longer admired and those who claim to have lost it become 'an object of amusement rather than sympathy' (Berger et al. 1977, 78). Given the success of Morosi and Cairns and the Abbotts and the Costellos, perhaps Berger et al. were hasty in their declaration that chastity is one of the 'ideological leftovers in the consciousness of obsolete classes' (Berger et al. 1977, 78). Notions of sexual propriety remain protected by Australian defamation law, potentially proving the continuing '*embourgeoisement* of honour' (Berger et al. 1977, 81).

The reputations at issue in these cases are not simply the honour of the plaintiffs. Because, for a natural plaintiff, injury to reputation and injury to feelings are inextricably linked (as to the interrelationship of compensatory damages for injury to reputation and injury to feelings, see Chapter 3), the publication of defamatory matter about a plaintiff affects not only the plaintiff's reputation as honour but also his or her reputation as dignity. In the cases where the plaintiffs succeeded, it was clear that the award of damages for injury to feelings was a substantial component of the verdict. Indeed, in Morosi's proceedings against Mirror Newspapers and the other media outlets, the New South Wales Court of Appeal suggested that, even if her reputation were bad, she could still recover substantial damages for injury to her feelings. In *Costello*, the concept of reputation as dignity was further engaged not only by the award of damages for injury to feelings but also for aggravated damages (as to aggravated damages, see Chapter 3). Random House's conduct towards the Abbotts and the Costellos aggravated their subjective experience of the defamation.

The concept of reputation as property also manifests itself in these cases in part. As politicians, Cairns, Costello and Abbott had clearly created and cultivated professional reputations. The defamatory publications in question do not merely relate to these plaintiffs in their private capacity. They also reflect upon them in their public lives, and it seems clear they were intended to do so by their publishers. Indeed, as Beaumont J observed in the *Costello* case, Ellis's anecdote reflected upon both politicians' professional and personal reputations ((1999) 94 FCR 296 at 306 per Beaumont J). The defamatory publications against Morosi can also be viewed as involving aspersions on her professional reputation, entailing as they do innuendos about her fitness to be a member of Cairns's staff. Post also suggests that the reputation a plaintiff cultivates in his or her social interactions also answers the description of reputation as property (Post 1986, 694–5). In this way, Mrs Abbott's and Mrs Costello's defamation proceedings might be construed as involving reputation as property as well.

Thus, the concepts of reputation as honour, dignity and property can be applied to the defamation proceedings brought by Morosi and Cairns and the Abbotts and the Costellos. However, there is an additional element common to these plaintiffs. These plaintiffs were the subject of intense media scrutiny as a result of their public (and sometimes, by extension, their private) activities. It is suggested that the defamation proceedings were brought in part to control the way in which the plaintiffs were portrayed in the media. It is instructive to examine the media's treatment of these cases in order to ascertain what insights this might yield about the nature of the reputations at issue and the concept of reputation generally.

Morosi, Cairns and the Media

From late 1974, when 'the Morosi affair' began, there was intense media interest surrounding Morosi and her relationship with Cairns. This media interest has waxed and waned over the subsequent three decades. Morosi and Cairns evidently objected to the way in which they had been treated by and portrayed in the media because they instituted defamation proceedings against a significant number of media outlets. Thus, the defamation proceedings were one means by which they sought to control their reputations.

It is submitted that these plaintiffs had other means available to them to control – to create, to cultivate and to repair – their reputations. Such means are unavailable to plaintiffs without a high profile. For instance, as a parliamentarian, Cairns had the forum of the parliament, wherein he could, under privilege, defend his own reputation and that of Morosi – an opportunity of which he availed himself (House of Representatives 1975). He also gave interviews to the Sydney tabloid newspaper, *The Sun*, which were sympathetic to him (McRae 1975).

Although Morosi's public profile only really arose because of the media attention which generated 'the Morosi affair', it nevertheless gave her access to a range of media opportunities through which she could promote her own version of her reputation and attempt to refute and repair damage done to it. The range of media opportunities available to Morosi in late 1974 and throughout 1975 were substantial. At the outbreak of 'the Morosi affair', media interest in Morosi, her activities and her background was intense. In this initial phase, Morosi refused to give interviews (Hills 1974, 1, 3; Stannard 1974, 1). Instead, she eventually held a press conference (Stannard 1974, 1). Whether intended or not, the effect of Morosi's decision to delay talking to the press until a time of her own choosing was to heighten the media interest in her eventual statement. Significantly, at the press conference, she denied she was having a sexual relationship with Cairns (Waugh 1974, 1, 15). In late 1974 and early 1975, Morosi and her husband, David Ditchburn, gave a series of interviews to *The Sun* newspaper, to the same journalist who had interviewed Cairns, Toni McRae. They received similarly sympathetic treatment in the articles (McRae 1974a; McRae 1974b; McRae 1974c; McRae 1974d). Morosi subsequently found further outlets for her side of the story. She provided women's weekly magazine, *Woman's Day*, with a 'world exclusive' three-part interview in February 1975 (Craig 1975a; Craig 1975b; Craig 1975c). Finally, in October 1975, Morosi released her book, *Sex, Prejudice and Politics*, consisting of reflections on her experiences over the preceding year and ruminations about the implications for Australian society and politics. This again provided Morosi with another forum in which to present her own version of her reputation. It also provided Cairns with another forum – he wrote the foreword (Morosi 1975).

Given the nature of the allegations levelled against them, it is arguable that Cairns and Morosi instituted their defamation proceedings to vindicate their honour and to assuage their wounded dignity. They wished to be perceived by the community as faithful spouses and they sought to make themselves feel better about the many publications that suggested otherwise. However, this provides only a partial explanation for the vigorous stance taken by Cairns and Morosi particularly. Arguably, Cairns and Morosi were concerned about how they were portrayed in the media and sought through their defamation proceedings to exert some degree of control over the manner in which they were presented. To some extent, they succeeded. For instance, as late as early July 2002, journalists writing about 'the Morosi affair' referred to Cairns's 'unconsummated infatuation' with Morosi (Crisp and Margo 2002, 24). What is interesting about the Morosi and Cairns defamation litigation is that one of the parties admitted that they had lied about the allegations for which they brought defamation proceedings.

Three months later and nearly thirty years after the event, Cairns revealed in a radio interview with John Cleary that he had had a [consummated] affair with Morosi (Crabb 2002; Charlton 2002a; Charlton 2002b; Walker and Gale 2002; Stephens 2002). He expressed no regrets about it. Asked why he had not made this admission earlier, he claimed that he had never been asked whether he had had sex with Morosi (Stephens 2002, 2). For her part, Morosi commented that discussion of her affair with Cairns was 'distracting to [her] professionalism' (Walker and Gale 2002, 11; Stephens 2002, 2). After more than twenty-five years, the memories of 'the Morosi affair' were revived. Press coverage of these revelations referred to the fact that Cairns and Morosi had sued various media outlets for defamation over allegations, *inter alia*, that they had been having an affair (Charlton 2002a, 3). As recently as late February 2005, the then editor of the Sydney tabloid newspaper, *The Daily Telegraph*, Campbell Reid, was quoted as saying: 'Sadly, the cheques are not back in the mail' (Maclean 2005, 23).

When Cairns died in October 2003, the media coverage again concentrated on his affair with Junie Morosi (see, for example, Bolt 2003; Legge 2003; Baird 2003; Price 2003b). Her absence from his funeral was noted (Legge 2003; McLachlan and Skulley 2003; Ryan 2003). In his eulogy, close friend and former ministerial colleague, Tom Uren, described Cairns's relationship with Morosi as 'fatal' to his political career. Uren was quoted as making the following statement in his eulogy for Cairns:

> The tragedy of this relationship was that he wouldn't listen to other people's opinion of her. Cairns would take criticism better than anyone in politics, but he was vulnerable in defence of Morosi. He wasn't honest about his relationship with her and those who had put him on a pedestal couldn't understand the relationship. (Ellingsen 2003, 6)

As a corrective, some commentators deliberately elected to emphasise another aspect of Cairns's public life (Moore 2003; Harris 2003) or downplay the importance ascribed to Morosi (Botsman 2003; Strangio 2003, 76). Both strategies proceeded from the basis that Morosi was an important part of Cairns's public life – his reputation – and that a departure from that premise needed to be justified, implicitly or explicitly.

The range of views on Cairns's posthumous reputation can also be gleaned from the condolence speeches made in parliament after his death. Some were hagiographic, some were uncharitable (Senate 2003 (Senator George Brandis; see also Senator Bob Brown and Senator Kim Carr)) some were neutral. Cairns's relationship with Morosi was also mentioned (House of Representatives 2003

(Mark Latham; Tanya Plibersek); see also Senate 2003 (Senator John Faulkner; Senator Peter Cook)).

There have not been any real adverse consequences for Cairns and Morosi flowing from the revelations that their defamation proceedings were brought in part to protect an unwarranted reputation. The relatively sympathetic treatment Morosi and Cairns have received may be contrasted with the difficulties experienced by litigants in a similar position in Great Britain. For instance, Jeffrey Archer, now Baron Archer of Weston-super-Mare, was imprisoned for perjury arising out of false evidence that he gave in his libel proceedings against *The Star*. In late October 1986, *The Star* published an article under the headline, 'POOR JEFFREY: VICE-GIRL MONICA TALKS ABOUT ARCHER – THE MAN SHE KNEW', claiming that Archer had slept with a prostitute, Monica Coghlan. Archer sued *The Star* for libel and was awarded £500,000 by a jury. He also received £50,000 plus £30,000 costs in respect of the same allegations published in the tabloid newspapers, *The News of the World*. In April 2000, Archer was arrested on charges of perjury. In July 2001, he was sentenced to four years' imprisonment by Potts J. An appeal against his conviction and sentence was dismissed (*R v Archer* [2002] EWCA Crim 1996). Understandably, both *The Star* and *The News of the World* announced their intention to seek the return of their damages – with interest – a substantial amount of money after the passage of almost fifteen years (see generally Hooper 2001, 121–35). However, even with the exposure of his undeserved victory in his libel proceedings against *The Star* and, more importantly, the dishonour of his criminal conviction, Archer still retained the capacity to rebuild his reputation and to finesse his celebrity – Archer published three volumes of his prison memoirs during his sentence (Archer 2003; Archer 2004a; Archer 2004b). Thus, whilst Archer's reputation as honour may have been diminished, his reputation as a form of property and celebrity, or more accurately, notoriety, still subsists.

Somewhat less spectacular than Jeffrey Archer's fall from grace is the fate of John Major. John Major sued *The New Statesman* for defamation over allegations that he was having an adulterous relationship with Downing Street caterer, Claire Latimer. Major particularly campaigned on an electoral platform of traditional moral values in the early 1990s. Clearly, an adulterous relationship would have been inconsistent with that. He settled his claim against *The New Statesman* on favourable terms. However, in 2002, former Conservative Minister, Edwina Currie, admitted that she had had a four-year adulterous relationship with Major (Edwina Currie's revelations were contained in Currie 2002). *The New Statesman* was correct that Major was an adulterer; it simply had the name of the partner wrong. The ensuing public outcry led *The New Statesman* to consider legal action in order to retrieve damages and costs (Milmo 2002; Kelso and White 2002; Morris 2002; Wells 2002). In comparison to Archer and Major, Morosi and Cairns escaped with their reputations comparatively unscathed.

The Abbotts, the Costellos and the Media

As with Morosi and Cairns, Tony Abbott's and Peter Costello's litigation against Random House and Ellis has become part of their reputation. Like Morosi and Cairns, their public profiles allow them greater opportunities to create, to cultivate and to defend their reputations. The integration of their defamation case into part of their reputation was achieved by the fact that the trial (Dore 1998a; Marr 1998a; Dore 1998b; Marr 1998b; Marr 1998c; Barker 1998; Marr 1998d; Gordon 1998; Jackson et al. 1998; Gare 1998; Grattan 1998a; Marr 1998e; Milne 1998; Pearson 1998a; Henderson 1998; Pearson 1998b; Dore 1998c; Armitage 1998a; Marr 1998f; Dore 1998d; Armitage 1998b; Marr 1998g; Devine 1998), verdict (Wright 1999; Dore 1999; McGregor 1999; Martin 1999; Armitage 1999a; Mapstone 1999; Marr 1999a; Ackland 1999a; Campbell 1999a) and appeal (Armitage 1999b; Sheehan 1999; Marr 1999b; Marr 1999c; Green 1999; Campbell 1999b; Marr 1999d; Marr 1999e; Waldren 1999; Marr 1999f) attracted considerable media attention. This has ensured that, notwithstanding their other achievements in public life, this aspect of their public life is consistently referred to in the media (see, for example, Grattan 1998b; Snow 2000; Macdonald 2001; Taylor 2004). Furthermore, even though Tanya Costello has elected to adopt a relatively low public profile, whenever she does make a media appearance, a reference to her part in the litigation against Random House remains obligatory (Loane 1998; Hudson 2000; McGregor 2000). The defamation litigation has similarly formed an integral part of Bob Ellis's reputation (Este and Leak 1998). Ellis complained that the case caused him 'collateral defamation', with witnesses under the protection of absolute privilege making accusations against Ellis, notably drunkenness (Este and Leak 1998). Indeed, on appeal, Miles J opined that 'at the end of the litigation, one might note, almost in passing, that the person whose reputation is in tatters is the author' (94 FCR 296 at 302 at 321 per Miles J).

Yet, in reality, reputation is not static. Ellis himself has available the means to repair his own reputation without recourse to defamation law (Ellis did, however, observe appositely: 'Litigation of this kind is the pursuit of the already rich' (Este and Leak 1998)). At the outset of his judgment, Higgins J made his view of the anecdote abundantly clear. Under a heading, 'The story is false', Higgins J stated that 'the story about Mr Abbott, Mr Costello and Mrs Costello (or Mrs Abbott if she is taken to be referred to), is untrue, has no foundation in fact, and should be totally deleted from the annals of Australian political mythology, if, indeed, it still lingers there' (137 ACTR 1 at 6 per Higgins J).

Higgins J's stated hope was forlorn. The defamation case itself, the subsequent appeal and the taking up of cudgels by the Australian *literati* on both sides ensured that the substance of the defamation remained in the public consciousness. Not only has it remained in the public consciousness, it has in fact become integrated into the reputations of the plaintiffs as well as that of the author.

Moreover, the author, Bob Ellis, has used a number of opportunities to restate the libel. For example, writing a review of Michael Warby's tract, *Ellis Unplugged*

(Ellis 2001), principally to correct its approximately two hundred errors in over two hundred pages (Ellis 2001, 41), Ellis reiterated the substance of the defamation:

> It's not hard to imagine Rodney Cavalier, a neighbour of Tanya Coleman and the political destroyer of her father, denying for all he was worth what he said. Not hard to imagine at all. If it was untrue that he'd said it, he would have rung me up and said so the minute he read it, on the first day of its publication. And he never has. We were business partners then and he would have. (Ellis 2001, 42)

In his sequel to *Goodbye Jerusalem*, *Goodbye Babylon*, Ellis incorporates the defamation trial into his own reputation (Ellis 2002, 331–40, 346–52). In doing so, he again restates his belief in the anecdote, albeit indirectly:

> And her husband, Peter Costello, began the legal action, I think. This was because he had changed his politics from Labor to Liberal soon after meeting, and deciding to marry, Tanya Coleman, daughter of the Leader of the Liberal Party in New South Wales, a proposition uncontested in two biographies. And Abbott would not have been keen, I think. He had, after all, known Tanya Coleman well at the time, and collaborated with her in student politics, and she had defended him in print.
>
> And he and Costello probably quarrelled about it.
>
> I wouldn't know. (Ellis 2002, 332–3).

As with Morosi and Cairns, it is useful to contrast the relative success of the plaintiffs with the loss of defamation plaintiffs elsewhere in respect of similar allegations. Abbott and Costello elected to sue for defamation in the Supreme Court of the Australian Capital Territory, a jurisdiction where defamation proceedings are conducted entirely before a judge. This was a fortuitous decision, as a contemporaneous example demonstrated. The Victorian Premier, Jeff Kennett, sued the publishers of *The Australian* newspaper, Nationwide News Pty Ltd, over an article printed in January 1998, repeating rumours that Kennett had had affairs with former Australian Grand Prix executive officer, Judith Griggs, and arts administrator, Maude Palmer. He brought his defamation proceedings in the Supreme Court of Victoria, where such cases are tried before a jury. In Kennett's case, it took the jury of six less than forty minutes to find that the imputations of adultery were not defamatory (Ackland 1999b; Ackland 1999c). Commenting on the outcomes in these cases, the New South Wales Solicitor-General, Michael Sexton SC, an experienced defamation barrister, observed that 'it seems likely, however, that the middle class is rather more blasé about these matters than Mr Doolittle … A Melbourne jury may have taken a more robust view of modern morals' (Sexton 1999, 23).

Perhaps Hutley JA's views expressed regarding *Cairns* about changes in social attitudes to sexual morality were right after all.

Celebrity and Imputations of Unchastity

Certainly Hutley JA's views seemed apposite when dealing with defamation proceedings brought by entertainment celebrities, such as film stars, as opposed to the more serious political celebrities (as to the definition of celebrity, see Chapter 8). Recent defamation proceedings brought by Nicole Kidman illustrate this.

It was previously thought that, in the marriage of Tom Cruise and Nicole Kidman, Cruise was the more litigious (see, for example, Reynolds 2002). Cruise has been vigorous in defence of his reputation for heterosexuality (as to Tom Cruise's defamation proceedings, see Chapter 6). However, following the dissolution of their marriage, Kidman has demonstrated that she too is not averse to suing newspapers for defamation. In late July 2003, Kidman settled her defamation proceedings against Associated Newspapers over an article published in *The Daily Mail* in March 2003, imputing that she had had an adulterous relationship with her co-star in *Cold Mountain*, Jude Law, during filming and that this relationship had contributed to the disintegration of Law's marriage to Sadie Frost. Kidman received 'substantial' damages and an apology from *The Daily Mail* (Milmo 2003; *The Times* (1 August 2003), 6). Again, in mid-October 2003, Kidman settled further defamation proceedings, this time against the London tabloid newspaper, *The Sun*, for printing the same allegation in March 2003. She received 'a five-figure payout' and an apology (Verkaik 2003, 4). Kidman reportedly donated this award of damages to a charity assisting abandoned children in Romania, the country in which the filming of *Cold Mountain* occurred (*The Times* (15 October 2003), 6). In relation to both these articles, Kidman claimed that they injured her personal and professional reputation, as well as causing her embarrassment and distress (Milmo 2003; *The Times* (1 August 2003), 6). She also argued that their timing, in the weeks preceding the Academy Award ceremony, was designed to injure her chance at winning an Oscar (Milmo 2003, Verkaik 2003). Kidman in fact subsequently won the Best Actress Oscar for her portrayal of Virginia Woolf in *The Hours*.

Given that the powerful and glamorous might be enhanced by imputations of sexual immorality, as suggested by Hutley JA in *Cairns*, and moreover that movie stars, such as Elizabeth Taylor, Zsa Zsa Gabor and Lana Turner onwards, have built their reputations on serial marriages and affairs, finding no real injury caused to them, it is difficult to view Kidman as seeking only to vindicate her honour and in part to assuage her insulted dignity. Kidman may not wish to be portrayed as committing adultery but it is becoming increasingly difficult to accept that social attitudes towards sexual morality would adopt an adverse view. Furthermore, the reputational interests of Kidman cannot be confined to the concepts of reputation as honour, dignity and property. Kidman's public profile, her reputation, is a creation of the media *par excellence*. The presence of her celebrity as part of her reputation is clearly engaged in the defamation proceedings she has brought.

Public attitudes on adultery may have changed so much that it is now possible for a woman to receive damages for defamation for failing to be recognised as a man's mistress. In July 2002, *The Evening Standard* published an article about a woman called Marie Josette Capece Minutolo. Minutolo claimed she was the mistress of the playwright Anthony Shaffer, and that, at the time of his death in 2001, she was co-habiting with him. Minutolo was not mentioned in the will and commenced proceedings seeking family provision. *The Evening Standard* article stated that Shaffer's relatives thought that Minutolo was 'a carpetbagger, anxious to cash in on her association with Anthony Shaffer, for whom she was nothing more than a researcher working on his memoirs' (Blackhurst 2002, 5). Although unsuccessful in her family provision claim with the argument that Shaffer was domiciled in England at the time of his death (*Morgan (as Attorney of Sir Peter Shaffer) v Cilento* [2004] EWHC 188 (Ch). See further *Morgan (as Attorney of Sir Peter Shaffer) v Cilento* [2004] EWCA Civ 631 Ch D), Minutolo settled her defamation proceedings advantageously with *The Evening Standard*, receiving 'substantial damages' (reportedly £35,000) (Barkham 2004, 6) and an apology (Lawson 2004).

Chapter 6

Reputation as Honour: Part II

Introduction

Just as imputations of unchastity in their various forms, explored in the previous chapter, have been held to be capable of being defamatory and have in fact been found to be defamatory, so too have imputations of homosexuality. Whether or not an imputation of homosexuality is capable of being defamatory is currently the subject of conflicting authority at first instance in the Supreme Court of New South Wales. However, as with imputations of unchastity, the defamatory sting of imputations of homosexuality has been challenged by significant shifts in social mores. Several high-profile cases have demonstrated the disparity between what judges think is capable of being defamatory and what society generally and the media particularly think is in fact defamatory.

This chapter seeks to examine this divided authority and place it in the context of recent instances where plaintiffs, overwhelmingly male,[1] have used defamation proceedings to assert their heterosexuality or their right to privacy. In doing so, it aims to illuminate specifically how the concept of reputation as honour manifests itself in such cases. In terms of reputation as honour, these cases fundamentally involve an assertion by the plaintiffs that they identify with the (hetero-)normative characteristics of the ordinary, reasonable reader. However, they may also raise other competing notions of reputation. This case study seeks to identify the range of concepts of reputation involved in such cases.

1 The case study on the imputation of homosexuality deals with cases involving male plaintiffs. There are at least two examples in Anglo-Australian law of female plaintiffs complaining of an imputation of homosexuality. Importantly, in both cases, an allegation of lesbianism was expressly linked to an allegation of unchastity. See *Kerr v Kennedy* [1942] 1 KB 409; *Harrison v Galuszko* (unreported, SC(WA), No. 1490/91, Adams AM, 8 November 1991). For an earlier instance of an imputation of lesbianism, see the Scottish case of *Woods and Pirie v Gordon*. The documents are usefully collected in Parr (ed.) 1975.

Case Study 3: Imputations of Homosexuality – Case Law

Horner v Goulburn City Council (unreported, SC(NSW), No. 21287/97, Levine J, 5 December 1997); Horner v Goulburn City Council [2000] NSWSC 1012

The first recent decision dealing with the capacity of an imputation of homosexuality to be defamatory is *Horner v Goulburn City Council*. In mid-March 1997, the General Manager, Ronald Horner, and the Human Resources Manager, Neville Usher, of Goulburn City Council commenced defamation proceedings against the council and its Director of Corporate Services. The proceedings arose out of a letter by the Director to the General Manager relating to Usher's performance review. In the letter, the Director of Corporate Services detailed why he thought that staff morale at the council was low. The reasons he provided were, *inter alia*:

- The General Manager is seen to spend his day in smoking or drinking coffee, playing with his PC, or closeted with Human Resource Manager.
- The unusual relationship between the General Manager and the Human Resources Manager, which extends outside work hours.
- Staff reluctant to confide in the Human Resource Manager because of his closeness to the General Manager. The Human Resource Manager considers himself to be the Assistant General Manager …
- The General Manager's shows of petulance in storming out of meetings.
- The perceived refusal of the General Manager to speak with certain members of the public. (*Horner v Goulburn City Council* (unreported, SC(NSW), No. 21287/97, Levine J, 5 December 1997) at 3)

In their defamation proceedings in the Supreme Court of New South Wales, the plaintiffs claimed that the letter conveyed the imputations that they were engaged in a homosexual relationship and that that relationship had an adverse impact on staff morale at the council (unreported, SC(NSW), No. 21287/97, Levine J, 5 December 1997 at 3). In addition, they claimed that the letter insinuated that Horner inappropriately allowed Usher to become the *de facto* Assistant General Manager and that Usher exploited their subsisting homosexual relationship to achieve this end.

At an interlocutory stage, the council challenged the capacity of an allegation of homosexuality, the unifying feature of the pleaded imputations, to be defamatory. Levine J found that the letter was capable of conveying the imputation of homosexuality (unreported, SC(NSW), No. 21287/97, Levine J, 5 December 1997 at 4). His Honour then had to determine whether the imputation of homosexuality was capable of being defamatory. Levine J held that it was, reasoning thus:

> Community attitudes to an assertion of a homosexual relationship may range from sympathetic tolerance and understanding to an irrational abhorrence. Whether the former represents a perception from the 'ivory tower' and the latter an 'avidity for scandal'

> cannot be concluded. I do not consider that it can be conclusively said that even towards the end of the this century's last decade that there can be, among ordinary members of the community, a view that to say of a person that that person is in a homosexual relationship is not disparaging or is not likely to lower that person in the estimation of such people. I do not hold that the imputations of a homosexual relationship are not capable of being defamatory. (Unreported, SC(NSW), No. 21287/97, Levine J, 5 December 1997 at 5)

The matter was subsequently transferred to the District Court of New South Wales (*Horner v Goulburn City Council* [2000] NSWSC 1012 at [18] per Levine J).

Rivkin v Amalgamated Television Services Pty Ltd [2001] NSWSC 432; Rivkin v Amalgamated Television Services Pty Ltd [2002] NSWSC 496

A different approach to the issue was taken by Bell J in her judgment in *Rivkin v Amalgamated Television Services Pty Ltd*, the second recent decision dealing with the defamatory capacity of imputations of homosexuality.

In *Rivkin*, the plaintiff, formerly a prominent 'celebrity' stockbroker (*John Fairfax Publications Pty Ltd v Rivkin* (2003) 201 ALR 77 at 116; 77 ALJR 1657; Aust Torts Reports ¶81-711 per Callinan J), brought defamation proceedings against the commercial television network, Channel Seven, arising out of a report on its current affairs programme, *Witness* ([2001] NSWSC 432 at [3]). The report concerned the open finding of a coronial inquest into the death of Sydney model, Caroline Byrne, whose body was found at the bottom of The Gap in Watsons Bay. The report suggested that Byrne's partner, Gordon Wood, was involved in her death. Wood was described as Rivkin's chauffeur and personal assistant. Wood acknowledged that Rivkin purchased an apartment, furniture, clothes and a car for him. In his evidence to the coronial inquest, Wood stated that Byrne was suspicious of his relationship with Rivkin ([2001] NSWSC 432 at [5]). In the report, the journalist, Paul Barry, interviewed Wood, suggesting to him that the police had received information that Byrne had had Wood placed under surveillance prior to her death and that Byrne had interrupted Wood and Rivkin having sexual intercourse ([2001] NSWSC 432 at [6]). In the interview, Wood strenuously denied any involvement in Byrne's death and any engagement in sexual intercourse with Rivkin ([2001] NSWSC 432 at [7]).

In his defamation proceedings against Channel Seven, Rivkin alleged that the report conveyed the following relevant imputations:

> (c) That the plaintiff had engaged in homosexual intercourse with Gordon Wood;
>
> (d) That the police had reason to suspect that the plaintiff had engaged in homosexual intercourse with Gordon Wood. ([2001] NSWSC 432 at [3])

Prior to the empanelment of the jury, Channel Seven challenged the capacity of these imputations to be defamatory of Rivkin ([2001] NSWSC 432 at [1]). It argued that, whilst an imputation of homosexual intercourse may have been disparaging 'until relatively recent times' ([2001] NSWSC 432 at [18]) and may still be viewed as such by certain sectors of the community, the test for defamatory meaning is the view of 'right thinking members of the society generally' ([2001] NSWSC 432 at [17]). In the identification of the normative view of homosexuality in contemporary Australian society, Channel Seven referred to the decriminalisation of homosexual intercourse in New South Wales in 1984, the prohibition on discrimination against and vilification of persons on the basis of sexual orientation under the *Anti-Discrimination Act* 1977 (NSW) and the *Workplace Relations Act* 1996 (Cth) and the expansion of the definition of '*de facto* relationship' and 'interdependent relationship' to encompass homosexual relationships for the purposes of the *Property Relations Act* 1984 (NSW) and the *Migration Regulations* 1994 (Cth) respectively ([2001] NSWSC 432 at [19]–[20]).

In response, Rivkin submitted that Federal and State legislative provisions conferring rights and protections on homosexuals did not deal definitively with the issue of what the 'ordinary right thinking member of the community' would think about a person who engages in homosexual intercourse ([2001] NSWSC 432 at [21]). He also argued that 'many reasonable persons holding religious convictions' would consider homosexual intercourse 'a sin' ([2001] NSWSC 432 at [22]). Ultimately, Rivkin submitted that the proper approach would be to allow the jury to determine whether or not the imputation was in fact defamatory ([2001] NSWSC 432 at [23]).

Bell J accepted Channel Seven's submission that the legislative changes at a Federal and a State level signalled a change in the community's attitudes towards homosexuality. Her Honour held the imputation of homosexual intercourse, of itself, was incapable of being defamatory. However, Bell J acknowledged that, depending on the context, the imputation of homosexuality or homosexual intercourse may convey the imputation of 'hypocrisy', 'the abuse of a position of power or trust' or 'infidelity' ([2001] NSWSC 432 at [30]. See also *Quilty v Windsor* [1999] SLT 346 at 355 per Lord Kingarth. During Jason Donovan's proceedings against *The Face* magazine (see below), the presiding judge, Drake J, suggested from the bench that it may no longer be defamatory for an imputation of homosexuality alone to be defamatory: Boseley 1992b).

Bell J granted Rivkin leave to re-plead its imputations in respect of this part of its case. In light of Bell J's reasons for judgment, Rivkin pleaded its imputations in the following terms:

> (c) That the plaintiff engaged in homosexual intercourse with Gordon Wood, a man who was an employee of his, much younger than him, who viewed him as a father figure, upon whom he lavished gifts and who was engaged to be married;

(d) That the police had reason to suspect that the plaintiff engaged in homosexual intercourse with Gordon Wood, a man who was much younger than him, an employee of his, who viewed him as a father figure, upon whom he lavished gifts and who was engaged to be married;

(e) That the plaintiff procured a male employee to have sexual intercourse with him by lavishing presents on him; an abuse of his wealth and power.' ([2001] NSWSC 432 at [32])

It pleaded imputations (c) and (d) in the alternative ([2001] NSWSC 432 at [34]). Despite Channel Seven's objections, Bell J left these three imputations to the jury ([2001] NSWSC 432 at [33]–[36]).

In late May 2001, at the s 7A jury trial before Bell J (*Rivkin v Amalgamated Television Services Pty Ltd* [2002] NSWSC 496 at [11]), the jury of four found that only imputation (c) was conveyed to the ordinary, reasonable viewer and was defamatory of the plaintiff ([2002] NSWSC 496 at [13]. See also Reucassel 2001). Dealing with the issues relating to defences in mid-June 2002, as required under the *Defamation Act* 1974 (NSW) s 7A(4)(a), Cripps AJ rejected the defences of unlikelihood of harm,[2] as well as common law ([2001] NSWSC 432 at [22]) and statutory qualified privilege.[3] In one of the rare cases where damages have actually been assessed for imputations of homosexuality (cf. *Kerr v Kennedy* [1942] 1 KB 409 at 413 per Asquith J (award of £300 damages for imputation of lesbianism committed by way of slander in presence of one person); *Harrison v Galuszko* (unreported, SC(WA), No. 1490/91, Adams AM, 8 November 1991) at 9 (award of $11,000 damages for imputation of lesbianism committed by way of slander in presence of four persons)), his Honour awarded Rivkin $150,000 compensatory and aggravated damages for Channel Seven's publication ([2001] NSWSC 432 at [65]), as well as costs (*Rivkin v Amalgamated Television Services Pty Ltd* [2002] NSWSC 587).

Rivkin also sued John Fairfax Publications Pty Ltd over three articles published in *The Sydney Morning Herald* and *The Australian Financial Review* (Chenoweth 1998; Hills 1998; Webb 1998). (The three articles are reproduced in their entirety in the judgment of Callinan J in (2003) 201 ALR 77; (2003) 77 ALJR

2 [2001] NSWSC 432 at [20]. The defence of unlikelihood of harm was created by the *Defamation Act* 1974 (NSW) s 13 (repealed). See now the defence of triviality: *Civil Law (Wrongs) Act* 2002 (ACT) s 139D; *Defamation Act* 2006 (NT) s 30; *Defamation Act* 2005 (NSW) s 33; *Defamation Act* 2005 (Qld) s 33; *Defamation Act* 2005 (SA) s 31; *Defamation Act* 2005 (Tas) s 33; *Defamation Act* 2005 (Vic) s 33; *Defamation Act* 2005 (WA) s 33.

3 [2001] NSWSC 432 at [42]–[43]. The defence of statutory qualified privilege was created by the *Defamation Act* 1974 (NSW) s 22 (repealed). See now *Civil Law (Wrongs) Act* 2002 (ACT) s 139A; *Defamation Act* 2006 (NT) s 27; *Defamation Act* 2005 (NSW) s 30; *Defamation Act* 2005 (Qld) s 30; *Defamation Act* 2005 (SA) s 28; *Defamation Act* 2005 (Tas) s 30; *Defamation Act* 2005 (Vic) s 30; *Defamation Act* 2005 (WA) s 30.

1657; (2003) Aust Torts Reports ¶81-711.) The articles dealt with the same subject matter as Rivkin's defamation proceedings against Channel Seven. Rivkin pleaded 17 imputations arising out of these three articles, including six imputations that Rivkin had engaged or was suspected of engaging in homosexual intercourse with Wood (*Rivkin v John Fairfax Publications Pty Ltd* [2002] NSWCA 87 at [31], [33] per Grove J; (2003) 201 ALR 77 at 126–7 per Callinan J). No preliminary challenge was made to the capacity of these imputations to be defamatory.

At the s 7A trial conducted before Simpson J in late April 2001, the jury took less than ninety minutes to find that none of the 17 pleaded imputations was conveyed by the articles ([2002] NSWCA 87 at [7] per Foster AJA; (2003) 201 ALR 77 at 97 per Kirby J. See also Kux 2001). It therefore did not need to consider whether any of the pleaded imputations were defamatory.

Rivkin appealed against the jury verdict. The New South Wales Court of Appeal found that the jury verdict was perverse and unreasonable and ordered a new trial in relation to all 17 imputations ([2002] NSWCA 87 at [1] per Meagher JA, at [3] per Foster AJA, at [113] per Grove J). This was one of a number of recent cases in which the New South Wales Court of Appeal has intervened to set aside a jury verdict in defamation proceedings on the basis of 'perversity' or unreasonableness.[4] Fairfax appealed to the High Court of Australia. By majority, the High Court found that the jury's answers in relation to five of the 17 imputations were unreasonable ((2003) 201 ALR 77 at 78 per Gleeson CJ, at 131–4 per Callinan J, at 136 per Heydon J). However, rather than allowing a retrial on all 17 imputations, including those in respect of which the jury verdict was not unreasonable, the High Court limited the scope of the retrial to the five challenged imputations ((2003) 201 ALR 77 at 79 per Gleeson CJ, at 136 per Callinan J, at 138 per Heydon J).

4 See also *Cinevest Ltd v Yirandi Productions Ltd* (2001) Aust Torts Reports ¶81-601; *Mularczyk v John Fairfax Publications Pty Ltd* [2001] NSWCA 467; *Buck v Jones* [2002] NSWCA 8; *Pavy v John Fairfax Publications Pty Ltd* [2002] NSWCA 46; *Sarma v The Federal Capital Press of Australia Pty Ltd* [2002] NSWCA 93; *Charlwood Industries Pty Ltd v Brent* [2002] NSWCA 201; *Channel Seven Sydney Pty Ltd v Parras* (2002) Aust Torts Reports ¶81-675; *Nationwide News Pty Ltd v Warton* [2002] NSWCA 377; *Harvey v John Fairfax Publications Pty Ltd* [2003] NSWCA 70; *Beran v John Fairfax Publications Pty Ltd* [2004] NSWCA 107; *Sonda v Signorelli* [2004] NSWCA 134; *Maitland v Nationwide News Pty Ltd* [2004] NSWCA 155; *Pavy v John Fairfax Publications Pty Ltd* [2004] NSWCA 177; *Saffron v John Fairfax Publications Pty Ltd* [2004] NSWCA 254; *Gorman v Barber* [2004] NSWCA 402; *Australian Broadcasting Corporation v Reading* [2004] NSWCA 411; *Harvey v John Fairfax Publications Pty Ltd* [2005] NSWCA 255; *Bennette v Cohen* (2005) 64 NSWLR 81; *Saunders v Nationwide News Pty Ltd* [2005] NSWCA 404; *Ramrakha v Chaudhry* [2006] NSWCA 42; *Mahommed v Channel Seven Sydney Pty Ltd* [2006] NSWCA 213; *Boniface v SMEC Holdings Ltd* [2006] NSWCA 351; *Gardener v Nationwide News Pty Ltd* [2007] NSWCA 10; *Echo Publications Pty Ltd v Tucker* [2007] NSWCA 73; *Habib v Nationwide News Pty Ltd* [2007] NSWCA 91; *John Fairfax Publications Pty Ltd v Gacic* (2007) 235 ALR 402. As to the position in Great Britain, see *Grobbelaar v News Group Newspapers Ltd* [2002] 4 All ER 732; [2002] 1 WLR 3024.

In the course of his judgment, Kirby J commented, *obiter*, on the issue of the defamatory capacity of imputations of homosexuality, observing:

> In most circumstances, it ought not to be the case in Australia that to publish a statement that one adult was involved in consenting, private homosexual activity with another adult involves a defamatory imputation. But whether it does or does not harm a person's reputation to publish such an imputation is related to time, personality and circumstance. Once, it was highly defamatory in many countries to allege, or suggest, that a person was a communist. Now, in most circumstances, it would be a matter of complete indifference. The day may come when, to accuse an adult of consenting homosexual activity is likewise generally a matter of indifference. However, it would ignore the reality of contemporary Australian society to say that that day has arrived for all purposes and all people. At least for people who treat their sexuality as private or secret, or people who have presented themselves as having a different sexual orientation, such an imputation could, depending on the circumstances, still sometimes be defamatory. ((2003) 201 ALR 77 at 109 per Kirby J)

Kelly v John Fairfax Publications Pty [2003] NSWSC 586

Also *obiter*, in *Obermann v A.C.P. Publishing Pty Ltd* [2001] NSWSC 1022, Levine J expressed his agreement with Bell J's reasons for the decision in *Rivkin v Amalgamated Television Services* on the issue of the defamatory capacity of an imputation of homosexuality *simpliciter* ([2001] NSWSC 1022 at [20]–[21]), seemingly departing from his own judgment in *Horner*.

In *Kelly v John Fairfax Publications Pty Ltd*, the issue of the capacity of an imputation of homosexuality to defame the plaintiff was squarely raised for reconsideration by Levine J. His Honour appeared to move away from the position of Bell J towards the position of Kirby J and back to his own original position in *Horner*.

In *Kelly*, the plaintiff, Robert Kelly, sued Fairfax for defamation arising out of an article published in the 16 February 2003 edition of *The Sun Herald*. In the column, 'Naked City', written by Alex Mitchell and Candace Sutton, under the headline, 'Solicitor lays down the law', a photograph of a half-naked man strapped to the top of a piano in Hyde Park was reproduced, with the caption, 'Rob Kelly accepts a brief on bondage'. The photograph was accompanied by the following text:

> No, it's not John Brogden's latest 'I'll do anything to get elected' strategy, it's lawyer Rob Kelly in Hyde Park practicing (sic) his piano-top bondage display as part of this year's street performance at the Gay and Lesbian Mardi Gras.

> Kelly, the Queensland Performing Arts Trust chairman, is a senior partner with law firm Gadens. Truly. Demonstrators at today's anti-war march take note: Hands off! Rob is a peaceful guy. ([2001] NSWSC 1022 at [5])

Unfortunately for Fairfax, the person in the photograph was not the plaintiff, 'Mr Robert Kelly, the (former) senior partner at Gadens, … a happily married heterosexual and a person who holds himself out as a happily married heterosexual' ([2001] NSWSC 1022 at [8]). Even at an interlocutory stage, it was clear that the case was one of 'mistaken identity' ([2001] NSWSC 1022 at [7]), in which 'something went dreadfully wrong' in the pre-publication process ([2001] NSWSC 1022 at [8]).

Kelly pleaded eight imputations arising from the article and the accompanying photograph. Relevantly, he claimed that the publication conveyed the following defamatory imputation: '(f) the Plaintiff is a homosexual.'

Fairfax challenged the capacity of the pleaded imputations to defame Kelly at all ([2001] NSWSC 1022 at [10]). The imputation of homosexuality *simpliciter* required the most detailed consideration.

Levine J noted that, contrary to Bell J's reasoning in *Rivkin v Amalgamated Television Services*, Kelly argued that the existence of legislative rights and protections for homosexual persons could be interpreted to mean that homosexuality was still stigmatised in contemporary Australian society – the need for legislative rights and protections suggesting that, without these, homosexual persons might suffer adverse consequences ([2001] NSWSC 1022 at [39]). Accepting this submission, his Honour found that the conferral of rights and protections by statute did not establish conclusively that homosexuality was socially acceptable, as opposed to lawful.

Having reviewed the authorities ([2001] NSWSC 1022 at [32]–[38]), Levine J declined to follow Bell J's decision in *Rivkin v Amalgamated Television Services*, instead allowing the jury to determine whether or not the imputation was in fact defamatory ([2001] NSWSC 1022 at [40]).

Case Study 3: Imputations of Homosexuality – Analysis

The Application of the Concepts of Reputation to Imputations of Homosexuality

Like imputations of 'unchastity', imputations of homosexuality exist at the vanguard of the debate about what is defamatory. However, more acutely than in cases involving imputations of 'unchastity', cases involving allegations of homosexuality raise the vexed issue of whether judges should reflect the best self of the community or whether judges should reflect more conservatively the views of the community. The consequence of a judge adopting an idealistic or optimistic view of community attitudes towards homosexuality is that it affirms the social acceptance of homosexuality, whilst at the same time potentially depriving a plaintiff who experiences real prejudice as a result of defamatory (and homophobic) publication of a remedy in defamation. Conversely, the consequence of a judge adopting a realistic or pessimistic view of community attitudes towards homosexuality allows a plaintiff to have a remedy in defamation but, in doing so, legitimises homophobic attitudes as socially acceptable and reinforcing homosexuality as aberrant behaviour. There is understandably a division of academic opinion about whether judges should lead or be led by changes in social attitudes towards homosexuality (for the spectrum of views on whether judges should lead or follow public opinion, see Fogle 1993, 185–7; Arend 1997, 113–14; Jones 2001, 100; McNamara 2001, 292–5; Yatar 2003, 151–8; Knight 2006, 267–79).

Ultimately, it ought to be from the decisions of juries, being the tribunal responsible for the determination of 'libel or no libel', not judges, on this matter that changes in social attitudes towards sexual matters are gleaned. There is a difference of opinion between judges and juries on the issue of the defamatory quality of an imputation of homosexuality (Ackland 2003). Whilst judges are willing as a matter of law to allow that imputations of homosexuality are capable of being defamatory, recent Australian juries have been less sympathetic to plaintiffs when determining whether imputations of homosexuality are in fact defamatory. In mid-February 1999, a jury found that racing odds assessor, Arthur Harris, had been defamed by Kevin Perkins's book, *The Gambling Man*, distributed by Gordon & Gotch. It found that a range of defamatory imputations were conveyed about Harris, including imputations of conspiracy to pervert the course of justice, dishonestly obtaining a financial reward and failure to honour contractual obligations and gambling debts. However, the jury found that the imputation of homosexuality was conveyed but was not defamatory (Good 1999. See also *Harris v 718932 Pty Ltd* [2000] NSWSC 784 at [5]–[6] per Windeyer J; *Harris v Perkins* [2001] NSWSC 258 at [12] per Newman AJ). In early November 2003, a jury at the s 7A trial in *Kelly v John Fairfax Publications Pty Ltd* found that the imputation of homosexuality was conveyed but was not defamatory. It also found that the imputation of exhibitionism was conveyed but was not defamatory. Kelly did, however, succeed in relation to several of his other imputations, relevantly the imputations of hypocrisy and lying, pleaded as true innuendos, relying on the extrinsic facts of his being a happily married heterosexual and his resolute non-participation in 'public displays of bondage' involving pianos (Kux 2003b). On the two recent occasions when Australian juries have been required to determine the issue, they have refused to accept the defamatory character of imputations of homosexuality. It is hardly a trend but it does offer at least a small insight into prevailing community attitudes.

Nevertheless, it is clear that the defamatory capacity of homosexuality, as well as jury verdicts as to the defamatory meaning of particular imputations of homosexuality, involve questions of reputation as honour. Judges and juries are concerned with negotiating the contours of acceptable and unacceptable sexual conduct and characteristics. It is pre-eminently a mediation of 'normative standards of personal conduct' (Post 1986, 701) (as to the definition of reputation as honour in this book, see Chapter 1).

The plaintiff's concern for his or her reputation as honour figures more prominently in some cases rather than others. For instance, it is not far-fetched to suggest that cases like *Horner v Goulburn City Council*, *Kerr v Kennedy*, *Harrison v Galuszko* and *Quilty v Windsor* are primarily concerned with the plaintiff seeking to vindicate his or her reputation in the form of honour. In each of these cases, the plaintiff sought, as Adams AM expressed it, to have 'the record set straight' (*Harrison v Galuszko* (unreported, SC(WA), No. 1490/91, Adams AM, 8 November 1991) at 8). They all aimed to have their heterosexuality (or the presumption of their heterosexuality) acknowledged and affirmed, thereby demonstrating their conformity to the '[hetero-]normative standards of personal conduct' prevailing in their communities. The effect of these cases, particularly in *Kerr v Kennedy* and *Harrison v Galuszko*, where the plaintiffs obtained a favourable verdict, is, in turn, to reaffirm and reinforce such standards.

Given that an award of damages for defamation serves not only as a vindication of the plaintiff but also a consolation for the injury to feelings inflicted by the publication of defamatory matter (as to the purposes for the award of damages in defamation cases, see Chapter 3), these cases also raise in part the plaintiff's concern for his or her reputation as dignity. A favourable defamation verdict, including an award of damages, forms part of the process whereby the plaintiff is not only restored to his or her former rightful position within the community but, as a consequence of that restoration, feels better about himself or herself. For example, in *Harrison v Galuszko*, Adams AM noted that Harrison's feelings, self-esteem, personal security and confidence had been eroded by the false imputations of lesbianism ((unreported, SC(WA), No. 1490/91, Adams AM, 8 November 1991) at 9). The award of $11,000 damages aimed in part to assuage that injury.

In addition, three of these cases involve imputations of homosexuality which have an impact on the respective plaintiffs' professional reputation. The unifying feature of these cases is that the imputations of homosexuality were made by persons aggrieved with the plaintiff in a work-related context. Thus, in *Horner v Goulburn City Council*, the allegations were made in the course of Usher's work performance review ((unreported, SC(NSW), No. 21287/97, Levine J, 5 December 1997) at 1); in *Harrison v Galuszko*, the source of the allegations was a disgruntled former client of the social worker ((unreported, SC(WA), No. 1490/91, Adams AM, 8 November 1991) at 8); and in *Quilty v Windsor*, the source of the allegations was a disgruntled prisoner making a complaint about the pursuer prisoner officer ([1999] SLT 346 at 349 per Lord Kingarth). Similarly, in *Kelly v John Fairfax Publications*, Kelly, as a solicitor, was concerned not only about the social perceptions of others, and how the suggestion of hypocrisy about his sexual orientation made him feel about himself, but also how the potential impact that a widely-circulated and untrue allegation of homosexuality would have upon his professional reputation ([2003] NSWSC 586 at [7]–[8] per Levine J). A professional reputation necessarily involves both notions of reputation as honour and reputation as property (as to professional reputation, see Chapter 4).

Thus, even in these cases involving imputations of homosexuality, the concept of reputation sought to be protected by the plaintiff is not unitary and straightforward. It raises complex notions of honour, dignity and property. However, in cases like *Horner v Goulburn City Council*, *Kerr v Kennedy*, *Harrison v Galuszko* and *Quilty v Windsor*, the concepts of reputation as honour, dignity and property can be deployed to give a relatively complete understanding of the plaintiff's reputation as manifested in the defamation proceedings. In other cases, the plaintiff's reputation and the damage done to it are qualitatively different. In other cases, something more than honour, dignity and property is engaged. Rivkin's defamation proceedings against Channel Seven and Fairfax usefully demonstrate this.

One of the readily apparent differences between cases such as *Horner v Goulburn City Council*, *Kerr v Kennedy*, *Harrison v Galuszko* and *Quilty v Windsor* on the one hand and Rene Rivkin's defamation proceedings against Channel Seven and Fairfax on the other hand is that, in the former category of cases, the defamatory matter was not widely circulated. In *Kerr v Kennedy*, Lady Kennedy uttered the imputation of lesbianism against Mrs Kerr to only one mutual acquaintance ([1942] 1 KB 409 at 409); in *Horner v Goulburn City Council*, the imputation of homosexuality was contained in the Director of Corporate Services' comments on Usher's performance review and was seen only by Horner and Usher ((unreported, SC(NSW), No. 21287/97, Levine J, 5 December 1997) at 1); in *Quilty v Windsor*, the defender prisoner sent the letter containing, *inter alia*, the allegation of homosexuality against Quilty to the Deputy Chief Executive of the Scottish Prison Service only; ([1999] SLT 346 at 349 per Lord Kingarth); and, in *Harrison v Galuszko*, Galuszko made the allegation of lesbianism against Harrison in front of four people ((unreported, SC(WA), No. 1490/91, Adams AM, 8 November 1991) at 8). There was limited and localised damage done to the reputations of these plaintiffs by the defamatory publications, reflecting in turn the fact that the reputations themselves were limited and localised.

By contrast, the imputations of homosexuality made against Rivkin reached both an extensive readership and a wide viewing audience. The damage done to Rivkin's reputation occurred on a significantly larger scale than that done to any of the reputations of Horner, Kerr, Harrison and Quilty. The viewing audience for Channel Seven's *Witness* programme was more than one million people ([2002] NSWSC 587 at [13] per Cripps AJ). The readership for Fairfax's daily newspapers, *The Sydney Morning Herald* and *The Australian Financial Review*, is a similar figure. This gestures towards the fundamental difference between Rivkin's defamation proceedings and those of Horner, Kerr, Harrison and Quilty – and, in turn, the fundamental difference between their respective reputations.

It may be accepted that Rivkin's defamation proceedings, like those of Horner, Kerr, Harrison and Quilty, involved the concept of reputation as honour. As a married man with five children ([2002] NSWSC 496 at [53] per Cripps

AJ), Rivkin wanted to be viewed as heterosexual, thus conforming to '[hetero-]normative standards of personal conduct'. To be thought otherwise necessarily affected the way in which Rivkin felt about himself, having a particular impact on his relationship with his family ([2002] NSWSC 496 at [53]–[55] per Cripps AJ). Whilst the imputation of homosexuality itself did not appear to reflect adversely upon Rivkin's professional reputation in his defamation proceedings against Channel Seven, Rivkin did sue Fairfax for suggesting that he was not 'a sagacious and astute stockbroker' ((2003) 201 ALR 77 at 126 per Callinan J). He also brought defamation proceedings against Nationwide News in respect of an article directed to his honesty and integrity as an investment advisor (*Rivkin v Nationwide News Pty Ltd* [2002] NSWSC 798 at [7] per Bell J). Thus, Rivkin was also concerned to use defamation proceedings to protect his reputation as a form of property. Yet the concepts of reputation as honour, dignity and property alone do not explain the qualitative difference between Rivkin's reputation and those of Horner, Kerr, Harrison and Quilty.

It is submitted that Rivkin's celebrity provides the answer. Rivkin had used his access to the media from the 1970s onwards to create and cultivate his public persona as a 'celebrity stockbroker' ((2003) 201 ALR 77 at 116 per Callinan J). By virtue of this public profile, Rivkin's activities became newsworthy. Whilst Horner, Kerr, Harrison and Quilty all brought defamation proceedings essentially limited to imputations of homosexuality, Rivkin's defamation proceedings against three major media companies raised broader imputations. This suggests that not only does Rivkin have a greater reputation than Horner, Kerr, Harrison and Quilty, in the sense that he is known by more people than they are and his activities are deemed to be of greater public interest than theirs, but also that his reputation – his celebrity – is more complex.

The recognition that Rivkin's celebrity distinguishes him from other defamation plaintiffs necessarily affects his motivation for bringing his proceedings. Whereas Horner, Kerr, Harrison and Quilty sought to vindicate their reputations amongst family, friends and work colleagues, Rivkin additionally sought to control the way in which his image was portrayed in the mass media. To adopt Post's terminology, whilst Horner, Kerr, Harrison and Quilty were concerned to vindicate their reputations through the mechanism of society and to protect their reputations as they operate in the marketplace, Rivkin was also concerned to control his image as it was mediated through the mass media and was received by its audience.

The recognition of Rivkin's celebrity as the distinguishing feature of his defamation proceedings, separating them from those brought by Horner, Kerr, Harrison and Quilty, also provides a basis for comparing the relative success of such proceedings in vindicating, protecting and restoring the respective plaintiffs' reputations. Presumably, the defamation proceedings brought by Horner, Kerr, Harrison and Quilty, especially those brought by Kerr and Harrison where the plaintiffs obtained more than nominal damages, had the desired effect of vindicating and restoring the plaintiffs' reputations within their family, social and work circles. It is impossible to ascertain whether this in fact occurred for these plaintiffs – the reputations involved and the damage done to them were equally limited and localised. What is more readily apparent is that Rivkin's successful defamation proceedings against Channel Seven, which resulted in an award of substantial damages, did not have the effect that the law of defamation claims a favourable verdict should have, namely the vindication of the plaintiff (as to the importance of vindication as a purpose for the award of defamation damages, see Chapter 3). Notwithstanding the verdict in his favour, allegations of Rivkin's homosexuality, *inter alia*, continued to be made in the media and his reputation deteriorated significantly.

In this regard, the outcome of Rivkin's defamation proceedings against Channel Seven may be instructively contrasted with the outcome of his suit against Fairfax. In his successful defamation proceedings against Channel Seven, in addition to the award of $150,000 damages, Rivkin also successfully resisted an application to deprive him of costs. Notwithstanding the fact that his level of damages was below the jurisdictional minimum of $225,000, with the consequence that, under the *Supreme Court Rules* 1970 (NSW) (Pt 52A r 33), in order to obtain costs ([2002] NSWSC 587 at [9] per Cripps AJ), Cripps AJ found that it was reasonable for Rivkin to bring his defamation proceedings in the Supreme Court of New South Wales ([2002] NSWSC 587 at [13]). Moreover, his Honour found that Rivkin's reputation had been substantially vindicated by the award of damages made in his proceedings ([2002] NSWSC 587 at [10]). This entitled Rivkin to a favourable costs order (see also *John Fairfax & Sons Ltd v Palmer* (1987) 8 NSWLR 297 at 306–7 per Kirby P). Thus, for the purposes of defamation law, Rivkin's reputation was vindicated and restored not only by the award of substantial damages but also by a favourable costs order. In reality, Rivkin's reputation was much more precarious.

Following the favourable resolution of his defamation proceedings against Channel Seven and the prospect of a retrial, at least in relation to the most damaging allegations levelled against him in the Fairfax press, Rivkin should have been in a strong position to vindicate his reputation again. However, by the time Rivkin's retrial in his proceedings against Fairfax was listed for hearing in mid-May 2004, Rivkin's reputation had taken a severe battering in the press (Main 2005, 212). In 2003, Rivkin's conviction for insider trading, his sentencing to nine months' periodic detention (*R v Rivkin* (2003) 198 ALR 400; 45 ACSR 366; 21 ACLC 1092), his continuing exemption from serving that sentence on medical grounds (Main 2003; Milligan and Saunders 2003; Nicholls 2003a; Nicholls 2003b; Colman 2003) and his candid television interviews, ranging over issues such as hypomania, suicide, obesity and teenage nudism (Casimir (ed.) 2003, 1–19), ensured that Rivkin's name was constantly in the headlines. In 2004, his media prominence continued, with his unsuccessful appeal against his insider trading conviction and sentence (*R v Rivkin* (2004) 59 NSWLR 284), the eventual enforcement of his sentencing to periodic detention (O'Malley 2004; Colman et al. 2004; Glendinning et al. 2004) and further damaging revelations attracting headlines.

Indeed, it was those subsequent revelations in the media about various aspects of Rivkin's life that made his defamation proceedings unsupportable. The State Coroner indicated that he would re-open the verdict and order a new inquest into the cause of Caroline Byrne's death (Sutton and Benns 2003; Harvey 2003). In addition, further investigative journalism undertaken by *The Australian Financial Review* uncovered more details about the mystery Swiss investors in Offset Alpine Press (Chenoweth et al. 2003). This led to the Australian Securities and Investments Commission re-opening its own investigations into the Offset Alpine Press affair (O'Loughlin 2003; Pheasant 2003; Askew et al. 2003; Fabro 2003; Lampe 2004; Elam and Chenoweth 2004). The allegation of arson as the cause of the Offset Alpine Press factory fire was also revived with fresh media revelations (Whittaker 2004; O'Brien et al. 2004), which, in turn, led to the police re-opening the investigation into this matter (Wainwright 2004b). The New South Wales Police then recommended to the Director of Public Prosecutions that Rivkin's former chauffeur and personal assistant, Gordon Wood, be charged with the murder of Caroline Byrne, sparking a police and media hunt for Wood in Europe (O'Brien and Colman 2004; Main 2004; McClymont and Cornford 2004). Following this, there were further salacious anecdotes reported in the newspapers about Rivkin and his circle of 'good-looking young men' (O'Brien 2004; McClymont 2004; Gerard 2004; McClymont and Fray 2004; Wainwright 2004a). The media coverage of Rivkin's activities in the first half of 2004 was intense. The cumulative effect of this treatment was to damage Rivkin's reputation precisely in relation to those matters which were raised in his defamation proceedings against Fairfax.

In light of these revelations, on the date listed for the retrial of the five imputations ordered by the High Court, Rivkin unsurprisingly settled his claim against Fairfax with judgment being entered for Fairfax (*Rivkin v John Fairfax Publications Pty Ltd* [2004] NSWSC 671 at [1], [30]–[31] per Kirby J. See also Chenoweth 2004; Ackland 2004). He was ordered to pay two-thirds of Fairfax's costs of the first jury trial and all of Fairfax's costs incurred since the High Court appeal ([2004] NSWSC 671 at [1], [53] per Kirby J), although he successfully avoided having them awarded on an indemnity basis ([2004] NSWSC 671 at [42]–[43] per Kirby J) Rivkin also settled his defamation proceedings against Nationwide News (Cameron 2004). In the light of subsequent revelations about Rivkin, legal commentator, Richard Ackland, described Rivkin's defamation litigation against Channel Seven, Fairfax and Nationwide News as 'audacious' and ultimately 'a massive try-on' (Ackland 2004).

Speaking on the television programme, *Australian Story*, prior to Rivkin's death, Rivkin's wife, Gayle, claimed that the family had lost many friends as a consequence of the defamation proceedings brought against various media outlets (*Australian Story: The Damage Done* 2004). This is entirely contrary to what defamation law claims as the consequences for a successful defamation verdict.

It is submitted that the concept of reputation as celebrity, as it exists in a media-saturated society like contemporary Australia, helps explain the tortuous course of Rivkin's defamation litigation and why it differed so markedly from

Maybe, or maybe substance of R's behaviour + reach of activities.

the more straightforward claims presented by Horner, Kerr, Harrison and Quilty. The reputations of Horner, Kerr, Harrison and Quilty remain relatively fixed, closer to the concept of reputation as honour, in contrast to Rivkin's reputation. Consequently, their reputations are more amenable to the vindicatory purpose of defamation damages. Rivkin's reputation was, however, more dynamic. Being the product of the media, it was less amenable to vindication by the courts and to control by Rivkin himself.

The Concept of Reputation as Celebrity and Imputations of Homosexuality

Liberace The concept of celebrity also illuminates defamation proceedings brought by other high-profile litigants to resist imputations of homosexuality levelled against them by the press. Notoriously, in the 1950s, Liberace was a serial litigant, vigorously contesting public insinuations of his homosexuality. In the mid-1950s, the English comedian, Jimmy Thompson, performed a skit, both on television and in long-running theatrical revues, in which he impersonated Liberace. As part of the skit, Thompson sang a song, which included the following lines:

> My fan mail is really tremendous,
> It's going so fast my head whirls;
> I get more and more,
> They propose by the score –
> And at least one or two are from girls.

Liberace sued Thompson for defamation arising out of his skit. Thompson settled the matter out of court (Pyron 2000, 193–4).

In September 1956, *The Daily Mirror* columnist, 'Cassandra' (the pseudonym for William Conner), wrote an article about Liberace, infamously describing the pianist thus:

> He is the summit of sex – the pinnacle of masculine, feminine and neuter. Everything that he, she and it can ever want … This deadly, winking, sniggering, snuggling, chromium-plated, scent-impregnated, luminous, quivering, giggling, fruit-flavoured, mincing, ice-covered heap of mother love has had the biggest reception and impact on London since Charlie Chaplin arrived at the same station, Waterloo, on September 12, 1921.

None of the defamatory matters in the decided cases approaches this as a denunciation of homosexuality (see *Horner v Goulburn City Council* (unreported, SC(NSW), No. 21287/97, Levine J, 5 December 1997) at 4 n 1). Liberace sued *The Daily Mirror* for defamation in respect of these comments (Pyron 2000, 200–201). The trial itself occurred almost three years after the date of publication (Pyron 2000, 223–33). Liberace instituted his defamation proceedings to perpetuate a lie and himself lied under oath (Pyron 2000, 229). The jury awarded Liberace £8,000.

In July 1957, the tabloid magazine, *Hollywood Confidential*, presented a cover story under the headline, 'Why Liberace's Theme Song Should Be "Mad About the Boy"!' It related an incident in which Liberace was alleged to have made an unwanted, aggressive sexual advance toward a male publicity agent. Liberace brought defamation proceedings in California, eventually settling the matter for US$40,000 (Pyron 2000, 221–3).

In terms of his reputation, Liberace clearly wanted to be perceived as heterosexual in conformity with the prevailing sexual attitudes of the 1950s, however undeserved that perception was. In this sense, Liberace's defamation proceedings engage the concept of reputation as honour. Given that he brought his defamation proceedings to perpetuate a lie and to prevent the truth being told, it is somewhat difficult to accept that the insinuations of homosexuality made against Liberace hurt his feelings and diminished his subjective sense of self. An obvious motivation for Liberace's defamation proceedings was to protect the reputation he and his management had assiduously created and cultivated, camp as it was, from damaging allegations of homosexuality. Liberace brought his defamation proceedings to police his image, to control his portrayal in the media, to protect his celebrity.

Tom Cruise Clearly, since the 1950s, social attitudes to homosexuality have shifted significantly. In the 1950s, the revelation that Liberace, Rock Hudson or Tab Hunter was homosexual would have been detrimental, if not destructive, to their careers. Nowadays, there are a number of high-profile actors, such as Sir Ian McKellen and Rupert Everett, comedians, such as Ellen de Generes and Rosie O'Donnell, and musicians, such as Melissa Etheridge, Sir Elton John, k.d. lang and George Michael, who are openly homosexual. Yet social attitudes to homosexuality have not shifted so decisively that judges have been prepared to find that a bare imputation of homosexuality is no longer defamatory. Similarly, certain celebrities still have recourse to defamation law to resist rumours of homosexuality.

For instance, Tom Cruise has notably demonstrated his vigilance in protecting his heterosexual reputation. Both Cruise and Nicole Kidman sued *The Sunday Express* over allegations that their marriage was a sham to conceal their respective homosexual orientations (*Cruise v Express Newspapers Ltd* [1998] EMLR 780. As to Kidman's defamation proceedings in relation to imputations of adultery, see Chapter 5). They settled their claim reportedly for £200,000, which they again donated to charity (*The Financial Times* (30 October 1998)); Rush and Molloy 1998; *The Australian* (31 October 1998); Hooper 2001, 535). They also sued the American tabloid magazine, *The Star*, over allegations that they required sex therapists to instruct them on how to represent (heterosexual) love convincingly on the set of *Eyes Wide Shut*, insinuating that they are homosexual (Gentleman 1999; Quinn 1999; Walter 1999). Cruise sued gay 'erotic wrestler', Chad Slater (a.k.a. Kyle Bradford), for US$100 million for defamation over Slater's claims to

French magazine, *Actustar*, that he had a sexual relationship with Cruise whilst Cruise was still married to Nicole Kidman. Slater settled his claim with Cruise for US$10 million (Ellison 2001a; Giles 2001; Associated Press, 2003; Wallace 2003). Cruise sued, again seeking US$100 million, over claims made by Michael Davis in *Bold* magazine that there was a videotape in existence showing Cruise having sex with a man but settled when the publisher retracted the claims (Schermerhorn 2001; Ellison 2001b).

Unlike Liberace, it may be accepted that Cruise objects to being falsely portrayed as a homosexual when he is heterosexual and that the related suggestions of homosexuality and hypocrisy affect him personally. Yet, given Cruise's status as a major film star and the fact that the defendants in his defamation proceedings are frequently tabloid publications that trade on gossip, real or fabricated, it is difficult to avoid the fact of Cruise's celebrity when considering the nature of his reputation and his purpose for bringing defamation proceedings.

Jason Donovan Even more vividly than Cruise's multiple defamation suits against media outlets, Jason Donovan's libel proceedings against *The Face* magazine illustrate the problematic nature of reputation as celebrity. As with Cruise's defamation claims, whilst it may be accepted that Donovan resented being falsely presented as homosexual when in fact he is heterosexual and that this had an adverse personal impact on him, the reputation at issue necessarily involves Donovan's celebrity. Even more clearly than Rivkin's compromised defamation claims, Donovan's case also demonstrates the perils of seeking to vindicate reputation as celebrity by means of defamation law.

In the northern summer of 1991, a group called FROCS ('Faggots Rooting Out Closet Sexuality'), planned to engage in a campaign of 'outing' approximately 200 prominent 'closeted' homosexuals. 'Outing', a decidedly early 1990s phenomenon, is the process of publicly identifying celebrities who conceal their homosexual or bisexual orientations against their wishes ('outing' is a controversial topic with a burgeoning legal and ethical literature. For a range of views on the subject of 'outing', see Grant 1991; Wick 1991; Mohr 1992; Pollack 1992; Elwood 1992; Moretti 1993; Becker 1994; Austen and Wellington 1995; MacDougall 1995; Ware 1997). As part of the campaign, posters featuring a photograph of the young Australian soap opera actor and pop singer, Jason Donovan, were posted around London. Donovan's public profile was pre-eminently the product of the media, created and cultivated through his acting on the top-rating television serial, *Neighbours*, and his recordings with leading popular music production team, Stock Aitken Waterman, and finessed by professional public relations and image management.

The photograph in question was doctored to show Donovan wearing a T-shirt emblazoned with the words, 'Queer as Fuck'. Donovan reacted badly to the posters and threatened legal action. He immediately gave a widely syndicated interview in which he flatly rejected the suggestion that he was homosexual and vigorously asserted his heterosexuality (Iley 1991a; Iley 1991b; Iley 1991c). He described his response to FROCS's conduct to journalist, Chrissy Iley, thus:

> 'I do not take this lightly. How dare people say: "I think he's gay". I know exactly what I am.
> 'I have never had a homosexual relationship in my life. These accusations have happened because no one has been able to link me with one girlfriend for some time. I am not obligated to tell the public what I do sexually.
> 'I have a busy life and I am in and out of relationships all the time.
> 'When they become public they become trouble. I don't want people reminding me in the street who I've broken up with.' (Iley 1991a; Iley 1991b; Iley 1991c)

The planned campaign of outing did not eventuate (O'Neill 1991) but, in August 1991, the high-profile style magazine, *The Face*, contained an article on the phenomenon of outing. A leading member of FROCS, Shane Broomhall, allegedly briefed *The Face*. As part of the article, *The Face* reproduced the controversial photograph of Donovan (*The Herald Sun* (1 April 1992); Borrill 1992b).

Donovan was embarrassed by the article. He was concerned that friends and acquaintances, including past, current and prospective (female) partners, might read it and shun and avoid him as a consequence (Jenkins 1992). So he commenced libel proceedings against the publishers of *The Face*, Nicholas Logan and Wagadon Ltd, and the freelance journalist responsible for the article, Benjamin Summerskill.

Just as the article in *The Face* ensured that the imputation of Donovan's homosexuality reached a wider audience than the localised poster campaign in London, Donovan's election to sue *The Face* for libel ensured an even wider audience for the damaging allegation. Donovan's defamation proceedings attracted considerable media attention both in the United Kingdom and in Australia (see, for example, Millington 1992a; Borrill 1992a; Millington 1992b; Borrill 1992b; Boseley 1992a; Borrill 1992c; Boseley, 1992b; Borrill 1992d).

The jury found in favour of Donovan, awarding him £200,000 damages (Borrill 1992e; Borrill 1992f; Clancy 1992). In principle, such a substantial verdict ought to have effected a complete vindication of Donovan's heterosexual reputation. In reality, it almost irreparably damaged his reputation and, more importantly, his career.

The size of the award of damages threatened to bankrupt *The Face* (Boseley 1992c; Whitworth 1992). Donovan later waived most of his damages in order to allow *The Face* to remain financially viable (Mitchell 1992a; Boseley 1992d; Myers 1992). This gesture, reported but not emphasised, did not detract from the fact that Donovan had still sued the style bible. Right-thinking members of society may have thought less of Donovan because it was suggested that he was homosexual, but right-thinking (and self-appointed) 'cool' members of society thought less of Donovan because he had bothered to care.

One of Jason Donovan's two major audiences – gay men (the other being teenage girls) – was understandably alienated by his decision to sue *The Face* over their repetition of allegations that he was homosexual. As a consequence of his libel proceedings, gay men began to shun and avoid Donovan (Mitchell 1992b). His career suffered accordingly.

Donovan made several attempts to rehabilitate his reputation with the gay community in the United Kingdom and Australia. For instance, in one spectacularly unsuccessful attempt, Donovan agreed to act as a compere for the Mr Gay UK competition in late May 1996. He appeared onstage dressed in a black garbage bag, clearly anticipating a particularly bruising reception. He was booed and hissed (Corbett 1996).

In November 1996, he posed for the Australian gay art magazine, *Blue*, near naked in leather fetish wear, in part to promote his then-current role as Frank'N'Furter in *The Rocky Horror Show* (Gow 1996). The natural starting-point for the interview was Donovan's libel proceedings against *The Face*. Donovan again explained why he sued:

> I didn't take them to court because they said I was gay, but because they said I was lying. I have never lied about who I am. I'm straight and they said I wasn't and that I was lying about it. Never. I have a lot of gay friends, I go to gay venues. And I'm straight. (Gow 1996, 47)

Four years after the event, Donovan expressed his regret at suing for defamation:

> When I look back on the whole thing now I see I was pretty naïve, but I really thought I could finally stop all the bullshit and publicly state that I was not a liar about my sexuality. It didn't work of course. Here I was, this cheesy blond (sic) soap star from down-under taking on the coolest magazine in the world. I won the case, but there was no way they were going to let me have the last word. So it's still going on. (Gow 1996, 49)

Demonstrating a keen insight into the reality of reputation as celebrity in a media-saturated society and the vexed nature of the allegedly defamatory quality of imputations of homosexuality, the journalist, Michael Gow, editorialised thus:

> If your sexuality has ever been open to question, if you've experienced any of the doubts and fears that are still part of being gay, then you would never use the courts to make a mere point of honour. And you would never be the tiniest bit surprised that people who had actually experienced those doubts and fears would see your legal point of honour at least as a condemnation and certainly a betrayal … Donovan demanded the right to be heard and he got it. And then he was jaw droppingly amazed that the gay world reacted the way it did. And that the press, which has to have the last word no matter what, won't ever forgive him. (Gow 1996, 49)

Donovan's decision to pose nude for *Blue* itself attracted further media attention (Corbett and Symons 1996; Kent 1996).

Donovan's defamation proceedings against *The Face* continue to be mentioned in interviews with him after the passage of more than a decade (Wilmoth 1995; Trioli 1996; Hattenstone 1996; Leith 1996; Jardine 1998; Manly 1999; Vincent 1999; Sullivan 2000; Yeaman 2002; Curtis and Wilson 2003; Ross 2004; Button 2004). They have in fact become an integral part of his reputation, explaining as it does the decline of Donovan's spectacularly promising career. The imputation of homosexuality, Donovan's response to it, the trial and its outcome, the subsequent impact on Donovan's celebrity career – all these elements are firmly integrated into Donovan's public profile.

Donovan's litigation against *The Face* magazine was integrated into *The Face*'s reputation as well (Cosgrove 1994; Reeves 1999). Notwithstanding that it was published continuously over 24 years, when it finally closed in April 2004, it was Donovan's defamation case that was routinely mentioned as its most significant event (Milmo and Martinson 2004; Kirby 2004; Brown 2004; McGavin 2004). Indeed, it was rumoured that Donovan was intending to finance *The Face* in order to keep it in circulation – thus perhaps paying the ultimate penance (Barrett 2004; Toy and Connolly 2004). Donovan's reputation and that of *The Face* are and will presumably remain inextricably linked.

In his recent memoirs, *Between the Lines: My Story Uncut*, Donovan explains, in his own words and in some detail, his reasons for bringing his defamation proceedings against *The Face*. His principal concerns were the suggestions that he was a liar and a hypocrite (Donovan 2007, 174, 178). However, Donovan also described his decision to sue as the biggest mistake of his life, because he did not understand the adverse impact in his daily life that would result from his success at trial (Donovan 2007, 181, 185).

As with Cairns and Morosi, as with Abbott and Costello, press coverage of Jason Donovan's career still refers to his defamation litigation against *The Face* magazine. Some of it is sympathetic; some of it is not. In theory, a favourable defamation verdict is intended to restore or vindicate a plaintiff's reputation, to demonstrate to the world at large that there is no basis upon which to think less of the plaintiff and no basis upon which to shun and avoid the plaintiff. In practice, the vagaries of celebrity suggest the outcome may be quite different. In January 2004, a profile of Donovan in the Sydney newspaper, *The Daily Telegraph*, referred to the case, describing the consequences for him thus: '[t]he beautiful people sided with the magazine and nobody wanted Jason at their parties any more' (Hardy 2004, 5).

Chapter 7
Reputation as Dignity

Introduction

The focus of this chapter is the concept of reputation as dignity. Although Australian law has not embraced what Feldman describes as 'legal humanism' (Feldman 1999, 682), in the sense that it has not adopted a comprehensive constitutional or statutory regime of explicit protections for human rights founded upon a belief in the importance of human dignity (as to the concept of reputation as dignity generally, see Chapter 1), it is submitted that Australian defamation law nevertheless incorporates the concept of reputation as dignity through its protection of plaintiffs from publications that tend to expose them to ridicule (as to the defamatory capacity of ridicule, see Chapter 3). As Hand J observed in *Burton v Crowell Publishing Co* 82 F (2d) 154 (1936) at 156, the gist of defamation based on ridicule is not really the injury to the plaintiff's reputation but rather the subjective, negative experience of the plaintiff in response to the publication and any 'repulsion' or 'light esteem' such may engender. The place of reputation as dignity in Australian defamation law will be explored principally through a case study comparing two cases, in both of which the photographic exposure of the plaintiffs' bodies exposed the plaintiffs to ridicule and consequently was held to be defamatory. As with the examination of the concept of reputation as property and as honour, this chapter concludes that the concept of reputation as dignity does manifest itself in Australian defamation law but that, again, there may be scope for a further concept of reputation – reputation as celebrity – to be identified.

Case Study 4

Exposure to Ridicule – Introduction

The definition of what is defamatory is expansive and includes exposing a person to ridicule. Making a plaintiff an object of ridicule, to more than a trivial degree, does not impute any moral fault to the plaintiff. It amounts to not so much an affront to his or her honour, but rather to an attack on his or her dignity (as to the defamatory capacity of ridicule, see Chapter 3).

This case study will focus primarily on two cases, *Ettingshausen* and *Shepherd v Walsh*. There are certain similarities between these cases. Fundamentally, both concern plaintiffs who had naked photographs of them published without their consent.[1] There are also important differences between these cases. An analysis of these differences will illuminate the applicability of reputation as dignity, as well as the limitations of such an understanding in interpreting Australian defamation law.

Case Study 4(a): Ettingshausen v Australian Consolidated Press Ltd

In 1990, freelance journalist and self-described 'cappuccino-drinking copywriter from Paddington' (Kerr and Cochrane 1991a, 95), James Kerr, and photographer, Brett Cochrane, were given permission to accompany the Kangaroos, the Australian representative rugby league team, on their English tour. Kerr and Cochrane were granted 'unqualified access' (Kerr and Cochrane 1991a, 96) to the players – at their hotels, at their training sessions, in the locker-rooms, and in the showers after matches. The purpose of Kerr and Cochrane accompanying the Kangaroos to England was to obtain material for a photo book (Kerr and Cochrane 1991a, 95), which would be sold to raise money for a charity, the Children's Leukaemia and Cancer Foundation (Kerr and Cochrane 1991a, 99). The resulting book, *Twenty Eight Heroes: Inside the 1990 Kangaroo Tour*, was published and released in 1991 (Kerr and Cochrane 1991b). As part of the promotion of the book, *H.Q.* magazine published an article under the title, 'Hunks', with text by Kerr and photographs by Cochrane. The text and eight of the nine accompanying photographs were unobjectionable (for contrasting characterisations of the nature of the article and the treatment of its subject matter, compare Gleeson CJ (at 1–2) and Kirby P (at 2–4) in *Australian Consolidated Press Ltd v Ettingshausen* (unreported, CA40079/93, CA(NSW), Gleeson CJ, Kirby P and Clarke JA, 13 October 1993)). One photograph, however, the photograph used on the first double-page spread of the article, proved especially controversial and ultimately gave rise to one of the largest Australian defamation trials of the early 1990s.

The photograph in question, a grainy black-and-white image captioned 'Shower power', depicted three Kangaroos, Ben Elias, Laurie Daley and Andrew Ettingshausen in the showers. Elias is shown facing Daley and Ettingshausen. He is bent over slightly, soaping himself down. Daley stands side on, facing towards Elias. Ettingshausen stands, arms folded, with his back against the wall, facing the camera (Kerr and Cochrane 1991a, 94–5. See also *Ettingshausen v Australian Consolidated Press Ltd* (1991) 23 NSWLR 443 at 444 per Hunt J). Amidst the grainy shadows of the photograph and beneath the superimposed text of the article is, according to Hunt J, 'a shape between the plaintiff's legs which (despite the

---

1 The defence of consent was specifically raised by the publisher, Australian Consolidated Press Ltd, in *Ettingshausen* but was not placed before the jury due to lack of evidence. See *Ettingshausen v Australian Consolidated Press Ltd* (unreported, SC(NSW), No. 12807/91, Hunt CJ at CL, 11 March 1993) at 12. The defence of consent was not raised in *Shepherd v Walsh* because it was clear that the plaintiff had never consented to the photograph or the publication. See *Shepherd v Walsh* [2001] QSC 358 at [4] per Jones J.

defendant's submission to the contrary) is certainly capable of being interpreted as a penis' (*Ettingshausen v Australian Consolidated Press Ltd* (1991) 23 NSWLR 443 at 445 per Hunt J. See also (unreported, CA40079/93, CA(NSW), Gleeson CJ, Kirby P and Clarke JA, 13 October 1993) at 1 per Gleeson CJ: 'The photograph included the respondent's penis.' Explicitly, rather than impliedly. See also Miller 1995). Because of the lighting and the manner in which the photograph has been cropped, the penises of Elias and Daley are not visible to the naked eye.

Ettingshausen immediately commenced defamation proceedings against the publisher of *H.Q.* magazine, Australian Consolidated Press Ltd (ACP). The terms in which the pleading of his imputations was originally cast suggests the way in which he viewed the publication:

> (a) The plaintiff is an indecent and lewd person in that he freely posed for a photograph of his naked body with genitals exposed for publication to the readers of the defendant's magazine, H.Q.
>
> (b) The plaintiff willingly pandered to the prurient interest of the readers of the defendant's magazine, H.Q., in that he freely posed for a photograph of his naked body with genitals exposed for publication to the readers of that magazine.
>
> (c) The plaintiff is an indecent and lewd person in that he freely allowed a photograph to be taken of his naked body with genitals exposed for publication to the readers of the defendant's magazine, H.Q.
>
> (d) The plaintiff willingly pandered to the prurient interests of the defendant's magazine, H.Q., in that he freely allowed a photograph to be taken of his naked body with genitals exposed for publication to the readers of that magazine. ((1991) 23 NSWLR 443 at 445 per Hunt J)

Hunt J, as his Honour then was, described these imputations as 'an egregious breach' of the requirement that the pleaded imputations differ in substance from each other ((1991) 23 NSWLR 443 at 445 per Hunt J). The requirement that the pleaded imputations differ in substance is found in the *Supreme Court Rules* 1970 (NSW) (Pt 67 r 11(3)). Recognising this, Ettingshausen recast the imputations, instead pleading the following imputations:

> (a) The plaintiff deliberately permitted a photograph to be taken of him with his genitals exposed for the purposes of reproduction in a publication with a widespread readership.
>
> (b) The plaintiff is a person whose genitals have been exposed to the readers of the defendant's magazine 'H.Q.', a publication with a widespread readership. ((1991) 23 NSWLR 443 at 445 per Hunt J)

These imputations were pleaded in the alternative ((1991) 23 NSWLR 443 at 445, 449 per Hunt J). (Ettingshausen also pleaded, as a true innuendo, the imputation that 'he is unfit to hold [his position as a schools and junior development promotions officer by the New South Wales Rugby League] because of having posed for or allowed a photograph to be taken exposing his genitals for publication in the defendant's magazine' ((1991) 23 NSWLR 443 at 445 per Hunt J). The proof of this true innuendo required proof of the extrinsic fact that Ettingshausen was known to have held such a position ((1991) 23 NSWLR 443 at 445).)

At a separate trial, ACP challenged the capacity of the matter complained of to convey these two imputations and the capacity of imputation (b) to be defamatory ((1991) 23 NSWLR 443 at 445). Examining the article in question, Hunt J had no difficulty in concluding that the ordinary, reasonable reader could find that imputation (a) was conveyed. His Honour found that there was ample evidence from the text to conclude that Kerr and Cochrane were accompanying the tour with the permission of the Australian Rugby League and that the players were made aware of the purpose for which Kerr and Cochrane were accompanying them. His Honour also pointed out that there was considerable evidence of the author's growing familiarity with the players. Hunt J rejected ACP's submission that Ettingshausen was unaware that Kerr and Cochrane intended to reproduce any photograph taken in 'a publication with a widespread readership'. His Honour pointed out that the imputation did not specify ACP's *H.Q.* magazine and that the book Kerr and Cochrane intended to write satisfied the description of 'a publication with a widespread readership'. Hunt J also dismissed ACP's submission that *H.Q.* was not 'a publication with a widespread readership', observing that the magazine sold advertising in five Australian states and in New Zealand, suggesting that it had a not insubstantial Australasian readership ((1991) 23 NSWLR 443 at 449 per Hunt J). There was, therefore, evidence in the article such as to allow the ordinary, reasonable reader to find the imputation was conveyed.

In relation to imputation (b), Hunt J had no difficulty in finding that it was capable of being conveyed by the article. The more complicated question was whether it was capable of defaming the plaintiff. Hunt J acknowledged that the imputation did not purport to ascribe any moral blame to Ettingshausen ((1991) 23 NSWLR 443 at 447 per Hunt J). Nevertheless, his Honour found that the imputation could be defamatory of Ettingshausen because, applying *Burton v Crowell Publishing Co* 82 F (2d) 154 (1936), 156, it was 'capable of subjecting the entirely blameless plaintiff to more than a trivial degree of ridicule' ((1991) 23 NSWLR 443 at 449 per Hunt J. As to the issue of the defamatory character of ridicule and what this suggests about the nature of reputation, see Chapter 3).

Following this interlocutory decision of Hunt J, ACP published a 'qualified and seemingly reluctant' apology to Ettingshausen in the Summer 1991 issue of *H.Q.*. The apology purported to withdraw imputation (a). Not only was the apology couched in 'qualified and seemingly reluctant' terms, it was unfortunately placed on the same page as a large advertisement for condoms, 'Discrete Objects of Desire' ((unreported, CA40079/93, CA(NSW), Gleeson CJ, Kirby P and Clarke JA, 13 October 1993) at 6 per Kirby P. See also Hickie 1993h: counsel for Ettingshausen, Tom Hughes QC, characterised ACP's apology as 'obviously insincere' because of its proximity to an advertisement for condoms, a characterisation Kirby P rejects).

At the trial itself, ACP maintained that the photograph in question did not show Ettingshausen's penis. On appeal, Gleeson CJ described this as 'a disingenuous attempt to deny the obvious' ((unreported, CA40079/93, CA(NSW), Gleeson CJ, Kirby P and Clarke JA, 13 October 1993) at 2). The unusual forensic position adopted by ACP did, however, provide one of the most famous pieces of cross-examination in Australian legal history. Tom Hughes QC, counsel for Ettingshausen, cross-examined the editor of *H.Q.*, asking her for her opinion about the photograph. He used the opportunity to make a joke at the expense of her New Zealand accent:

> HUGHES: It is a penis isn't it?
> MARTYN: I assume if it is in that part of the body, may be it could be or it might not be.
> HUGHES: What else could it be ... is it a duck?
>
> (Hickie 1993c; Casimir and Squires 1993b; O'Neill 1993. See also Miller 1995, 111–12)

In contrast, the photographer, Brett Cochrane, readily conceded in cross-examination that Ettingshausen's penis was present and visible in the photograph (Hickie 1993d).

During the trial, Hunt CJ at CL refused to allow the defences of consent and statutory qualified privilege, pursuant to the *Defamation Act* 1974 (NSW) s 22, to be presented to the jury.

In relation to the defence of statutory qualified privilege, Hunt CJ at CL was prepared to accept, for the purpose of argument, that there was a legitimate public interest in receiving the information about the subject matter of the article, as required by the *Defamation Act* 1974 (NSW) s 22(1)(a), although it was clear that ACP had difficulty identifying the requisite interest (*Ettingshausen v Australian Consolidated Press Ltd* (unreported, No. 12807/91, SC(NSW), Hunt CJ at CL, 11 March 1993) at 2–3). ACP variously suggested that the public interest in the subject matter was the use of sex in marketing rugby league ((unreported, No. 12807/91, SC(NSW), Hunt CJ at CL, 11 March 1993) at 2), the performance and training methods of rugby league teams ((unreported, No. 12807/91, SC(NSW), Hunt CJ at CL, 11 March 1993) at 3) and 'the physical appetites, prowess and physical fitness' of rugby league players and, by extension, the physiques of individual players ((unreported, No. 12807/91, SC(NSW), Hunt CJ at CL, 11 March 1993) at 3). Hunt CJ at CL was also willing to accept, again for the purpose of argument, that the article conveyed information to its readership about one of these matters of public interest. However, his Honour held that there was no evidence that, in publishing the imputations, the 'lowest common denominator' of which was, according to Hunt CJ at CL, the exposure of the plaintiff's penis, ACP's conduct was reasonable in all the circumstances, as required by the *Defamation Act* 1974

(NSW) s 22(1)(c) ((unreported, No. 12807/91, SC(NSW), Hunt CJ at CL, 11 March 1993) at 7).

In relation to the defence of consent, Hunt CJ at CL noted that Ettingshausen had conceded that he knew that Brett Cochrane was the official team photographer, that Cochrane was taking photographs for the purpose of using them in a forthcoming book for charity and that material from the book would be used to promote it in magazines ((unreported, No. 12807/91, SC(NSW), Hunt CJ at CL, 11 March 1993) at 7). However, his Honour held that there was no evidence that Ettingshausen had consented to the use of the particular photograph in the particular magazine. Because Ettingshausen was complaining that the photograph was published in a context that suggested he consented to the exposure of his penis, the consent ACP was required to establish was the consent to the photographic exposure of his penis ((unreported, No. 12807/91, SC(NSW), Hunt CJ at CL, 11 March 1993) at 11). On the evidence, ACP was clearly unable to do this. Hunt CJ at CL found that ACP's submission that Ettingshausen had effectively consented to the publication of the photograph, relying on the facts conceded, was based upon an erroneous conflation of the defences of consent and voluntary assumption of risk ((unreported, No. 12807/91, SC(NSW), Hunt CJ at CL, 11 March 1993) at 8).

The only defence Hunt CJ at CL allowed ACP to present to the jury therefore was the defence of unlikelihood of harm, pursuant to the *Defamation Act* 1974 (NSW) s 13. Unsurprisingly, given the onerous requirements of this defence and its infrequent success (see *Morosi v Mirror Newspapers* [1977] 2 NSWLR 749; *Singleton v John Fairfax & Sons Ltd [No 1]* [1983] 2 NSWLR 722; *Chappell v Mirror Newspapers* (1984) Aust Torts Reports ¶80-691; *King and Mergen Holdings Pty Ltd v McKenzie* (1991) 24 NSWLR 305; *Jones v Sutton* (2004) 61 NSWLR 614), the jury rejected it.

At the first trial before Hunt CJ at CL, conducted over eight days in early February 1993, the jury found that imputation (a) and the true innuendo pleaded by Ettingshausen were conveyed and were defamatory. It was therefore unnecessary for the jury to consider imputation (b). The jury needed to deliberate for only an hour ((unreported, CA40079/93, CA(NSW), Gleeson CJ, Kirby P and Clarke JA, 13 October 1993) at 7 per Kirby P) in order to award Ettingshausen $350,000 damages (*The Sydney Morning Herald* (12 February 1993); see also Ackland 1993).

The media response to the decision was one of incredulity and derision (O'Neill 1993; Strong 1993). Given the media response, Hunt CJ at CL felt compelled, two days after the jury verdict, dealing with an application brought by ACP for a stay pending an appeal, to take the somewhat unusual course of castigating the media for their reporting and analysis of the jury verdict, accusing them of unbalanced reporting of the outcome of the case arising out of their vested interests (Hickie 1993h).

ACP appealed to the New South Wales Court of Appeal, which, by majority, dismissed the appeal as to liability ((unreported, CA40079/93, CA(NSW), Gleeson CJ, Kirby P and Clarke JA, 13 October 1993), (Gleeson CJ and Clarke JA, Kirby

P dissenting)) but unanimously agreed that the quantum of the jury's award of damages was manifestly excessive ((unreported, CA40079/93, CA(NSW), Gleeson CJ, Kirby P and Clarke JA, 13 October 1993) at 3 per Gleeson CJ, at 45 per Kirby P, at 32 per Clarke JA). A new trial was ordered, limited to the question of damages ((unreported, CA40079/93, CA(NSW), Gleeson CJ, Kirby P and Clarke JA, 13 October 1993) at 4 per Gleeson CJ, at 33 per Clarke JA).

A retrial was conducted before Badgery-Parker J in early 1995. At the second trial, the jury awarded Ettingshausen only $100,000 damages (Dean 1995b).

Commenting after the second trial, Ettingshausen stated that he was satisfied with the outcome. He felt that the jury's verdict indicated to himself and the world at large that his 'morals', as well as his reputation, were intact. Ettingshausen claimed that the case demonstrated emphatically that he did not and would never pose nude for a magazine. Counsel for Ettingshausen, Tom Hughes QC, opined that '[s]elf-respecting people don't like being seen as a sort of a hunk of human flesh, a plaything'. Counsel for ACP, Bruce McClintock, understandably expressed a markedly different view. He claimed that the publication of the offending photograph in *H.Q.* magazine had no effect whatsoever on Ettingshausen's reputation. McClintock also asserted that the article accompanying the photograph was overwhelmingly positive. Finally, McClintock noted that the nature and quality of the photograph meant that many readers may not have noticed the exposure of Ettingshausen's penis in the photograph until the publicity of the proceedings brought it to their attention (Dean 1995b).

Case Study 4(b): Shepherd v Walsh

The decision of the Supreme Court of Queensland in *Shepherd v Walsh* provides a neat contrast to *Ettingshausen* in a number of respects. In *Shepherd v Walsh*, the plaintiff, Sonia Shepherd, sued over the publication of a naked photograph of her, accompanied by some lewd commentary, in the 'Home Girls' section of the 1 November 1995 edition of *The Picture* magazine ([2001] QSC 358 at [1] per Jones J). *Picture* was characterised by the trial judge in *Shepherd v Walsh* as 'a picture magazine of a salacious bent' ([2001] QSC 358 at [17] per Jones J), comprised 'mainly of photographs of naked women and crass, and essentially inane, stories relating to the photographs' ([2001] QSC 358 at [18] per Jones J). More succinctly, in similar proceedings, another judge described *Picture* as 'soft-core pornography' (*Obermann v ACP Publishing Pty Ltd* [2001] NSWSC 1022 at [4] per Simpson J). The 'Home Girls' section publishes naked photographs of ordinary women who send them in for that purpose. It is the most popular segment of this magazine (Albury 1997, 19, 25 n 1). For their efforts, women who submit photograph can elect to have their faces obscured, in which case they are dubbed 'Bag Girls' and paid $75, or they can have their faces displayed, in which case they qualify as 'Home Girls' and are paid $150. Shepherd appeared as a 'Home Girl' with her face clearly visible ([2001] QSC 358 at [18] per Jones J. See also Albury 1997, 19).

The corresponding 'Home Blokes' section in the same magazine is less popular and less lucrative. It also has stricter identification requirements for its participants. Men who submit naked photographs of themselves must send a copy of some form of photographic identification, such as a driver's licence. Women simply clip and sign a coupon, indicating their consent, with no additional proof required. Jones J described the risk of misrepresentation as 'obvious' ([2001] QSC 358 at [18]).

Such a misrepresentation occurred in this case – and it occurred deliberately. As an act of revenge ([2001] QSC 358 at [4]), Shepherd's disgruntled ex-boyfriend, Anthony Patterson, encouraged his current girlfriend, Sonja de Vries, to submit the photograph with a coupon. De Vries then conducted a telephone interview with the editor to confirm her details ([2001] QSC 358 at [4]).

Accompanying the photograph of Sonia Shepherd was the following text, which in no way reflected the *persona* of the plaintiff but instead substantially reflected the *persona* of Sonja de Vries ([2001] QSC 358 at [4]):

> **SONJA: Hervey Bay, Qld**
> Age 22 and single with one girl ruggie [Jones J helpfully notes that '[t]he term "ruggie" in the patois of the magazine means "child"': [2001] QSC 358 [3] n 1]. Sonja rates her favourite things as Pet Shop Boys, tenpin bowling, *Chicago Hope*, spaghetti and getting smashed on tequila slammers at the Pie every weekend. '*Where did you score your weirdest root, Son?*' 'At the end of the jetty at high tide.' '*Who would you like to get naked with?*' 'My next door neighbour.' ([2001] QSC 358 at [3])

Shepherd did not consent to the original taking of the photograph. In fact, she claimed she was unaware of its existence ([2001] QSC 358 at [4]). In the early 1990s, her boyfriend at the time, Anthony Patterson, surprised Shepherd in their bedroom and took the photograph in spite of her protestations. He assured Shepherd that there was no film in the camera when in fact there was. Shepherd believed him and did not check the camera for herself because Patterson quickly packed the camera away in their holiday luggage ([2001] QSC 358 at [13]). Clearly, Shepherd did not consent to the publication of the photograph ([2001] QSC 358 at [4]), nor did she give the brief interview which was attributed to her in *Picture*.

The publication of the offending photograph was exposed in this way. Mark Douglas, a friend of Shepherd's brother-in-law, first saw the photograph of Shepherd when he purchased the magazine prior to a fishing trip in November 1995 ([2001] QSC 358 at [33]). He telephoned his friends, and Shepherd's relatives, the Jeppesens, to alert them to the contents of the magazine ([2001] QSC 358 at [34]). Shepherd first became aware of the existence of the photograph when she was informed by a letter from her sister, Helen Jeppesen, in December 1995 in the following terms: 'We saw that photo of you in that girlie magazine, and you call yourself a Christian. I don't believe anything you say' ([2001] QSC 358 at [31]).

Shepherd commenced defamation proceedings in the Supreme Court of Queensland against the publisher, printer and distributor of *Picture*, as well as her ex-boyfriend, the fifth defendant. ACP attempted to commence third party proceedings against de Vries. Jones J refused the application, given that it was made only three weeks before the matter itself was set down for hearing (*Shepherd v Walsh* (unreported, SC(Qld), No. S49/96, Jones J, 8 May 2001) at 3). Had his Honour acceded to the application, Shepherd's defamation hearing would have to be adjourned to allow time for de Vries to prepare her case. Jones J ruled that this would cause substantial and unnecessary injustice and hardship to Shepherd.

The publishing defendants admitted that they published the photograph ([2001] QSC 358 at [1]) and that the photograph was 'of and concerning the plaintiff' ([2001] QSC 358 at [5]). All the defendants denied, however, that the publication of the photograph with the accompanying text was capable of being defamatory and that it was in fact defamatory of Shepherd ([2001] QSC 358 at [7]). Otherwise, the defendants raised no defence (the publishing defendants abandoned the defence of 'non-publication by reason of their lack of knowledge that the words and picture was of a character likely to contain defamatory material' prior to the trial: [2001] QSC 358 at [8]). Given the nature of publication, Jones J unsurprisingly found in favour of Shepherd.

His Honour proceeded to assess Shepherd's damages. The publishing defendants relied principally upon their apology to Shepherd in mitigation. In late February 1996, Shepherd, through her solicitors, sought an apology from the publishing defendants. This did not occur, however, until the close of the cross-examination of the plaintiff in her defamation proceedings ([2001] QSC 358 at [61]). Jones J found that this late apology had no real mitigating effect on the assessment of damages ([2001] QSC 358 at [62]).

His Honour awarded Shepherd $50,000 compensatory damages against all five defendants ([2001] QSC 358 at [67]) but found that there were no grounds for an award of aggravated damages ([2001] QSC 358 at [71]). However, his Honour did find that the fifth defendant, Shepherd's ex-boyfriend, had acted in contemptuous disregard of Shepherd's rights and, as such, deserved to have an award of exemplary damages imposed upon him ([2001] QSC 358 at [75]). Jones J assessed the appropriate level of exemplary damages at $20,000 ([2001] QSC 358 at [76]). Shepherd may experience difficulty recovering these damages from Patterson as he did not file an appearance at the hearing ([2001] QSC 358 at [1]).

Case Study 4: Exposure to Ridicule – Analysis

The Application of the Concepts of Reputation to Imputations of Exposure to Ridicule

Both *Ettingshausen* and *Shepherd v Walsh* centrally involve the concept of reputation as dignity. Both Andrew Ettingshausen and Sonia Shepherd felt that they had been portrayed in a ridiculous light by having naked photographs of themselves published without their consent and reacted adversely to the publications in question. At his first trial, Ettingshausen gave evidence that he found the photograph 'very offensive' and 'pornographic' (Hickie 1993a). At his second trial, he gave evidence that, almost four years after the photograph was originally published, he was still experiencing the repercussions. He was subjected to comments from team-mates, opponents and spectators; he was the subject of graffiti; he had been dubbed 'The Nudist' by radio sports commentators, 'Rampaging' Roy Slaven and H.G. Nelson. Ettingshausen gave evidence that he felt that he was compelled to overachieve on the sportsfield in order to obliterate the public memory of the photograph. He did, however, admit in the course of cross-examination that the publication had not harmed his football, television or radio career (Dean 1995a). Similarly, in her defamation proceedings, Sonia Shepherd gave evidence that she was 'shocked', 'upset', 'totally disgusted', almost suicidal, when she learned of the publication ([2001] QSC 358 at [31], [58] per Jones J). She claimed, and it was accepted by Jones J, that the publication was a significant stressor on her already fragile marriage and it hastened the decline of that relationship ([2001] QSC 358 at [53]–[54]). Her distress was revived first when she had to disclose the publication to her fiancé in order to explain her conduct of the defamation proceedings ([2001] QSC 358 at [58]) and again when she had to give evidence in her defamation proceedings ([2001] QSC 358 at [62]). Thus, both Ettingshausen and Shepherd were complaining that the respective defendants' publications exposed them to ridicule and that this diminished their sense of self. In this way, both cases directly engage the concept of reputation as dignity.

The concept of reputation as dignity also arises in both *Ettingshausen* and *Shepherd v Walsh* by virtue of the fact that both publications may be construed as an invasion of privacy. Ettingshausen particularly viewed the publication of the photograph as 'a gross invasion of [his] privacy' ((unreported, CA40079/93, CA(NSW), Gleeson CJ, Kirby P and Clarke JA, 13 October 1993) at 32 per Clarke JA; see also at 14. See further O'Neill 1993; Kent 2000) and brought his defamation proceedings in part to seek redress for it. This is problematic for a number of reasons, both at the level of principle and according to the particular facts of the case. At the level of principle, it is perhaps inappropriate to use defamation proceedings to vindicate a right to privacy, given that the sole interest directly protected by defamation law is the right to reputation (Watterson 1993, 812–13; Barendt 1999, 112–14; Beverley-Smith 2002, 249–50; Rogers 2002, [12.1]). The current contested status of an independent, enforceable right to privacy in Australian law tends to reinforce this.[2] Defamation proceedings may, however, provide an incidental measure of protection for the plaintiff's privacy, but this is

2 *Australian Broadcasting Corporation v Lenah Game Meats Pty Ltd* (2001) 208 CLR 199; 185 ALR 1 at 11–13 per Gleeson CJ, at 31–7 per Gummow and Hayne JJ, at 54–6 per Kirby J, at 93–5 per Callinan J; 76 ALJR 1; 54 IPR 161; Aust Torts Reports ¶81-627. Compare *Grosse v Purvis* [2003] QDC 151 at [415]–[447] per Skoien DCJ; *Kalaba v Commonwealth* [2004] FCA 763; *aff'd* [2004] FCAFC 326; *Giller v Procopets* [2004] VSC 113 at [187]–[189] per Gillard J; *Doe v Australian Broadcasting Corporation* [2007] VCC 281 at [101]–[164] per Judge Hampel.

premised upon damage to the plaintiff's reputation being at issue (*Chappell v TCN Channel Nine Pty Ltd* (1988) 14 NSWLR 153 at 165–8; (1988) Aust Torts Reports ¶80-187 per Hunt J). In *Ettingshausen*, the plaintiff's interest in his reputation and his 'right' to privacy were unhelpfully confused.

On the facts of the case, Ettingshausen's claim that his 'privacy' had been invaded is also problematic. In cross-examination, Ettingshausen gave evidence that he objected to the photograph because 'it shows my genitals which I believe to be a very personal part of my body which I do not want to be shown to anybody' (Hickie 1993a).

He subsequently qualified that statement, acknowledging that he did not object to his wife seeing him naked. Likewise, he did not object to his team-mates seeing him naked. He also accepted that he knew of Cochrane's role as official team photographer and that Cochrane was taking photographs of the Kangaroos in the locker-rooms and the showers. Nor did Ettingshausen object to all displays and representations of the penis. For instance, he accepted in cross-examination such displays and representations of the penis may be appropriate or inoffensive, depending on the context, citing a medical encyclopaedia as an example (Hickie 1993a). What Ettingshausen essentially objected to was the selection of the particular photograph for use in *H.Q.* magazine. It was this act, not the other acts which entailed the exposure of his penis, that seemed to have constituted the invasion of privacy.

This starkly reveals two interrelated features of *Ettingshausen*. Firstly, it demonstrates the problematic nature of discourses surrounding privacy. Like dignity, notions of privacy are highly subjective. Moreover, the boundaries of what is private (and, by implication, what is public) are not rigidly defined. For Ettingshausen, his body was not entirely private – some could look, some could not. The activity he was engaging in, showering after a game, was private but this did not occur in an entirely private space – it was a communal shower to which team officials, including photographers, were allowed access (See also *Vernonia School Dist v Acton* 515 US 646 (1995); 115 S Ct 2386 (1995), 2392–3 (Scalia J) (right to privacy in sporting showers and change-rooms qualified because expectation that one might be viewed naked)). Ettingshausen wanted to control for himself what personal aspects of his body, his activities and his spaces were private and public (McKee 2001, 286). ACP's conduct was an interference with his autonomy as well as his reputation, his dignity and his privacy.

Secondly, as Miller argues, *Ettingshausen* demonstrates a fundamental cultural anxiety surrounding the exposure of the penis (Miller 1995, 132–7). This 'cultural anxiety' does not extend to female nudity. It is largely absent from *Shepherd v Walsh*. Whilst judges and advocates strongly condemned the invasion of privacy Ettingshausen was subjected to by having a grainy, black-and-white photograph of his body, including his visually indistinct penis, published in a magazine, particularly ACP's conduct ((unreported, CA40079/93, CA(NSW), Gleeson CJ, Kirby P and Clarke JA, 13 October 1993) at 2 per Gleeson CJ, at 32 per Clarke JA. Gleeson CJ states, somewhat cryptically, that there was 'an emphasis on male nudity that was calculated to attract and amuse a certain type of reader'. See also Dean 1995b), the same censure was not evident in *Shepherd v Walsh*, where a more revealing colour photograph of the plaintiff had been reproduced and circulated again by ACP. Yet the defendants' conduct in *Shepherd v Walsh* equally amounted to an invasion of Shepherd's privacy with adverse consequences for Shepherd's dignity.

Both Ettingshausen and Shepherd were also complaining about an intrusion on their dignity and autonomy in another related sense. Neither Ettingshausen nor Shepherd apparently objected to nudity *per se*. The gist of their complaints was that a naked photograph of them had been published without their consent. They were fundamentally objecting to the way in which they had been portrayed. By publishing the naked photographs of the plaintiffs, the defendants had interfered with the plaintiffs' dignity and autonomy, their right or desire to control the manner in which they are portrayed. Whilst Ettingshausen, with his higher public profile, clearly had more at stake, Shepherd, through her defamation proceedings, also manifested this desire.

Yet the concept of reputation as dignity only provides a partial explanation for the reputation and the damage done to it involved in these two cases. By a judge or jury, as relevant, finding that the physical exposure of the plaintiff's body by the defendant was defamatory, the judge or jury is reflecting and at the same time imposing a value judgment about the morality of publicly mediated nudity. This explains, in part, the nature and the vehemence of Ettingshausen's subjective reaction to the photograph in *H.Q.* magazine – he would not have willingly participated in a photograph he characterised as 'very offensive' and 'pornographic' (Hickie 1993a). Indeed, Ettingshausen himself stated that he felt that his 'morals' had been vindicated by the jury verdict (Dean 1995b), suggesting that he generally viewed such photographs as immoral. Likewise, Shepherd would not have consented to the taking and the publication of the photograph. Indeed, in addition to the imputations based on portrayal in a ridiculous light, Shepherd also pleaded that the publication conveyed the imputation that she would expose herself for financial gain and that she was promiscuous ([2001] QSC 358 at 50 at [29], [52] per Jones J. As to imputations of 'unchastity' generally, including promiscuity, see Chapter 5).

Yet both of these value judgments are contestable in contemporary Australian society. For example, Ettingshausen's claim that the publication of the naked photograph adversely affected his reputation seems inconsistent with the increasing use of the physical attractiveness of sportsmen to market professional sport – including the liberal use of male nudity. At the time, *Ettingshausen* itself caused a division of opinion amongst sportspeople about whether this trend is a desirable development, as two different reactions to Ettingshausen's litigation by former rugby league players attest. Whilst former Balmain Tigers captain, Wayne Pearce, may agree with Ettingshausen's view, other rugby league players, such as the former Western Suburbs stalwart, Tommy Raudonikis, adopt a markedly different view. Pearce gave evidence at the first trial in *Ettingshausen* that he was 'repulsed' by the sight of Ettingshausen's penis in *H.Q.* magazine. Asked to explain his reaction, Pearce responded: 'I wouldn't want my pecker in the paper' (Hickie 1993b; O'Neill 1993).

Responding to Ettingshausen's claim and Pearce's evidence, Raudonikis, made the following offer: 'I'll drop my ol' fella out anytime anywhere for that kind of money' (O'Neill 1993).

Yet the professionalisation and commercialisation of sport has led, since the mid-1980s, to the commodification and exploitation of the bodies of sportspeople, both men and women. Importantly, this process of commodifying and exploiting the bodies of sportspeople explicitly involves the sexualisation of their bodies. The logic is clear enough – sex sells, as the advertising adage goes, so use sex to sell sport. Fortunately, with sportspeople, there is generally the advantage of having healthy and attractive bodies to exploit.

The trend towards marketing professional sport based on the physical attractiveness of its participants has been particularly noticeable in relation to male-dominated sports, such as rugby league. The impetus for this development was the need to expand the sport's market share by appealing to women, a group which generally felt excluded from the working-man's game, rugby league, thereby aiming to secure rugby league as a family-friendly sport (Yeates 1995, 39; Turner et al. 2000, 57–9). In order to attract female spectators, the public relations officer for rugby league, Brian Walsh, selected the photogenic Pearce to become the public face of rugby league. When Pearce retired, Ettingshausen, described by Walsh as 'young, great looking, articulate, clean image', replaced Pearce (Turner et al. 2000, 58). His task was 'giving a sexy image to the blokey sport' (Will 1997, 32). Brian Walsh also handled Ettingshausen's personal public relations (Walsh 1992, 68). With the assistance of his personal management and the management of the rugby league administration, Ettingshausen consciously exploited his physical attractiveness.

Thus, Ettingshausen was at the forefront of this trend. In 1991, Ettingshausen was on the front cover of the inaugural 'Men of League' calendar (Walsh 1992, 68). He also acknowledged in cross-examination that he had modelled extensively, often shirtless (Hickie 1993a). Since its inception, the 'Men of League' calendars have been regularly produced, helping to raise the public profiles of the individual players and the sport generally.

The list of sportsmen who have posed nude is long and growing longer. It is now seemingly *de rigueur* for professional sportsmen to produce 'beefcake' calendars. Another football code, Australian Rules, has produced an annual 'Men for All Seasons' calendar, for over a decade. Male and female Australian Olympians now line up to pose nude for a 'coffee table' book which precedes each summer Olympic Games (*The Atlanta Dream: A Photographic Tribute* 1996; *The Sydney Dream* 2000; *The Athens Dream* 2004). Australian Rules footballer Warwick Capper, cyclist Martin Vinnicombe and rugby league player Chris Caruana were all centrefolds for women's magazine, *Australian Women's Forum* (as to Warwick Capper, see *Australian Women's Forum* (March 1993). See also Casimir and Squires

1993a. As to Martin Vinnicombe, see *Australian Women's Forum* (May 1993). See also Borham 1993b; Casimir and Squires 1993c; Casimir and Squires 1993d. As to Chris Caruana, see *Australian Women's Forum* (1996). See also Smith 1996; Koch 1996). The attempt to attract women as an audience for traditionally male sports has had the incidental effect of attracting another audience normally excluded, gay men. When high-profile rugby league player, Ian Roberts, 'came out', he did so by posing nude for a gay magazine (see James 1995. See also Freeman 1997, 259ff. For a comparison of Ettingshausen's and Roberts' respective attitudes to nude photography, see Miller 2001, 72–3). The Australian Rugby League realised it could raise its profile (and its revenue stream) by specifically targeting gay men as a potential audience (Cunningham and Miller 1994, 69; McKee 2001, 284–5). Now even heterosexual footballers like the former Canterbury-Bankstown Bulldogs captain, Steve Price, married with children, will voluntarily pose nude for an Australian gay magazine with minimal public reaction (See Lord 1999). As Kirby P, as His Honour then was, noted, '[c]ommon experience demonstrates that male nudity is now much more frequently seen in books, magazines, television, video and film than was formerly the case' ((unreported, CA40079/93, CA(NSW), Gleeson CJ, Kirby P and Clarke JA, 13 October 1993) at 9).

Against this background, it is difficult to accept that the publication of a naked photograph of a sportsman is necessarily immoral. There is no uniform moral or social standard on the acceptability of publicly mediated nudity by sportsmen.

Equally, there is arguably no uniform moral or social standard in relation to publicly mediated nudity of ordinary people – or non-celebrities. Just as celebrities, in particular sportspeople, are more willing to pose nude (as to celebrity nudity, see Barcan 2004, 241–8), there is also a trend towards ordinary people participating in this phenomenon. As Barcan argues, *fora* such as the 'Home Girls' pages where the photograph of Sonia Shepherd appeared are designed to allow ordinary people to pose nude, just like celebrities increasingly do (see generally Barcan 2004, 262–8). For Barcan, the 'Home Girls' pages and its equivalents attest to the democratisation of celebrity that has occurred in a post-modern society – a celebration of celebrity, an emulation of celebrity, a participation in the production of celebrity and yet, in its ordinariness, an ambivalent rejection of celebrity (Barcan 2000, 145–6). The 'Home Girls' section of *Picture* is nominated by readers as their favourite part of the magazine and it attracts approximately fifty entries per week (Barcan 2000, 148), suggesting that there are a not insubstantial number of people within the community who have no particular moral problem with this activity. Thus, whilst both *Ettingshausen* and *Shepherd v Walsh* partly involve reputation as honour, the liberalisation and fragmentation of social attitudes towards publicly mediated nudity, by both celebrities and 'non-celebrities' alike, mean that it is difficult to posit a uniform moral or social standard by which to assess such conduct.

These cases also manifest in part a notion of reputation as property. Post suggests that the concept of reputation as property can be applied to the reputations acquired by individuals in non-professional contexts. He argues that social interactions with others is a form of labour requiring skill and effort and consequently the product of that labour, reputation, can be construed as an asset (Post 1986, 694–5). In this way, it could be suggested that Shepherd's reputation amongst her family, friends and work colleagues was an asset she possessed and could protect by means of defamation proceedings. Ettingshausen's reputation is more readily identifiable as a form of property. As journalists have noted, Ettingshausen has assiduously cultivated and vigilantly protected his public profile over a number of years (Kent 2000). Through his professional career in rugby league, Ettingshausen has obviously created a reputation as an elite sportsman. However, in addition to this profile, and as a consequence of it, Ettingshausen has been offered a range of other opportunities, often unrelated to sport, to enhance and diversify his reputation. Supported by professional personal management and the professional management of the rugby league administration, as well as by his own endeavours, Ettingshausen has clearly developed a valuable reputation. In this sense, Ettingshausen's reputation is also a form of property. The difference in value between Shepherd's and Ettingshausen's reputations, however, indicates a fundamental difference in their respective reputations, a difference that is best explained by recourse to the concept of reputation as celebrity.

The Concept of Reputation as Celebrity and Imputations of Exposure to Ridicule

Superficially, *Ettingshausen* and *Shepherd v Walsh* bear many similarities. Yet there is clearly a qualitative difference between the cases and, more fundamentally, the reputations of the respective plaintiffs. Whilst the concepts of reputation identified by Post might adequately explain the reputational interests of Sonia Shepherd involved in her defamation proceedings, they do not completely explain those of Andrew Ettingshausen. Consequently, they cannot explain why their reputations are qualitatively different. The differentiating factor lies in the fact that Ettingshausen is a celebrity – and Shepherd is not.

There are a number of ways in which Ettingshausen's celebrity distinguishes his defamation proceedings from those of Shepherd. For instance, there is a clear difference in the level of damages awarded. Ettingshausen was originally awarded \$350,000 damages, which was subsequently reduced to \$100,000 damages, comprising compensatory and aggravated damages; Shepherd received \$50,000 compensatory damages and \$20,000 exemplary damages. Given that exemplary damages are no longer available in Australia, the proper basis for comparison of these two awards requires the component of exemplary damages from Shepherd's award to be excluded. On the basis of the ultimate verdict (and not taking into account inflation), Ettingshausen's award was twice that of Shepherd's; on the basis of the original verdict, it was seven times that of Shepherd's.

Even taking Ettingshausen's favourable verdicts alone, there is a real issue as to whether the damage to any man's reputation as a consequence of a photograph of his penis was worth \$100,000, let alone the original verdict of \$350,000. The original verdict sparked criticism from the media, the public and members of the legal fraternity (Dixon 1993; O'Neill 1993; Strong 1993; Jurman

1993a; Jurman 1993b). On appeal, Kirby P, as his Honour then was, noted that plaintiffs claiming permanent, physical disfigurement and disability would have received substantially less damages than Ettingshausen did for his comparatively ephemeral injury ((unreported, CA40079/93, CA(NSW), Gleeson CJ, Kirby P and Clarke JA, 13 October 1993) at 39–42). Indeed, the verdict was cited as an impetus for defamation law reform (New South Wales Legislative Assembly 1994 (Mr Hatton; Mr Shaw; Mr Hannaford); New South Wales Legislative Assembly 1994), particularly in relation to the removal of the function of assessing damages from the jury (the now repealed *Defamation Act* 1974 (NSW) s 7A(4)(b)), and the introduction of the requirement for judges assessing defamation damages to take into consideration the level of personal injury damages (the now repealed *Defamation Act* 1974 (NSW) s 46A(2)). No such concern attended the quantum of damages awarded to Shepherd.

The difference between the damages awarded to Ettingshausen and Shepherd – whether they be distinguished by a multiple of two or seven – indicates the difference in reputation between the plaintiffs. As counsel for Ettingshausen, Tom Hughes QC, observed to the jury at the first trial, '[t]he bigger they are, the harder they fall' (O'Neill 1993). In other words, plaintiffs with high public profiles are likely to have greater damage done to their reputations than plaintiffs without high public profiles. The logic of defamation law on this point is not incontrovertible. It is equally plausible to argue that plaintiffs with high public profiles have greater access to *fora*, such as the media, by which they can rebuild their reputations or at least overwhelm any actual damage done to their reputations by the publication of defamatory matter.

Indeed, Raudonikis's observation about Ettingshausen's defamation proceedings, that Ettingshausen's celebrity status had allowed him greater access to justice than the average person, tends to support this: '[i]f (Ettingshausen) can get that much then good luck to him. But really the average person, a battler, can't go and sue a big company like that because he hasn't got the money to do it in the first place' (O'Neill 1993).

Raudonikis's point might be extended beyond the simple observation that 'the average person' confronts barriers to access to justice to further the point that he or she also confronts barriers to *fora*, not only the courts but also the media, wherein he or she might attempt to rebuild their reputations.

The sharp difference between the reputations of Ettingshausen and Shepherd – and the importance of Ettingshausen's celebrity – becomes noticeable in relation to the identification of the plaintiff in the respective cases. Named in the article, Ettingshausen is regarded by the judges, both at first instance and on appeal, as famous. The trial judge, Hunt J, described him as 'a well-known Rugby League footballer' who represented Australia in international competitions ((1991) 23 NSWLR 443 at 444) and the presiding appellate court judge, Gleeson CJ, described him as 'a prominent rugby league footballer' ((unreported, CA40079/93, CA(NSW), Gleeson CJ, Kirby P and Clarke JA, 13 October 1993) at 1). Ettingshausen was not only identifiable and identified but his reputation was also known. There was no such recognition for Shepherd. Shepherd was not sufficiently identified by the matter in question – only her given name was used and the accompanying description of her corresponded to the personality of Sonja de Vries. She was required to provide particulars of identification (*Shepherd v Walsh* [2000] QSC 177). Even when Shepherd had established the defendants' liability, including identification, the scope of identification became crucial to the assessment of damages. Whereas in *Ettingshausen*, there was simply reference made to the extent of publication through the citation of circulation figures for *H.Q.* magazine ((1991) 23 NSWLR 443 at 449. See also (unreported, CA40079/93, CA(NSW), Gleeson CJ, Kirby P and Clarke JA, 13 October 1993) at 43 per Kirby P), in *Shepherd v Walsh*, Jones J undertook an extensive review of the evidence in an attempt to establish the number and classes of persons who, actually or inferentially, identified Shepherd ([2001] QSC 358 at [31]–[45]). His Honour also geographically confined the areas in which damage to Shepherd's reputation may have occurred to those three locations where Shepherd had recently lived – Adelaide, Cairns and Hervey Bay – but ultimately finding that the greatest harm to Shepherd's reputation had occurred in Hervey Bay ([2001] QSC 358 at [40]–[41]). Unlike Ettingshausen, Shepherd's reputation was not known and recognised as such by the court and it was certainly not considered to be nationwide. The fact that Ettingshausen was immediately recognisable (and that Shepherd was not) further explains the difference in media attention the two litigants received.

There was a large amount of publicity surrounding the *Ettingshausen* trial (Hickie 1993a; Hickie, 1993b; Hickie 1993c; Hickie 1993d; Hickie 1993e. See generally Casimir and Squires, 1993b; Dixon 1993; *The Sydney Morning Herald* (12 February 1993); Borham 1993a), the appeal (Hickie 1993g; Hickie 1993h; Curtin 1993) and the retrial (Dean 1995a; Dean 1995b) of Ettingshausen's case. It even attracted international media attention (see, for example, Milliken 1993). As *The Sydney Morning Herald* observed in its editorial: '[a]ll court proceedings are part-theatre. But, as the daily reports of the Ettingshausen case vividly show, none is more theatrical than a defamation proceeding' (*The Sydney Morning Herald* (12 February 1993)).

However, contrary to the editorialist's view, not all defamation proceedings are 'theatrical'. *Shepherd v Walsh* does not meet this description. In contrast to *Ettingshausen*, there was apparently no publicity surrounding Shepherd's case and thus no 'media circus' similar to the one that attended Ettingshausen's proceedings.

The fact that Ettingshausen's defamation proceedings were conducted in the full glare of the media spotlight, whilst Shepherd's case was not, necessarily has an impact on the purposes served by the defamation proceedings and the effectiveness of the defamation trial in serving those purposes. Shepherd's defamation proceedings presumably achieved the vindication and consolation she desired (as to the purposes of defamation damages, see Chapter 3). Indeed, in Jones J's judgment, his Honour awarded damages at the lower end of the scale because the passage of time had negated, to some extent, the damage wrought to her family and social relationships by the publication of the photograph in *Picture* ([2001] QSC 358 at [60]). Ettingshausen's defamation proceedings have not had such finality. This suggests that Ettingshausen's reputation is fundamentally different. Not only is it larger, enjoyed on a wider scale, it is in part beyond Ettingshausen's control. It has a cultural significance in popular culture. It was created and cultivated in, by and through the media; it now belongs in part to that realm.

The media attention itself was the result of Ettingshausen's creation and cultivation of a public profile. Ettingshausen was not merely a footballer. He and his management had constructed a complex public profile – footballer, representing Australia and New South Wales (Heads 2000, 52–75. On Ettingshausen's representative rugby league career generally, see also Will 1997; Kent 2000), fiercely loyal to his Cronulla-Sutherland Sharks club team (Heads 2000, 20–43. See also Will 1997); family man (Heads 2000, 106–11. See also O'Neill 1993; Will 1997); sex symbol; model (Heads 2000, 76–7, 80–81); radio commentator (Walsh 1992); television presenter (Walsh 1992; Kent 2000); actor (Heads 2000, 84–5); businessman; gym owner (Borham 1993a); a role model and a paragon of 'clean living' (Kent 2000). The blurb of the authorised video produced to commemorate his retirement from professional rugby league, *The E.T. Story: The Life and Career of Andrew Ettingshausen*, reinforces the complexity of Ettingshausen's reputation as part of his own design, promising as it does an exploration of 'the amazing career of Andrew Ettingshausen the player, the role model, *the sex symbol*, the family man' (emphasis added).

Ettingshausen's reputation is complex because he has had so many opportunities over almost two decades which have allowed him to expand, diversify and exploit his reputation. In August 1992, readers of *Cleo* magazine, also owned by ACP, voted Ettingshausen the sexiest man alive. He was thus described: '[t]he hair is by Sampson (sic), the face by Rubens, the smile by Colgate and the body by Michelangelo' (*Cleo* (August 1992)). Over the years, Ettingshausen has endorsed a wide range of products, including Jeans West, Nissan, Shimano, Grace Bros, Aussiesoft Computers, Asics/Tiger, Hero Cologne, instant lotteries and Cebe (Heads 2000, 82). He has modelled extensively (Heads 2000, 82–3) and acted occasionally (Gambotto 1991; Heads 2000, 82). As a result of his widely-publicised interest in fishing, Ettingshausen has been a spokesperson for the state government body, New South Wales Fisheries. He has also been a spokesman for the Road Safety Council (Heads 2000, 106–20, 108). Upon his retirement from professional rugby league, there were bipartisan congratulations in the New South Wales Legislative Assembly (New South Wales Legislative Assembly (Messrs Collier and Watkins)). Ettingshausen is currently the presenter and executive producer of the long-running television fishing programme, *Escape with ET*.

Ettingshausen possesses a complex reputation, largely because he has constructed a complex reputation. Part of Ettingshausen's strategy for constructing and preserving his reputation was the defamation trial itself. It was unfortunately not entirely successful in focusing the public on the parts of his reputation that he considered rightfully to belong to the public realm. Nevertheless, Ettingshausen's public profile – his reputation – is not simply a piece of property, a piece of goodwill – it is more than that. Ettingshausen has acquired celebrity – something beyond property (for an exposition of the concept of reputation as celebrity generally, see Chapter 8). He has cultivated a reputation, which he exploits for gain, but that reputation is also public 'property' beyond his control.

A clear demonstration that his reputation is largely beyond his own control is provided by the fact that Ettingshausen's defamation proceedings have had a lasting impact, whereas Shepherd's case has not. For example, Ettingshausen's defamation proceedings have a continuing cultural resonance that Shepherd's defamation proceedings lack. In 1993, prolific Australian playwright, David Williamson, included a reference in his play, *Brilliant Lies*, alluding to the *Ettingshausen* case. One of the characters, Susy, has brought a sexual harassment claim against her employer, Gary, for fondling her breasts. During the mediation, she is asked how much she would settle the case for and responds by nominating $40,000 as the figure. When those present express their surprise, Susy responds thus: 'High figure? Why is it a high figure? Some football hero got three hundred and fifty thousand 'cause a magazine photographed his dick!' (Williamson 1993, 35). The fact that Williamson could include an allusion, rather than a direct reference, indicates that the incident had already achieved some cultural currency.

Over ten years after the publication of the original photograph, the left-leaning columnist, Tony Moore, writing about a perceived explosion in litigation, branded Australia 'a nation of sooks', citing as one of his examples Ettingshausen. In relation to *Ettingshausen*, he observed that:

> Defo remains a profitable way for the rich and famous to remain, well, rich and famous. Remember Andrew Ettingshausen earning a cool $100,000 on appeal when he took offence at a shower shot in *HQ* magazine? Would a factory worker's severed finger be worth as much as this photo-shy member? (Moore 2002, 6)

Ettingshausen's defamation proceedings have also been influential in legal terms. They encouraged others to sue and his imputations formed the precedent for prospective litigants' pleadings. Indeed, the central imputation in *Shepherd v Walsh* was explicitly based on the imputation of exposure to ridicule originally approved by Hunt J ([2001] QSC 358 at [27] per Jones J. As to the 'Ettingshausen' imputation, see (1991) 23 NSWLR 443 at 449). In addition to Sonia Shepherd, a number of other plaintiffs were influenced by Ettingshausen's precedent and thus commenced their own defamation proceedings. An accountant who had posed nude for prominent Australian artist, Donald Friend, sued the Australian Broadcasting Corporation over a documentary in which this event was portrayed (*Haines v Australian Broadcasting Corporation* (unreported, SC(NSW), No. 19417/93, Levine J, 9 May 1995)). Another rugby league player sued a local newspaper for publishing photographs in which part of his penis was exposed during a tackle (*McDonald v The North Queensland Newspaper Co Ltd* [1997] 1 Qd R 62). An Australian representative water polo player sued the *Picture* magazine over a photograph in which her breasts were accidentally exposed during the course of a match (*Obermann v ACP Publishing Pty Ltd* [2001] NSWSC 1022). All of these cases relied explicitly upon what was described as 'the *Ettingshausen* imputation'.

Ettingshausen hoped that *that* photograph would fade from the public memory and that he would be remembered for other things. In this regard, Ettingshausen has been particularly fortunate. As a celebrity, he has had a wide range of opportunities available to him whereby he can attempt to promote an image of himself which can overwhelm the memory of *that* photograph. Yet media commentary about Ettingshausen still routinely refers to his defamation proceedings, almost a decade after their resolution (Will 1997; Kent, 2000; Moore, 2002). Interestingly, in the authorised photo book celebrating Ettingshausen's 18-year first-grade rugby league career, the author, Ian Heads, makes no mention of the defamation trial (Heads 2000). However, in the accompanying video (*The ET Story: The life and career of Andrew Ettingshausen*), the defamation trial is mentioned, albeit only briefly. Thus, even Ettingshausen, reviewing his public profile over 18 years, is compelled to acknowledge that his defamation proceedings not only occurred but now form part of his reputation.

Paul Hasleby

The *Ettingshausen* imputation and the popular memory of Ettingshausen's defamation litigation were recently revived yet again when, in mid-May 2003, a photograph of an Australian Rules footballer, Paul Hasleby, from the Fremantle Dockers, was published in the early edition of *The West Australian* newspaper. The photograph, taken of Hasleby during play in a game against the North Melbourne Kangaroos (Coghlan 2003a) and published as part of a preview of an upcoming fixture against the Western Bulldogs (O'Donoghue 2003), showed the tip of Hasleby's penis protruding slightly from his football shorts (Timms 2003a; *The Mercury* (14 May 2003)). *The West Australian* realised its mistake and airbrushed the photograph for its late edition but not before it was noticed by other media outlets. The circulation of the early edition of *The West Australian* was estimated to be approximately 175,000 copies (Coghlan 2003a). In the days following, the incident was the subject of intense discussion on Perth talkback radio (Timms 2003b). Then Channel Ten's nationwide light entertainment television programme, *The Panel*, showed the photograph, uncut as it were, and used it as the fodder for banter (Beacham 2003). Hasleby threatened defamation proceedings against West Australian Newspapers Ltd, based on the *Ettingshausen* precedent, but settled out of court, allegedly for the sum of $30,000 (Beacham 2003), which Hasleby promptly donated to an unnamed Perth children's medical charity. *The West Australian* also published an apology to Hasleby and any offended readers (*The West Australian* (14 May 2003)). Less impressed by *The Panel*'s conduct, Hasleby considered launching defamation proceedings against the show's producers, Working Dog Productions, presumably for substantially more money (Beacham 2003). Hasleby's embarrassing incident even reached the British (*The Daily Star* (18 May 2003)), American (Hoffmann 2003) and German (*Deutsche Presse-Agentur* (14 May 2003)) press. Hasleby's threat of defamation proceedings attracted some supportive editorial comments (Price 2003a) but also received some savage ones (*The Sunday Tasmanian* (18 May 2003); Salusinszky 2003).

Significantly, in Australia, the reporting of Hasleby's unfortunate slip referred extensively to Ettingshausen's defamation proceedings (*Courier-Mail* (13 May 2003); Coghlan 2003a; Williams and Hurt 2003; *The Sunday Tasmanian* (18 May 2003); Salusinszky 2003). This is understandable, given that Hasleby was another footballer, albeit from a different code, complaining that a publisher had printed a photograph of (at least part of) his penis. However, the approach to this situation adopted by Hasleby and his management was clearly influenced by Ettingshausen's case. Having witnessed the adverse public reaction to Ettingshausen's defamation proceedings, Hasleby's manager, Wayne Loxley, adopted the prudent course of negotiating a speedy settlement rather than embarking on the fraught course of lengthy, contested litigation, which would only have provided fodder for the media. As such, it seems unlikely that this incident will occupy as central a place in Hasleby's reputation – in Hasleby's celebrity – as Ettingshausen's defamation proceedings occupy in his.

The occasion of Hasleby's threatened defamation proceedings caused the media to ask how Ettingshausen himself felt about his own litigation after the passage of almost a decade. Speaking after the second jury verdict in early February 1995, Ettingshausen was emphatic that he had adopted the correct course, further stating 'if it ever happened again, I definitely would do exactly the same' (Dean 1995b).

Although Ettingshausen himself refused to comment at the time of the Hasleby incident, a close friend of Ettingshausen, John Dunphy, told a newspaper that 'although Ettingshausen believed he made the right choice at the time, justice had come at a significant price' (Coghlan 2003b). Dunphy continued: '[w]ith hindsight, I'm not sure he would do it again … But he wanted to make a point. He felt his privacy had been invaded' (Coghlan 2003b).

It appears that Ettingshausen and sporting penises have become inextricably linked. His defamation proceedings – the photograph, the first trial, the excessive jury verdict, the retrial – have now become part of his reputation. Yet the use of the defamation trial in part to police the presentation of one's image is paradoxical. Ettingshausen succeeded, so the verdict vindicated his position. Yet the defamation trial itself and the extensive publicity which attended it necessarily becomes part of Ettingshausen's reputation, such that any balanced, complete account of his career cannot avoid reference to it. The trial itself, as well as the publicity, as public events, therefore become part of the public domain, to be debated and discussed. Ettingshausen cannot control this debate – and thus cannot control his reputation.

Overview

It is perhaps paradoxical that plaintiffs who complain that a publication of a naked photograph exposed them to more than a trivial degree of ridicule seek to assuage the insult to their dignity by agitating the issue, and thereby re-agitating the insult, in the very public forum of the courtroom. This observation was first made almost seventy years ago in *Burton v Crowell Publishing Co*, when Hand J concluded his judgment, cynically or realistically, depending on one's point of view, by presciently noting that '[p]ossibly any one who chooses to stir such a controversy in a court cannot have been very sensitive originally, but that is a consideration for the jury …' (*Burton v Crowell Publishing Co* 82 F (2d) 154 (1936), 156).

For a plaintiff like Sonia Shepherd, defamation proceedings are presumably effective. Even if they are not, Shepherd has few other alternatives. For a plaintiff like Andrew Ettingshausen, defamation proceedings are less effective as a means of 'vindicating' and 'protecting' his reputation. He may have been awarded substantial damages for what he perceived was a photograph that damaged his reputation, yet the real damage to his reputation seems not to have arisen from the publication of the photograph but from his decision to pursue the matter through the courts. However, whilst defamation proceedings may prove to be an ineffective means of restoring reputation for celebrities like Ettingshausen, they can seek solace in the fact that they have other *fora*, such as the media, in which to begin the process of rebuilding their own reputations.

Like Donovan and Rivkin, *Ettingshausen* appears to be an example of winning the defamation battle but losing the reputational war. As Kate Gleeson has observed, 'ET simply made too much fuss. He wasn't a good sport' (Gleeson 2003, 7).

PART III

Chapter 8
Reputation as Celebrity

> As it is, the law takes reputations as they are, and does not ask how they were acquired. It thereby provides unmerited protection to those who have the capacity and resources to mould their personal images to their own advantage.
>
> (Gibbons 1996, 597)

> In the future everyone will be world-famous for fifteen minutes.
>
> (Andy Warhol)

Introduction

In the preceding chapters, the ways in which concepts of reputation have manifested themselves in Australian defamation law have been examined through a series of case studies. The conclusion has been that no one concept of reputation adequately explains the reputation at stake in most cases in Australian defamation law. Reputation is necessarily a complex, and composite, construct. Moreover, these case studies suggest that there may be viable explanations for the concept of reputation beyond those advanced by Post, which can augment the concepts of reputation he identified. Post himself allowed that other types of reputational interests may be protected by the law of defamation. This chapter is devoted to an exposition of such a type – reputation as celebrity.

Although the impact of the concept of celebrity on defamation law has not been considered in legal scholarship, the academic literature on celebrity in other disciplines is burgeoning. The concept of celebrity has been analysed from a number of critical perspectives – cultural studies (see, for example, Marshall 1997; Turner 2004), film studies (see, for example, Schickel 1986), economics (Cowen 2000), history (see, for example, Braudy 1997; Ponce de Leon 2002), media studies (see, for example, Turner et al. 2000), psychology (see, for example, Giles 2000; Maltby et al. 2002; Maltby et al. 2003; McCutcheon et al. 2003; Giles and Maltby 2004; Maltby et al. 2004), sociology (see, for example, Gamson 1994; Rojek 2001). These understandings of celebrity have not been brought to bear upon the law of defamation, yet arguably, given that celebrities are bringing actions for defamation, it is important to understand this aspect of reputation.

This chapter argues that there needs to be an understanding of reputation which explicitly acknowledges the essentially mediated nature of reputation. Other accounts of reputation have argued that reputation is a social or an economic interest and, more importantly, is a social or an economic construct (Bellah 1986,

643; Lidsky 1996, 6). In addition, this chapter argues that reputation is a media construct, dependent on the medium of communication between the plaintiff and his or her audience (Rojek 2001, 10–12). Just as the notion of reputation as honour relies upon a notion of the individual interacting with his or her society, and just as the notion of reputation as property relies upon a notion of the individual interacting with his or her consumers through the marketplace, so too the notion of reputation as celebrity relies upon a notion of the plaintiff interacting with his or her audience through the media. As Rojek observes, 'media representation is the basis of celebrity' (Rojek 2001, 16). The concept of celebrity thus illuminates one aspect of the concept of reputation that pervades the law of defamation – the fact that all reputation, and consequently all damage to reputation, is mediated, that is, it occurs through some form of medium of communication.

What is Celebrity?

It is useful to commence this analysis of reputation as celebrity by attempting to define what is meant by celebrity. *The Oxford English Dictionary* defines the term 'celebrity' thus:

> 1. Due observance of rites and ceremonies; pomp solemnity …
> 2. A solemn rite or ceremony; a celebration …
> 3. The condition of being much extolled or talked about; famousness; notoriety …
> 4. A person of celebrity; a celebrated person; a public character … (*The Oxford English Dictionary* 1989, 1019)

The first and second definitions indicate that the term 'celebrity', in its original usage in English, was used as a synonym for 'honour' (cf. the original meaning of the term 'dignity' in Chapter 1). The third and fourth meanings are more consistent with the contemporary understanding of celebrity. It is instructive to contrast this definition of the term 'celebrity' with that in the *Macquarie Dictionary*, wherein it is defined thus:

> 1. a famous or well known person. 2. fame; renown. (*The Macquarie Dictionary* 1997, 355)

The etymology of the term 'celebrity' also illuminates its meaning (for academic discussions of the etymology of the term 'celebrity', see Boorstin 1992, 57; Marshall 1997, 5–7; Rojek 2001, 9). Celebrity derives from the Latin word '*celebrem*', which not only has the connotation of 'famous' but also of 'thronged'. P. David Marshall suggests that this gestures towards the democratic nature of celebrity. He observes that '[t]he celebrity, in this sense, is not distant but attainable – touched by the multitude. The greatness of the celebrity is something that can be shared and, in essence, celebrated loudly and with a touch of vulgar pride. It is the ideal representation of the triumph of the masses' (Marshall 1997, 6).

Unlike honour, with its historical origins in feudal and aristocratic modes of social organisation, celebrity is a form of reputation which has developed and flourished in democratic societies.

Celebrity also derives from the Latin word '*celere*', meaning 'swift', and is thus related to 'celerity'. This suggests that celebrity is fleeting and ephemeral. For Rojek, 'the Latin roots indicate a relationship in which a person is marked out as possessing singularity, and a social structure in which the character of fame is fleeting' (Rojek 2001, 9). This reinforces Warhol's oft-quoted dictum on the temporal limitations of fame but contradicts the view implicitly adopted in defamation law. The notion of reputation protected by defamation law is fixed or at least relatively stable. For example, in the English Court of Appeal's judgment in *Dingle v Associated Newspapers Ltd* [1961] 2 QB 162 at 181 Holroyd Pearce LJ opined that '[a] man's reputation in the sense in which the word is used in civil or criminal courts does not alter daily as good or bad deeds are ascribed to him. It is the judgment of his fellows on his general life over a period of time.'

It is somewhat difficult to reconcile his Lordship's statement of principle with the realities of reputations in a culture of celebrity.

The most influential modern commentator on celebrity (Gamson 1994, 9; Marshall 1997, 11; Giles 2000, 4; Turner 2004, 5–6), Daniel Boorstin, famously described the term thus: '*The celebrity is a person who is known for his well-knownness*' (Boorstin 1992, 57 (original emphasis)).

He also devised the withering shorthand designation of the celebrity as 'the human pseudo-event' (Boorstin 1992, 45ff). This definition conveys another important aspect of celebrity as a form of reputation. Whereas the concept of honour presupposes that reputation is sustained by reference to pre-ordained status and social roles, and whereas the concept of property presupposes that reputation is sustained by reference to the exertions of the plaintiff in the marketplace, celebrity appears to suggest that reputation can be self-sustaining. In fact, the sustenance of celebrity, the ongoing '*well-knownness*', is provided by the media. According to Boorstin, the media create and sustain 'the human pseudo-event' (Boorstin 1992, 60). As Boorstin and the subsequent scholarship on celebrity indicate, it is impossible to discuss celebrity – and, by extension, reputation – in contemporary society without reference to the formative role of the media.

The Historical Development of Celebrity

The concept of reputation as celebrity is largely an historical development of the late twentieth century. Whilst some academic commentators identify earlier historical antecedents of the concept of celebrity, there is a general scholarly consensus that celebrity, deriving as it does from the confluence of a number of important factors, is a distinctly modern phenomenon (see, for example, Rojek 2001, 28–9).

Braudy argues that the concept of celebrity has a long and distinguished history. In his history of fame, he traces the origin of celebrity from Alexander the Great, whom he designates as the first famous person (Braudy 1997, 28). According to Braudy, famous figures in Western European history, such as Julius Caesar (Braudy 1997, 80ff), Augustus (Braudy 1997, 90ff) and Jesus Christ (Braudy 1997, 151ff) can also be construed as 'celebrities'.

However, it is not possible to characterise earlier periods of history, as Schickel has characterised contemporary society, as embodying or incorporating a 'culture of celebrity'. Indeed, Rojek argues that Alexander the Great and the other great men and women of history discussed by Braudy are properly understood as 'prefigurative celebrities' (Rojek 2001, 19). The emergence of celebrity as a distinct form of reputation occurred in the late twentieth century. Firstly, it was predicated upon the political conditions of democracy. Again, as Rojek observes, 'celebrity only becomes a phenomenon in the age of the common man' (Rojek 2001, 28). Indeed, celebrity has been characterised as the democratisation of reputation (Rojek 2001, 14; Lumby 2004, 113). Secondly, it was premised on the economic conditions of capitalism. Celebrity has also been characterised as the commodification of reputation (Marshall 1997, x; Rojek 2001, 10; Turner 2004, 34–41). However, the confluence of these factors alone is insufficient to explain the emergence of celebrity as an important and distinct form of reputation in the late twentieth century.

The crucial additional factor that explains the emergence of celebrity is the development and spread of mass media technologies and formats (Rojek 2001, 16). The historical development of these developments ought to be noted. Boorstin provides a history of the technological developments that facilitated the emergence of celebrity as a distinct form of reputation. Boorstin traces the beginning of what he styles 'the Graphic Revolution' to the early nineteenth century (Boorstin 1992, 13). He observed that, between the early nineteenth century and the late twentieth century, the media technologies used have developed 'from the daguerrotype to color television' (Boorstin 1992, 13). He identifies some of the technological milestones driving the Graphic Revolution: the introduction of dry-plate photography in 1873; the patent of the telephone in 1876; the invention of the phonograph in 1877; motion pictures and radio transmission in 1900; and the introduction of television and later colour television (Boorstin 1992, 13). To this might be added the most significant technological developments of the last decades, the advent of internet technologies (Boorstin 1992, 13). Mirroring these technological developments of media were developments in media formats, such as the development of the interview (Boorstin 1992, 14–16) and the news or press release (Boorstin 1992, 18ff).

However, as the High Court itself has recognised, the pervasive influence of mass media technologies and formats did not crystallise until the middle of the twentieth century when cinema, radio and television were widely accessible to ordinary people (*Dow Jones & Co Inc v Gutnick* (2002) 210 CLR 575 at 603; 194 ALR 433; 77 ALJR 255; Aust Torts Reports ¶81-682 per Gleeson CJ, McHugh,

Gummow and Hayne JJ). What then has facilitated the emergence of celebrity in contemporary society is not merely the existence of mass media communications but their unprecedented ubiquity (Rojek 2001, 12). The pervasiveness of the mass media in creating, cultivating and damaging reputations, as demonstrated in the preceding case studies, is the crucial element that has allowed celebrity to emerge as a distinct category of reputation.

Perhaps the most important development towards entrenching the pervasiveness of celebrity, thereby ensuring the emergence of celebrity as a distinct form of reputation, was the creation of the Hollywood studio system in the 1920s and 1930s. The Hollywood studio system provided the prototype for the manufacture of a new commodity – celebrity. It relied upon erecting and investing in a vast, expensive industrial structure to construct and exploit celebrity. As a consequence of the formative work done by the Hollywood studio system, demonstrating that reputation could be wholly created and cultivated by the media, Rojek correctly observes that 'no celebrity now acquires public recognition without the assistance of cultural intermediaries who operate to stage-manage celebrity presence in the eyes of the public' (Rojek 2001, 10).

Rojek defines 'cultural intermediaries' as 'the collective term for agents, publicists, marketing personnel, promoters, photographers, fitness trainers, wardrobe staff, cosmetics experts and personal assistants' (Rojek 2001, 10–11. See also Turner et al. 2000, 5). Consequently, it should be recognised that, when high-profile plaintiffs, like Jason Donovan (as to Jason Donovan's defamation proceedings, see Chapter 6) and Andrew Ettingshausen (as to Andrew Ettingshausen's defamation proceedings, see Chapter 7), approach the courts to vindicate their reputations, the interest in their reputation is not purely personal; it is the work of many hands.

However, the emergence of celebrity itself has its own distinctive history. The democratising tendency which led to the emergence of celebrity as a distinctive category of reputation has itself been applied to the concept of celebrity in its industrial form. During the 1990s, mass media technologies, like webcams (see, for example, Barcan 2004) and weblogs (see, for example, Cook 2004), and formats, such as reality television (see, for example, Lumby 2003; Andrejevic 2004; Holmes and Jermyn (eds) 2004) and the 'Home Girls' pages of *Picture* and similar magazines (see, for example, Albury 1997; Barcan 2004), have allowed 'ordinary' people to create and cultivate their own celebrity, thereby fulfilling Warhol's 'prophecy'. The rigid demarcation between the celebrity and the audience is eroding.

Nonetheless, celebrities supported by the institutionalised machinery of celebrity still wield greater influence than home-made celebrities. As Marshall appositely observes '[c]elebrity status also confers on the person a certain discursive power: within society, the celebrity is a voice above others, a voice that is channeled into the media systems as being legitimately significant' (Marshall 1997, x).

This 'discursive power' of celebrities – the power to generate, shape and participate in public discourses – is evident in the preceding case studies. Specifically, this 'discursive power' can be, and has been, deployed by high-profile defamation plaintiffs to create, cultivate and defend their reputations. For example, Jason Donovan immediately gave a widely-syndicated interview to refute allegations circulating about his sexuality (Iley 1991a; Iley 1991b; Iley 1991c). Throughout the 1990s, Andrew Ettingshausen was able to exploit a number of media opportunities, through radio, television, modelling and advertising, allowing him to develop his reputation in such a way as to minimise any damage done to his reputation by the publication of the nude photograph (as to Ettingshausen's defamation proceedings, see Chapter 7). Such 'discursive power' even allows defamation plaintiffs to withhold their 'discursive power', temporarily or permanently. For instance, at the height of 'the Morosi affair', Morosi was pursued by the media seeking a comment from her. Morosi refused to comment, instead holding a press conference at a time of her own choosing in order to deal with allegations made through the press. In doing so, she intensified the media interest in her press conference when it was eventually held (as to Morosi's defamation proceedings, see Chapter 5). A further example is provided by the political journalist, Maxine McKew, who had a regular column in *The Bulletin* magazine in which she broke several important political news stories. McKew's articles were essentially records of conversations she had with prominent public figures over lunch. Peter Costello repeatedly turned down an invitation, much to the chagrin of McKew (Simons 2003; McKew 2003). However, it is important to note that, whilst celebrities have 'discursive power', it is not a monopoly – the media and the audience have power as well.

Celebrity and the Common Law of Defamation

Central to the notion of celebrity is the use of the media to enlarge the range of one's reputation. Prior to the development of mass media technologies, opportunities for the cultivation and dissemination of one's reputation on a wider scale were limited. This is reflected by the preponderance of instances of slander in the early historical development of the law of defamation. It is useful to consider whether the common law of defamation has attempted to accommodate or even to acknowledge the existence of reputation as celebrity. There is at least apparent a nascent notion of celebrity – of reputation moving beyond the confines of one's immediate social circle into the wider world – that has been implicitly recognised by the law of defamation, albeit in a limited way, for over almost two centuries.

In *De Crespigny v Wellesley* (1829) 5 Bing 391 at 402; 130 ER 1112 at 1116, attempting to justify the common law's differential treatment of slander and libel, Best CJ made the following observation:

> If the person receiving a libel may publish it at all, he may publish it in whatever manner he pleases; he may insert it in all the journals, and thus circulate the calumny through every region of the globe. The effect of this is very different from that of the repetition of oral slander. In the latter case, what has been said is known only to a few persons, and

> if the statement be untrue, the imputation cast upon any one may be got rid of; the report is not heard beyond the circle in which all the parties are known, and the veracity of the accuser, and the previous character of the accused, will be properly estimated. But if the report is to be spread over the world by means of the press, the malignant falsehoods of the vilest of mankind, which would not receive the least credit where the author is known, would make an impression which it would require much time and trouble to erase, and which it might be difficult, if not impossible, ever completely to remove.

In *Plato Films Ltd v Speidel* [1961] AC 1090 at 1138, Lord Denning observes:

> In short, his 'character' is the esteem in which he is held by others who know him and are in a position to judge his worth. A man can sue for damage to his character in this sense, even though he is little known to the outside world … But a man's 'character', so understood, may become known to others beyond his immediate circle. In so far as the estimate spreads outwards from those who know him and circulates among people generally in an increasing range, it becomes his 'reputation', which is entitled to the protection of the law just as much as his character. But here I speak only of a reputation which is built upon the estimate of those who know him. No other reputation is of any worth. The law can take no notice of a reputation which has no foundation except the gossip and rumour of busybodies who do not know the man.

What both of these understandings indicate implicitly is a recognition that reputation can move beyond the confines of one's immediate social circle. The vehicle by which the dissemination and enlargement of reputation occurs is principally through the media. Historically, the development of basic principles of liability for defamation, including the common law's differential treatment of libel and slander, became fixed in the late seventeenth century. Following that time, technological developments led to the development of mass communication technologies – newspaper, journals and magazines, radio, cinema, television, internet technologies – each of which facilitated the spread of information about individuals and therefore the spread of reputations. These developments in turn facilitated the emergence of a new form of reputation, reputation as celebrity. Indeed, in *De Crespigny v Wellesley*, Best CJ specifically acknowledges that the media is integral to the infliction of damage to reputation. By extension, the media is also integral to the creation and cultivation of reputation.

However, these extracts also indicate that defamation law has had difficulty integrating this recognition into an understanding of the concept of reputation. For instance, Lord Denning's analysis in *Plato Films v Speidel* demonstrates ambivalence in the common law – on the one hand, his Lordship is willing to recognise that a plaintiff's reputation may be established amongst persons who do not know the plaintiff personally, yet their assessment of the plaintiff's reputation is dismissed as being worthless. Lord Denning's dismissal of reputations founded upon 'the gossip and rumour of busybodies' sits awkwardly with a celebrity culture.

Whilst the common law has recognised the fact that a reputation can be disseminated beyond one's immediate social circle, it has not explored the implications of this recognition for the concept of reputation. Given the fact that the common law of defamation has generally eschewed analysis of the concept of reputation, it is unsurprising that it has not developed and integrated the refined concept of reputation as celebrity. There are nonetheless at least intimations of its sensitivity to the claims of celebrity.

Post's Concepts of Reputation and Reputation as Celebrity

Introduction

Given that Post is the leading theorist on the concept of reputation in defamation law, it is important to attempt to integrate the insights provided by reputation as celebrity into his reputational schema. One of the crucial insights Post brings to bear on his analysis of the concept of reputation is that reputation must be understood in the context of relationships, that a plaintiff's reputation exists only by the plaintiff's relationship with others. For Post, the concept of reputation as honour demonstrates that a plaintiff's reputation exists and must be understood in relation to the plaintiff's society. Likewise, the concept of reputation as property demonstrates that a plaintiff's reputation exists and must be understood in relation to the plaintiff's involvement in a marketplace (Post 1986, 695). This is why Post has difficulty explaining reputation as dignity. Reputation as dignity is not really predicated on a relationship between the plaintiff and the outside world (as to the problematic nature of the concept of dignity in Post's reputational schema, see Chapter 1).

Theorists of celebrity conceptualise celebrity in a similar way. An individual's celebrity exists and must be understood in relation to external forces. Just as reputation as honour presupposes that all people are connected through society and just as reputation as property presupposes that all people are connected through the marketplace, reputation as celebrity presupposes that all people are connected through the media. Furthermore, just as reputation as honour suggests that society forms its opinions of the plaintiff and just as reputation as property suggests that the marketplace forms its opinion of the plaintiff, reputation as celebrity suggests that the audience forms its opinion of the plaintiff. The audience's assessment of the information it receives from the media about the plaintiff thereby constitutes the plaintiff's celebrity (Gamson 1994, 5; Rojek 2001, 9).

It is instructive now to analyse the concept of celebrity by comparison with and contrast to the two most important of the concepts of reputation identified by Post: reputation as property and reputation as honour.

Reputation as Property and Reputation as Celebrity

Reputation as celebrity has certain similarities but more telling differences with Post's conception of reputation as property. Celebrity is contingent, not fixed, a characteristic it shares with the concept of reputation as property (Post 1986, 695–6). Like reputation as property, reputation as celebrity accepts that the personal identity of an individual is 'distinct from and anterior to' his or her social (or, more appropriately, media) identity (Post 1986, 696). Like reputation as property, reputation as celebrity is not 'a matter of either honor or dishonor' (Post 1986, 696). Indeed, notoriety, a sub-species of celebrity, suggests that a bad reputation can in fact confer a positive benefit on its possessor (Rojek 2001, 10). Celebrity may also be created and cultivated. It may, like reputation as property, be earned. It may, however, be serendipitous and undeserved. It is at this point that the concepts of reputation as property and reputation as celebrity markedly diverge.

The notion of reputation as property proceeds on the basis that the plaintiff enters the marketplace and through his or her skill, labour and effort acquires and develops a reputation. Although Post applies this analysis equally to natural persons in social contexts, it has been suggested that this notion of reputation as property provides at least a more appropriate explanation for professional reputation. Moreover, it provides an even more convincing explanation of the right to reputation enjoyed by various corporate entities. According to Post, reputation is an asset that is the product of an individual's or an entity's exertions. Crucial to Post's analysis therefore is that reputation, so defined, is deserved as the product of skill, labour and effort.

The concept of reputation as celebrity in its post-modern manifestation renders the understanding of reputation as property problematic. Unlike property, there is no necessary correlation between the input of skill, labour and effort and the output of celebrity (Rojek 2001, 14). It fragments the necessary relationship between the merit of the plaintiff and the reputation he or she acquires. There is an inherent tension in the concept of celebrity because, on the one hand, celebrity can arise from success and achievement, yet, on the other hand, can also arise from success without work (Marshall 1997, x–xi). Joshua Gamson articulates well the two competing but co-existing narratives of reputation in this media-saturated age:

> In one, the great and talented and virtuous and best-at rise like cream to the top of the attended-to, aided perhaps by rowdy promotion, which gets people to notice but do nothing to actually make the unworthy famous. In this story, fame is deserved and earned, related to achievement or quality. In the second story, the publicity apparatus itself becomes a central plot element, even a central character; the publicity machine focuses attention on the worthy and unworthy alike, churning out many admired commodities called celebrities, famous because they have been made to be. (Gamson 1994, 15–16)

More importantly, unlike reputation as property, reputation as celebrity does not suggest that all participants have equal access to the marketplace. There are in fact structural barriers to entry into the marketplace of reputation and into the means of vindicating or protecting reputation by legal means, as some jurists have been willing to recognise. In terms of the structural barriers presented to the vindication or protection of reputation by legal means, some judges have been willing to recognise that defamation proceedings, like most other forms of civil litigation, are expensive to commence and even more so to maintain and prosecute to conclusion (*R v Lucas* (1998) 157 DLR (4th) 423 at 450 per Cory J). As Ipp JA recognised, defamation litigation, with its complexities of principle and procedure, may function as an instrument of oppression by a wealthy plaintiff against a poor defendant (*Burden v Ainsworth* [2004] NSWCA 3 at [42]). All litigation is risky. Defamation litigation may or may not have a deterrent effect on the defendant. Cory J has suggested that civil defamation proceedings will have a negligible effect on impecunious defendants (*R v Lucas* (1998) 157 DLR (4th) 423 at 450 per Cory J). Callinan J has equally suggested that large media outlets with their deep pockets, which can fund protracted defamation litigation as well as any award of damages, and, more importantly, their prospects of financial gains through increased circulation or ratings, are undeterred by civil defamation proceedings (*Dow Jones & Co Inc v Gutnick* (2002) 210 CLR 575 at 648–9 per Callinan J).

In relation to the structural barriers to initial entry into the marketplace of reputation, it must be acknowledged the media are more interested in some individuals than others. Some individuals are better known than others. Some individuals have greater access to and therefore greater power deploying the media to create, cultivate and control their own reputations. In earlier times, there was a clearer barrier between the celebrity and his or her audience. With the development of media technologies and formats, the barrier between the celebrity and the spectator is disintegrating but it is untenable to suggest that it no longer exists.

Unlike reputation as property, reputation as celebrity does not suggest that an individual's reputation fluctuates on the basis of the conditions of a notional market and an individual's exertions within that market. Rather, reputation as celebrity suggests that an individual's reputation waxes and wanes according to the media's attention and the audience's interest he or she receives. The media's attention and the audience's interest can be the result of his or her own exertions, or the exertions of those employed on his or her own behalf, or this could be the result of the agenda of the media itself. It is, however, not a matter over which the individual has control. Whereas the locus of control in the concept of reputation as property appears to reside largely with the individual, it resides in the media and the audience in the concept of reputation as celebrity. This represents one of the most fundamental differences between reputation as property and reputation as celebrity (Turner 2004, 3).

This indicates a further difference between reputation as property and reputation as celebrity. Whilst it has been suggested that celebrity is a commodity, it is an unusual type of commodity. Celebrity exists not only in the market of commodities but also, as Rojek asserts, it exists and operates in the 'market of sentiments' (Rojek 2001, 14) – a market he characterises as 'fickle' and 'temporary' (Rojek 2001, 9). Thus, whilst the concept of reputation as property is purely economic, the concept of reputation as celebrity is partly economic and partly cultural.

Reputation as Honour and Reputation as Celebrity

Whilst there are many similarities and even more differences between reputation as property and reputation as celebrity, there are fewer similarities and yet more differences between reputation as honour and reputation as celebrity. This is because property and celebrity are more similar than honour and celebrity. For example, both property and celebrity are, in some senses, commodities.

Reputation as honour and reputation as celebrity are marked by contrasts. Whilst reputation as honour is fixed or at least relatively stable, reputation as celebrity is more dynamic. Reputation as honour may be more enduring than the more ephemeral celebrity. Whilst both reputation as honour and reputation as celebrity confer status on an individual, reputation as honour does so on the basis of social rank or role, whereas reputation as celebrity does so simply by reference to fame, as determined by the media and its audience. This reflects the fact that reputation as honour performs the function of creating and enforcing social norms, a task reputation as celebrity does not purport to fulfil. Indeed, given that the concept of celebrity can encompass notoriety, it occasionally performs the function of transgressing social norms. Whereas reputation as honour forms an integral part of the plaintiff's personality, reflecting the close identification of the public and private aspects of the plaintiff's self, reputation as celebrity, like reputation as property, proceeds on the basis that a plaintiff's private self is distinct from and anterior to his or her public (media) self (Post 1986, 696). Fundamentally, reputation as honour represents and reflects the feudal and aristocratic society from which it emerged, just as reputation as celebrity represents and reflects the liberal democratic society in which it developed. These are significant differences.

More fundamentally, there is a distinction between the three concepts of reputation expounded by Post and the concept of reputation as celebrity. Central to the concept of reputation as property, reputation as honour and reputation as dignity is the notion that the plaintiff's reputation is deserved. In terms of reputation as property, the plaintiff's reputation is merited by his or her exertion of skill, labour and effort in the marketplace. In terms of reputation as honour, the plaintiff's reputation is merited by the plaintiff's occupancy or fulfilment of a particular social rank or role. In terms of reputation as dignity, the plaintiff's reputation is merited by virtue of the plaintiff's humanity – it is an enforceable human right to which all natural persons are equally entitled. The fundamental challenge posed to reputation as property, reputation as honour and reputation as dignity by the concept of reputation as celebrity is to contest the notion that reputation is somehow deserved.

Thus, it is now perhaps possible to state, as the media studies expert, Catharine Lumby, has recently observed, that:

> Fame has no necessary relationship to wealth, natural ability, looks, intelligence, family, character or social charisma, although all those characteristics can be useful in acquiring it. Fame is both radically democratic and brutally random. Anybody can become famous, but there are no sure-fire ways of gaining admission to a club that now offers its members privileges (and obligations) once only bestowed on royalty. (Lumby 2004, 113)

Perhaps, as Julianne Schultz more pithily expressed it, 'we no longer live in a meritocracy, more a media "mediacracy", in which polished words and images are the key to recognition …' (Schultz 2004, 8).

The recognition of these developments, including the emergence of celebrity as a category of reputation, necessarily challenges basic principles of defamation law across the issues of liability and meaning, defences and damages. It remains to be seen how defamation law will respond to the challenges posed by its existence and operation in a culture of celebrity.

The Application of Reputation as Celebrity to Defamation Law

There is no single, coherent concept of reputation in Australian defamation law. Moreover, as the case studies have demonstrated, most defamation proceedings involve a complex interplay of reputational interests – reputation as property, reputation as honour, reputation as dignity. However, as the case studies also attest, not all defamation proceedings involve the same reputational interests. There is no aspect of reputation common to all defamation cases. Thus, it is to be expected, in applying the concept of reputation as celebrity to defamation proceedings brought before the courts, that celebrity will be apposite in certain cases and not in others.

For example, it is submitted that the distinguishing feature between Andrew Ettingshausen's proceedings against ACP Publishing and Sonia Shepherd's proceedings against the same entity is that Ettingshausen is a celebrity whereas Shepherd is not (see generally Chapter 7). Similarly, it is suggested that the defamation proceedings of Rene Rivkin, Liberace, Tom Cruise and Jason Donovan are fundamentally different from those brought by Ronald Horner, Neville Usher and Anna-Maria Harrison (as to these defamation proceedings, see generally Chapter 6). The reputations of the former category of plaintiffs are qualitatively different from the reputations of the latter category of plaintiffs.

Reputation as celebrity clearly manifests itself in many defamation cases, distinguishing those proceedings from those brought by non-celebrity plaintiffs. Celebrity may take many forms (Gamson 1994, 5) – it may be grounded in acting and music, like Jason Donovan; in sport, like Andrew Ettingshausen; or in politics, like Junie Morosi. The categories of celebrity are, however, not closed.

Prominent English defamation lawyer, David Hooper, has usefully catalogued all the defamation cases that have been brought in England since the late 1980s. Many of the cases he records involve plaintiffs with no real public profile. There are, however, a significant number of cases brought by celebrity plaintiffs. A selection of the cases will convey the flavour. He records that, in 1988, a jury awarded the former girlfriend of Prince Andrew, Koo Stark, £300,000 over false allegations that she had maintained her relationship with the prince whilst married to another man (Hooper 2000, 316–18). In 1989, the pop singer, George Michael, received £100,000 from *The Sun* over an allegation that he had gate-crashed Andrew Lloyd Webber's opening night party for *The Phantom of the Opera* (Hooper 2000, 504). In 1991, the late singer, Dusty Springfield, received £75,000 from TVS over a comedy sketch wherein she was portrayed as performing drunk (Hooper 2000, 513). In 1992, Jason Connery, the actor son of a more famous actor, Sean Connery, obtained £35,000 from *The Sun* over an article claiming that he was unable to fight in the first Gulf War (Hooper 2000, 514). In 1998, married acting couple, Liam Neeson and Natasha Richardson, obtained £130,000 from *The Daily Telegraph* and £50,000 from Mirror Group Newspapers over false allegations that their marriage was disintegrating (Hooper 2000, 535). In 1999, television hypnotist, Paul McKenna, reportedly received over £100,000 from each of *The National Enquirer* and *The Star* over allegations that a child he subjected to hypnosis had to be admitted to a psychiatric hospital (Hooper 2000, 537–8).

There are also a substantial number of celebrity plaintiffs in Australian defamation law. For example, in 1990, Jane Makim, the sister of the Duchess of York, received $300,000 from a jury over allegations that she was having an affair with an Argentinian polo player (*Makim v John Fairfax & Sons Ltd* (unreported, SC(NSW), No. 15264/88, Hunt J, 15 June 1990) at 1. See also Dean 1990; Dean 1991; Lewis 1991). More recently, in 2002, ex-model, television personality and socialite, Charlotte Dawson, sued A.C.P. Publishing over an interview given in *Woman's Day* by her ex-husband, Olympic swimmer, Scott Miller, wherein he alleged that she was emotionally and physically abusive towards her husband and sought to undermine his chances of qualifying for the Olympics because she resented his success (*Dawson v ACP Publishing Pty Ltd* [2002] NSWSC 712 at [2], Appendix A per Levine J; Kux 2003a. See also Dawson 2003, 130ff). In 2007, she settled her claim for a reported award of $225,000 damages (Byrnes et al. 2007). In 2004, Mark McGaw, a former rugby league player and personal trainer, best known as a television 'gladiator' under the moniker 'Hammer', sued television network, Channel Seven, over an interview conducted by tabloid current affairs programme, *Today Tonight*, with his ex-girlfriend, Louise Boucheron, claiming it portrayed him as prone to domestic violence (Kux 2004b). At trial, he was awarded $385,000 damages by Rothman J (*McGaw v Channel Seven Sydney Pty Ltd* [2006] NSWSC 1147).

In all of these cases, it is difficult to analyse the reputations at issue without having recourse to the fact that the plaintiffs are celebrities. This aspect of their reputations is inescapable. They came to public attention through the media; their profiles were sustained by the media's attention and the audience's interest; their activities remained of interest to the media and to the public. Their reputations are, in a significant sense, products of the media. It may be accepted that the concept of reputation as property, honour and dignity are involved, to varying degrees, in all of these cases. However, they do not offer a complete explanation of the reputations at issue. Celebrity provides the additional element.

Overview

Defamation law makes significant claims about its purposes. An award of defamation damages to a defamed plaintiff is intended to vindicate and to console (as to the purposes of an award of defamation damages, see Chapter 3). Yet many of the high-profile defamation plaintiffs discussed can hardly claim that they feel vindicated by their defamation victories. For example, Ettingshausen and Donovan clearly regret their decisions to sue. Those decisions, along with their eventual successes, have perhaps proven to be more injurious to their reputations than the defamatory matters about which they initially complained. Indeed, the defamatory matters, the imputations they conveyed, the trials and the verdicts have all been integrated into their reputations. Likewise, Rivkin may have won an award of substantial damages in one of his three defamation proceedings but that did not prevent the continuing deterioration of his reputation. Many of the high-profile defamation plaintiffs discussed would also have found negligible comfort from their favourable verdicts. Ettingshausen and Donovan are again in this category. Arguably the consolation the Abbotts and the Costellos ought to have enjoyed after obtaining a verdict against Random House was diminished by media criticisms about their decision to sue, the substance of their claim and the quantum of damages (as to the Abbotts' and the Costellos' defamation proceedings, see Chapter 5).

These then are successful defamation plaintiffs who are, in principle, entitled to vindication and consolation but, in fact, do not experience this or at least have their experience of vindication and consolation diminished. It is impossible to ascertain but presumably, for plaintiffs with a lower or non-existent public profile, a favourable defamation verdict operates more effectively to restore their reputations, where the plaintiffs' reputations and the damage done to them are more limited and more localised. This reinforces the suggestion that there is a qualitative difference between the reputations of defamation plaintiffs – and that this difference is explicable by reference to the concept of reputation as celebrity. Exploring the problematic nature of defamation proceedings for celebrity plaintiffs, Julianne Schultz tellingly observes that '[w]hen wealthy stars take legal action to protect their privacy or reputation, there is a feeling that they are not honouring the terms of the Faustian deal they made, that in a whirl of paparazzi, gossip and rumour, reputation is disposable …' (Schultz 2004, 9).

Conclusion

Although it is the central interest directly protected by defamation law, there is surprisingly little consideration of reputation in defamation jurisprudence. The need to explore the concept of reputation is frequently stated but the task itself is rarely undertaken. The consequence of this comparative neglect is that there are a number of assumptions, occasionally contradictory, made about the nature of reputation. This book has endeavoured to contribute to redressing this oversight in defamation jurisprudence.

Any attempt to explore the concept of reputation necessarily has to engage with the seminal article by Robert C. Post, 'The Social Foundations of Defamation Law: Reputation and the Constitution' (Post 1986). In this article, Post proposed a schema of reputational interests which manifest themselves in defamation law – reputation as property; reputation as honour; and reputation as dignity. According to Post, the most relevant concepts in contemporary defamation law are property and dignity. For Post, the most readily observable form of reputation is property, as a type of asset. He considered honour, founded upon rigid, institutional social roles characteristic of feudal and social modes of organisation, as outmoded, superseded by its democratic equivalent, dignity. He concluded that there is no single, coherent concept of reputation at the centre of defamation law.

In his analysis of defamation law, Post explicitly adopted a sociological approach. He did, however, suggest that different approaches to the analysis of reputation are possible, thereby yielding different types of reputation. Post specifically suggested an historical approach might yield important insights into the nature of reputation.

An historical approach to the concept of reputation does in fact illuminate important aspects of the concept of reputation. Firstly, the peculiar historical development of defamation law confirms that there is no unitary concept of reputation but, more importantly, reveals the reason for this. In early English law, liability for defamatory publications was recognised, to varying degrees, in a number of jurisdictions, such as the ecclesiastical courts, the local courts, the Star Chamber and the royal courts. It was also imposed by the statutory offence of *scandalum magnatum*. Each of these served different purposes and was directed towards protecting different reputational interests. Deriving as it did from a number of jurisdictions, each directed to the protection of different reputational interests, it is unsurprising that from its inception defamation law did not develop a single, coherent concept of reputation (as to the historical development of the tort of defamation and particularly the concept of reputation, see Chapter 2).

Secondly, an historical approach to defamation law indicates that the tort of defamation and its basic contours of liability emerged in its modern form in the latter half of the seventeenth century but did not really develop beyond that time. The peculiar history of the tort of defamation is characterised by stasis, rather than by evolution. Unlike almost every other area of the common law, defamation law has not been subjected to subsequent structural rationalisation and reform. There is therefore a fundamental disjunction between defamation law and contemporary political, economic, social and cultural realities.

This disjunction tends to explain the dissatisfaction lay observers, such as John Birmingham, Bob Ellis and Tommy Raudonikis, feel about defamation law. Another critic of the unreality of defamation law is the former chief executive officer of News Ltd, John Hartigan, who recently commented:

> In this day and age it is hard to believe that people can be held up to hatred, ridicule and contempt by a light-hearted gossipy paragraph. When did we last see someone drummed out of polite society because of something written about them? People go to jail these days and, when they come out, they blithely resume their place in society. People are awarded huge sums for what I think most folk would describe as a mere personal slight. (Hartigan 2004, 2)

Hartigan's observations underline the fact that this historical disjunction affects not only the principles of defamation law but, more importantly, the reputations defamation law purports to protect (for a critique of the basic principles of liability in light of the concepts of reputation identified by Post, see Chapter 3). Given the function of defamation law in creating and enforcing social norms, as well as the lingering importance of social roles and identities, and in light of the arrested historical development of defamation law, it is suggested that the concept of reputation as honour bears the heaviest imprint on defamation law, outmoded though it may be. The concept of reputation as property – reputation as an economic construct, an asset – achieved its greatest influence in the nineteenth century after the crystallisation of the basic contours of the tort of defamation. Likewise, the concept of reputation as dignity – reputation as a basic human right, democratic, individualistic and subjective – has achieved its greatest influence from the late twentieth century onwards. The emphasis on reputation as honour is indeed borne out by recent statements by Australian judges on the nature of reputation and the purposes for which defamation damages are awarded.

Nevertheless, aspects of the concepts of reputation identified by Post manifest themselves in contemporary Australian defamation law, as the case studies have sought to demonstrate. The case studies illuminate two aspects of the concept of reputation in particular. Firstly, they suggest that all reputations manifest more than one concept of reputation. Secondly, and related to this recognition, there is no common or unifying element of reputation, nor is there a set combination of reputational interests.

Even the simplest type of reputation involves composite elements. Corporate reputation is seemingly a clear example of reputation as property – a corporation, through its participation in the market in its business or trade, acquires a reputation that has a monetary value (as to corporate reputation, see Chapter 4). However, if a corporation seeks to sue for defamation, it is insufficient for it merely to point to an allegation that injures its business or trade. It must prove that the imputation made against it suggests unfitness or incompetence or in some other way disparages it. In other words, a corporation must satisfy the requirements of defamatory character and meaning, premised as they are upon a notion of reputation as honour (as to the requirements of defamatory character and meaning, see Chapter 3). However, because corporations are artificial persons, they are not awarded damages by way of a solatium. In other words, corporations do not experience subjective hurt as a result of a defamatory publication and, as such, do not manifest the concept of reputation as dignity.

The reputation of a professional person is even more complex than the reputation of a corporate entity (as to professional reputation, see Chapter 4). Unlike corporations, which manifest at most only two concepts of reputation, professional reputation can manifest all three concepts of reputation. *Crampton v Nugawela* (1996) 41 NSWLR 176 is a clear example of this. Through his education, training and practice, the plaintiff invested, created and exploited his good professional reputation. The allegation made against him of professional dishonesty severely undermined that reputation. It had quantifiable economic consequences which sounded in damages for economic loss. Yet it also reflected adversely on the plaintiff personally as well as professionally. It was impossible to extricate the personal and the professional aspects of the defamation. Equally inextricable was the harm to the plaintiff's reputation, in the sense of the opinion of others, and the harm to the plaintiff's feelings, his own subjective response to the defamatory publication. The concept of professional reputation can thus manifest all three concepts of reputation.

However, there are limits to the utility of the concepts of reputation as honour, dignity and property as explanation of all reputations protected by defamation law. In cases involving imputations of sexual 'immorality' – adultery, promiscuity, 'unchastity', homosexuality – there is clearly a notion of reputation as honour involved. The plaintiff wishes to be viewed by his or her society as complying with what Post describes as the 'normative standards of personal conduct' (Post 1986, 701. As to the definition of the concept of reputation as honour in this book, see Chapter 1). The defamatory publication suggests that the plaintiff has failed to do so. As with aspersions upon the professional reputation of natural persons, the publication of a defamatory matter about a natural person imputing sexual immorality will necessarily have an effect not only upon the ways in which others view the plaintiff but also on the way in which the plaintiff views himself or herself. The plaintiff's subjective reaction to the defamation, compensated as it is by an award of damages, reflects the concept of reputation as dignity (as to the purposes for the award of defamation damages and their relationship to Post's concepts of reputation, see Chapter 3). Depending upon the context, it is also possible for the concept of reputation as property to be engaged. In the abstract, all this seems tolerably clear. However, when applied to case studies, it emerges that, whilst the concepts of reputation identified by Post may explain the reputations of some plaintiffs entirely, they leave scope for a further concept of reputation to be identified and articulated, in order to provide a more complete account for other plaintiffs' reputations.

In relation to imputations of homosexuality, for instance, Rene Rivkin's defamation proceedings are qualitatively different to those undertaken by Horner and Usher. In relation to imputations of exposure to ridicule, for instance, Andrew Ettingshausen's defamation proceedings are qualitatively different to those undertaken by Sonia Shepherd. The imputations which they plead – the substance of their claims – are similar, yet it is clear that the cases are different. The concepts of reputation identified by Post can arguably provide a complete explanation for Horner's and Usher's and Shepherd's claims, yet they do not capture the essence of Rivkin's and Ettingshausen's claims. This is because the reputations of the plaintiffs are different, that Rivkin and Ettingshausen, for example, possess an aspect of reputation that Horner and Usher and Shepherd lack.

One of the central insights Post provided into the nature of reputation is that reputation is founded upon an interaction between the plaintiff and the outside world through a mechanism or a medium. The dialectic relationship between the plaintiff and the outside world is integral to the formation and maintenance of reputation and is also the locus in which damage to that reputation will occur and be experienced. Thus, Post's concepts of reputation as honour and as dignity are premised upon a relationship between the plaintiff and others through the mechanism of society. The concept of reputation as property is premised upon a relationship between the plaintiff and others through the mechanism of the marketplace. It is now apparent that, in addition to this mechanism, it needs to be recognised now that a plaintiff can relate to others through the mechanism of the media. Indeed, a significant proportion of all defamation cases now involve a mass media defendant. The acknowledgement that a plaintiff can relate to others through the mechanism of the media leads to the recognition of a distinct form of reputation – reputation as celebrity (for an exposition of the concept of reputation as celebrity, see Chapter 8). This is a form of reputation that is readily observable in contemporary society – styled, as it has been by Schickel as a 'culture of celebrity'. Moreover, it is a form of reputation that is readily observable in defamation cases. Morosi, Cairns, Abbott, Costello, Rivkin, Liberace, Cruise, Donovan, Ettingshausen – all of these defamation plaintiffs are celebrities of one variety or another. They, and their activities, are deemed 'newsworthy'. They possess 'discursive power' – power to shape and participate in public discourse. It should now be recognised that, in addition to the concepts of reputation as property, honour and dignity, there is equally a concept of reputation as celebrity that manifests itself in contemporary Australian defamation law. Just as reputation is a social and an economic construct, so too is it a media construct. By acknowledging the concept of reputation as celebrity, it then becomes possible to explain adequately the fact that not all defamation plaintiffs are created equal.

Bibliography

Books

The Athens Dream, Studio Magazines, Sydney (NSW), 2004.

The Atlanta Dream: A Photographic Tribute, Studio Magazines, Sydney (NSW), 1996.

The Sydney Dream, Studio Magazines, Sydney (NSW), 2000.

Andrejevic, Mark, *Reality TV: The Work of Being Watched*, Rowman and Littlefield Publishers, Lanham (MD), 2004.

Archer, Jeffrey, *A Prison Diary: Volume I – Hell*, Pan Macmillan, London, 2003.

Archer, Jeffrey, *A Prison Diary 2: Wayland – Purgatory*, Pan Macmillan, London, 2004a.

Archer, Jeffrey, *A Prison Diary: Volume 3 – Heaven*, Pan Macmillan, London, 2004b.

Baker, J. H., *An Introduction to English Legal History*, 4th edn, Butterworths LexisNexis, London, 2002.

Balkin, R. P. and Davis, J. L. R., *Law of Torts*, 3rd edn, LexisNexis Butterworths, Chatswood (NSW), 2004.

Barcan, Ruth, *Nudity: A Cultural Anatomy*, Berg, Oxford, 2004.

Barendt, Eric, *Freedom of Speech*, 2nd edn, Oxford University Press, Oxford, 2005.

Berger, Peter L., Berger, Brigitte and Kellner, Hansfried, *The Homeless Mind: Modernization and Consciousness*, Penguin Books, Ringwood (Vic), 1977.

Beverley-Smith, Huw, *The Commercial Appropriation of Personality*, Cambridge University Press, Cambridge, 2002.

Blackstone, Sir William, *Commentaries on the Laws of England*, Vol. 3, 1768, 123 (repr. University of Chicago Press, Chicago (IL), 1979).

Boorstin, Daniel, *The Image: A Guide to Pseudo-Events in America*, Vintage Books, New York, 1992.

Boswell, James, *The Journal of a Tour to the Hebrides*, Penguin Books, Ringwood (Vic), 1984.

Braudy, Leo, *The Frenzy of Renown: Fame and Its History*, rev. edn, Vintage Books, New York, 1997.

Brown, Raymond E., *The Law of Defamation in Canada*, 2nd edn, Carswell, Scarborough (ON), 1994.

Brydall, John, *Privilegia Magnatum apud Anglos*, London, 1704.

Butler, Des and Rodrick, Sharon, *Australian Media Law*, 2nd edn, Lawbook Co., Pyrmont (NSW), 2004.

Carroll, Robert and Prickett, Stephen, *The Bible: Authorized King James Version with Apocrypha*, Oxford University Press, Oxford, 1998.

Carter-Ruck, Peter F. and Starte, Harvey N. A., *Carter-Ruck on Libel and Slander*, 5th edn, Butterworths, London, 1997.

Casimir, Jon (ed.), *Enough Rope with Andrew Denton*, ABC Books, Sydney (NSW), 2003.

Chesterman, Michael, *Freedom of Speech in Australian Law: A Delicate Plant*, Ashgate, Aldershot, 2000.

Cowen, Tyler, *What Price Fame?*, Harvard University Press, Cambridge (MA), 2000.

Cunningham, Stuart and Miller, Toby, *Contemporary Australian Television*, University of New South Wales Press, Sydney (NSW), 1994.

Currie, Edwina, *Diaries 1987–1992*, Time Warner, London, 2002.

Dawson, Charlotte, *Charlotte's Secrets: Advice I Wish I'd Taken*, Penguin Books, Auckland, 2003.

Donovan, Jason, *Between the Lines: My Story Uncut*, HarperCollins, 2007.

Ellis, Bob, *Goodbye Jerusalem*, Vintage, Milsons Point (NSW), 1997a.

Ellis, Bob, *Goodbye Jerusalem*, 2nd rev. edn, Vintage, Milsons Point (NSW), 1997b.

Ellis, Bob, *Goodbye Babylon: Further Journeys in Time and Politics*, Viking, Camberwell (Vic), 2002.

Fleming, J. G., *The Law of Torts*, LBC Information Services, North Ryde (NSW), 1998.

Freeman, Paul, *Ian Roberts: Finding Out*, Random House Australia, Milsons Point (NSW), 1997.

Gambotto, Antonella, *Lunch of Blood*, Random House Australia, Milsons Point (NSW), 1994.

Gamson, Joshua, *Claims to Fame: Celebrity in Contemporary America*, University of California Press, Berkeley (CA), 1994.

Gardiner, Samuel Rawson (ed.), *Reports of Cases in the Courts of Star Chamber and High Commission*, London, 1886.

George, Patrick, *Defamation Law in Australia*, LexisNexis Butterworths, Chatswood (NSW), 2006.

Giles, David C., *Illusions of Immortality: A Psychology of Fame and Celebrity*, Macmillan Press, London, 2000.

Gillooly, Michael, *The Law of Defamation in Australia and New Zealand*, Federation Press, Leichhard (NSW), 1998.

Gillooly, Michael, *The Third Man: Reform to the Australasian Defamation Defences*, Federation Press, Annandale (NSW), 2004.

Goffman, Erving, *Interaction Ritual: Essays in Face-to-Face Behavior*, Aldine, Chicago (IL), 1967.

Greenblatt, Stephen et al., *The Norton Shakespeare*, W.W. Norton, New York, 1997.

Hargrave, F. (ed.), *Collectanea Juridica*, 2 vols, London, 1792, Vol. II.

Heads, Ian, *Andrew Ettingshausen*, Pan Macmillan Australia, Sydney (NSW), 2000.

Helmholz, R. M., *Select Cases on Defamation to 1600*, Selden Society, London, 1985.

Holdsworth, Sir William, *History of English Law*, 7th edn, Vol. VIII, Methuen, London, 1972.

Holmes, Susan and Jermyn, Deborah (eds), *Understanding Reality Television*, Routledge, London, 2004.

Hooper, David, *Reputations Under Fire: Winners and Losers in the Libel Business*, Warner Books, London, 2000.

Hudson, W., *A Treatise of the Court of Star Chamber*, *c.* 1620.

Ibbetson, D. J., *A Historical Introduction to the Law of Obligations*, Oxford University Press, Oxford, 1999.

Justinian, *Institutes* (transl. Peter Birks and Grant McLeod), Duckworth, London, 1994.

Justinian, *The Digest of Justinian*, rev. edn (ed. Alan Watson), Vol. 2, University of Pennsylvania Press, Philadelphia (PA), 1998.

Keeton, W. Page, Dobbs, Dan B., Keeton, Robert E. and Owen, David G., *Prosser and Keeton on the Law of Torts*, 5th edn, West Publishing, St Paul (MN), 1984.

Kermode, Sir Frank, *Shakespeare's Language*, Penguin Books, Ringwood (Vic), 2001.

Kerr, James and Cochrane, Brett, *Twenty Eight Heroes: Inside the 1990 Kangaroo Tour*, self-published, Surry Hills (NSW), 1991b.

Kiralfy, A. K. R., *The Action on the Case*, Sweet and Maxwell, London, 1951.

Kiralfy, A. K. R., *A Source Book of English Law*, Sweet and Maxwell, London, 1957.

Linden, Allen M., *Canadian Tort Law*, 7th edn, Butterworths, Markham (ON), 2001.

Luntz, Harold and Hambly, David, *Torts: Cases and Commentary*, 5th edn, LexisNexis Butterworths, Chatswood (NSW), 2002.

Main, Andrew, *Rivkin Unauthorised: The Meteoric Rise and Tragic Fall of an Unorthodox Money Man*, HarperCollins, Pymble (NSW), 2005.

Marshall, P. David, *Celebrity and Power: Fame in Contemporary Culture*, University of Minnesota Press, Minneapolis (MN), 1997.

McGregor, Harvey, *McGregor on Damages*, 17th edn, Sweet and Maxwell, London, 2003.

McKee, Alan, *Australian Television: A Genealogy of Great Moments*, Oxford University Press, South Melbourne (Vic), 2001.

McNab, Duncan, *The Usual Suspect: The Life of Abe Saffron*, Pan McMillan, Sydney, 2005.

Miller, Toby, *Technologies of Truth: Cultural Citizenship and the Popular Media*, University of Minnesota Press, Minneapolis (MN), 1998.

Miller, Toby, *Sportsex*, Temple University Press, Philadelphia (PA), 2001.

Milmo, Patrick and Rogers, W. V. H. (eds), *Gatley on Libel and Slander*, 10th edn, Sweet and Maxwell, London, 2004.
Milsom, S. F. C., *Historical Foundations of the Common Law*, Butterworths, London, 1981.
Mitchell, Paul, *The Making of the Modern Law of Defamation*, Hart Publishing, Oxford, 2005.
Mohr, Richard D., *Gay Ideas: Outing and Other Controversies*, Beacon Press, Boston (MA), 1992.
Morosi, Junie, *Sex, Prejudice and Politics*, Widescope International Publishers, Camberwell (Vic), 1975.
Nicholas, Barry, *An Introduction to Roman Law*, Clarendon Press, Oxford, 1962.
Orgel, Stephen and Goldberg, Jonathan (eds), *John Milton*, The Oxford Authors, Oxford University Press, Oxford, 1991.
Ormonde, Paul, *A Foolish Passionate Man*, Penguin, Ringwood (Vic), 1981.
Parr, Leslie (ed.), *Miss Marianne Woods and Miss Jane Pirie Against Dame Helen Cumming Gordon*, Arno Press, New York, 1975.
Plucknett, Theodore F. T., *A Concise History of the Common Law*, 5th edn, Butterworths, London, 1956.
Pollock, Sir Frederick, *The Law of Torts*, 13th edn, Stevens and Sons, London, 1929.
Pollock, Sir Frederick and Maitland, Frederic, *The History of English Law Before the Time of Edward I*, 2nd edn, Vol. II, Cambridge University Press, Cambridge, 1898.
Ponce de Leon, Charles L., *Self-exposure: Human-interest Journalism and the Emergence of Celebrity in America, 1890–1940*, University of North Carolina Press, Chapel Hill (NC), 2002.
Powicke, F. M. and Cheney, C. R. (eds), *Councils and Synods with Other Documents Relating to the English Church*, Vol. II (A.D. 1205–1313), Part I (1205–1265), Clarendon Press, Oxford, 1964a.
Powicke, F. M. and Cheney, C. R. (eds), *Councils and Synods with Other Documents Relating to the English Church*, Vol II (A.D. 1205–1313), Part II (1265–1313), Clarendon Press, Oxford, 1964b.
Price, David and Duodu, Korieh, *Defamation Law, Procedure and Practice*, 3rd edn, Sweet and Maxwell, London, 2004.
Pyron, Darden Asbury, *Liberace: An American Boy*, University of Chicago Press, Chicago (IL), 2000.
Reeves, Tony, *Mr Sin: The Abe Saffron Dossier*, Allen and Unwin, Crows Nest (NSW), 2007.
Rogers, W. V. H., *Winfield and Jolowicz on Tort*, 16th edn, Sweet and Maxwell, London, 2002.
Rojek, Chris, *Celebrity*, Reaktion Books, London, 2001.
Schickel, Richard, *Intimate Strangers: The Culture of Celebrity*, Fromm International Publishing Corporation, New York, 1986.

Sheppard, W., *Action upon the Case for Slander, Or A Methodical Collection under certain Heads, of Thousands of Cases Dispersed in the many Great Volumes of the Law, of what words are Actionable, and what not*, London, 1662.
Spencer Bower, George, *A Code of the Law of Actionable Defamation*, 2nd edn, Legal Books, Redfern (NSW), 1990.
Starkie, Thomas, *A Treatise on the Law of Slander, Libel, Scandalum Magnatum and False Rumours*, Collins and Hannay, New York, 1832.
Strangio, Paul, *Keeper of the Faith: A Biography of Jim Cairns*, Melbourne University Press, Melbourne (Vic), 2002.
Stuckey, Michael, *The High Court of Star Chamber*, Gaunt Inc., Holmes Beach (FL), 1998.
Tobin, Terence K. and Sexton, Michael G., *Australian Defamation Law and Practice* (loose-leaf service), Butterworths, Sydney (NSW), 1991.
Turner, Graeme, *Understanding Celebrity*, SAGE Publications, London, 2004.
Turner, Graeme, Bonner, Frances, and Marshall, P. David, *Fame Games: The Production of Celebrity in Australia*, Cambridge University Press, Cambridge, 2000.
Vidal, John, *McLibel: Burger Culture on Trial*, Macmillan, London, 1997.
Walker, Sally, *Media Law: Commentary and Materials*, LBC Information Services, Pyrmont (NSW), 2000.
Warby, Michael, *Ellis Unplugged: The Public Life of a Great Australian Eccentric*, Duffy and Snellgrove, Sydney (NSW), 2001.
Warby, Michael, *Ellis Unpulped: Bob Ellis and the Art of Celebrity*, Duffy and Snellgrove, Sydney (NSW), 2001.
Williamson, David, *Brilliant Lies*, Currency Press, Sydney (NSW), 1993.

Journal Articles

Ackland, Richard, 'Huge Verdicts for "Tasteful" Photo of Sex Symbol' (1993) 18 *Gazette of Law and Journalism* 16.
Adams, Norma, 'The Writ of Prohibition to Court Christian' (1936) 20 *Minnesota LR* 272.
Albury, Katherine, 'Homie-Erotica: Heterosexual Female Desite in *The Picture*' (1997) 84 *Media International Australia* 19.
Anderson, David A., 'Reputation, Compensation and Proof' (1984) 25 *William & Mary LR* 747.
Anderson, David A., 'First Amendment Limitations on Tort Law' (2004) 69 *Brooklyn LR* 755.
Anderson, David A., 'Rethinking Defamation' (2006) 48 *Arizona LR* 1047.
Arend, Patrice S., 'Defamation in an Age of Political Correctness: Should a False Public Statement that a Person is Gay be Defamatory?' (1997) 18 *Northern Illinois University Law Review* 99.

n, Andrea and Wellington, Adrian Alex, 'Outing: The Supposed Justification' (1995) 8 *Canadian Journal of Law and Jurisprudence* 83.

Barcan, Ruth, 'Home on the Rage: Nudity, Celebrity and Ordinariness in the Home Girls/Blokes Pages' (2000) 14 *Continuum: Journal of Media and Cultural Studies* 145.

Barendt, Eric, 'What is the Point of Libel Law?' (1999) 52 *Current Legal Problems* 110.

Becker, Susan J., 'The Immorality of Publicly Outing Private People' (1994) 73 *Oregon LR* 159.

Behrendt, Larissa, 'It's Broke So Fix It: Arguments for a Bill of Rights' (2003) 9 *AJHR* 257.

Bellah, Robert N., 'The Meaning of Reputation in American Society' (1986) 74 *California LR* 743.

Boivin, Denis W., 'Accommodating Freedom of Expression and Reputation in the Common Law of Defamation' (1997) 22 *Queen's LJ* 229.

Butler, Des, '*Lange* Revisited: Exploring the Implied Freedom of Political Communication Concerning Government or Political Matters' (2000a) 5 *MALR* 145.

Butler, Des, 'Media Negligence in the Information Age: A New Frontier for a New Century?' (2000b) 8 *Torts LJ* 159.

Calvert, Clay, 'Harm to Reputation: An Interdisciplinary Approach to the Impact of Denial of Defamatory Allegations' (1995) 26 *Pacific LJ* 933.

Charlesworth, Hilary, 'Human Rights in Australian Law' (2002) 13 *PLR* 155.

Cottrell, Jill, 'What Does "Defamatory" Mean? Reflections on *Berkoff v Burchill*' (1998) 6 *Tort LR* 149.

Cottrell, Jill, 'Courts, Freedom of Speech and Defamation' (1999) 7 *Asia Pacific LR* 205.

Courtney, James C., 'Absurdities of the Law of Slander and Libel' (1902) 36 *American LR* 552.

Davis, Megan and Williams, George, 'A Statutory Bill of Rights for Australia? Lessons from the United Kingdom' (2002) 22 *UQLJ* 1.

Debeljak, Julie, 'The *Human Rights Act* 2004 (ACT): A Significant, Yet Incomplete, Step Towards the Domestic Protection and Promotion of Human Rights' (2004) 15 *PLR* 169.

Donnelly, R. C., 'History of Defamation' [1949] *Wisconsin LR* 99.

Ellis, Bob, 'Warby Plugged' (2001) 163 *Overland* 41.

Elwood, John P., 'Outing, Privacy and the First Amendment' (1992) 102 *Yale LJ* 747.

Enonchong, Nelson, 'Contract Damages for Injury to Reputation' (1996) 59 *MLR* 592.

Evans, Simon and Evans, Carolyn, 'Legal Redress under the Victorian Charter of Human Rights and Responsibilities' (2006) 17 *Public Law Review* 264.

Feldman, David, 'Human Dignity as a Legal Value: Part 1' [1999] *PL* 682.

Fitzgerald, Brian, '*Dow Jones & Co Inc v Gutnick* – Negotiating "American Legal Hegemony" in the Transnational World of Cyberspace' (2003) 27 *Melb ULR* 590.

Fitzpatrick, Simon, 'The Imperial Expansion of Defamation' (2000) 8 *Torts LJ* 263.

Flahiff, G. B., 'The Use of Prohibitions by Clerics against Ecclesiastical Courts in England' (1941) 3 *Mediaeval Studies* 101.

Flahiff, G. B., 'The Writ of Prohibition to Court Christian in the Thirteenth Century: Part I' (1944) 6 *Mediaeval Studies* 261.

Flahiff, G. B., 'The Writ of Prohibition to Court Christian in the Thirteenth Century: Part II' (1945) 7 *Mediaeval Studies* 229.

Fogle, Randy M., 'Is Calling Someone "Gay" Defamatory?: The Meaning of Reputation, Community Mores, Gay Rights, and Free Speech' (1993) 3 *Law and Sexuality* 165.

Garnett, Richard, '*Dow Jones & Co Inc v Gutnick* – An Adequate Response to Transnational Internet Defamation?' (2003) 4 *MJIL* 196.

Gibbons, Thomas, 'Defamation Reconsidered' (1996) 16 *OJLS* 587.

Giles, David C. and Maltby, John, 'The Role of Media Figures in Adolescent Development: Relations between Autonomy, Attachment, and Interest in Celebrities' (2004) 36 *Personality and Individual Differences* 813.

Grant, Jon E., '"Outing" and Freedom of the Press: Sexual Orientation's Challenge to the Supreme Court's Categorical Jurisprudence' (1991) 77 *Cornell LR* 103.

Greig, Brian, 'Political Leadership on a Bill of Rights' (2003) 9 *AJHR* 21.

Hartigan, John, 'Press Freedom Under Attack', *Australian Press Council News*, Vol. 16, No. 1, February 2004, 1.

Heerey, Hon Justice Peter, 'Character and Personality: Where to for Protection in the Intellectual Property Area?' (2000) 39 *Intellectual Property Forum* 8.

Helmholz, R. M., 'Canonical Defamation in Medieval England' (1971) 15 *American Journal of Legal History* 255.

Helmholz, R. M., 'Writs of Prohibition and Ecclesiastical Sanctions in the English Courts Christian' (1976) 60 *Minnesota LR* 1011.

Helmholz, R. M., 'The Writ of Prohibition to Court Christian before 1500' (1981) 43 *Mediaeval Studies* 297.

Holdsworth, Sir William, 'Defamation in the Sixteenth and Seventeenth Centuries: Part I' (1924a) 40 *LQR* 302.

Holdsworth, Sir William, 'Defamation in the Sixteenth and Seventeenth Centuries: Part II' (1924b) 40 *LQR* 397.

Holdsworth, Sir William, 'Defamation in the Sixteenth and Seventeenth Centuries: Part III' (1925) 41 *LQR* 13.

Kenyon, Andrew, 'Problems with Defamation Damages?' (1998) 24 *Monash ULR* 70.

Kildea, Paul, 'The Bill of Rights Debate in Australian Political Culture' (2003) 9 *AJHR* 65.

Knight, Dean R., '"I'm Not Gay: Not That There's Anything Wrong With That": Are Unwanted Imputations of Gayness Defamatory?' (2006) 37 *Victoria University of Wellington Law Review* 249.

Lassiter, John C., 'Defamation of Peers: The Rise and Decline of the Action for *Scandalum Magnatum*, 1497–1773' (1978) 22 *American Journal of Legal History* 216.

Lidsky, Lyrissa Barnett, 'Defamation, Reputation, and the Myth of Community' (1996) 71 *Washington LR* 1.

Lloyd Jones, Marina, 'Imputations of Homosexuality in Defamation Actions' (2001) 5 *TeleMedia* 94.

Lovell, Colin Rhys, 'The "Reception" of Defamation by the Common Law' (1962) 15 *Vanderbilt LR* 1051.

Lumby, Catharine, 'Out of the Slipstream' (2004) 5 *Griffith Review: Addicted to Celebrity* 111.

MacDougall, Bruce, 'Outing: The Law Reacts to Speech about Homosexuality' (1995) 21 *Queen's LJ* 79.

Magnusson, Roger S., 'Freedom of Speech in Australian Defamation Law: Ridicule, Satire and Other Challenges' (2001) 9 *Torts LJ* 269.

Maltby, John, Day, Liz, McCutcheon, Lynn E., Martin, Matthew M. and Cayanus, Jacob L., 'Celebrity Worship, Cognitive Flexibility, and Social Complexity' (2004) 37 *Personality and Individual Differences* 1475.

Maltby, John, Houran, James and McCutcheon, Lynn E., 'A Clinical Interpretation of Attitudes and Behaviors Associated with Celebrity Worship' (2003) 191 *Journal of Nervous and Mental Disease* 25.

Maltby, John, Houran, James, Langer, Rense, Ashe, Diane and McCutcheon, Lynn E., 'Thou Shalt Worship No Other Gods – Unless They Are Celebrities: The Relationship between Celebrity Worship and Religious Orientation' (2002) 32 *Personality and Individual Differences* 1157.

McClelland, Robert, 'How is a Bill of Rights Relevant Today?' (2003) 9 *AJHR* 11.

McCutcheon, Lynn, Ashe, Diane D., Houran, James and Maltby, John, 'A Cognitive Profile of Individuals Who Tend to Worship Celebrities' (2003) 137 *Journal of Psychology* 309.

McNamara, Lawrence, 'Bigotry, Community and the (In)Visibility of Moral Exclusion: Homosexuality and the Capacity to Defame' (2001) 6 *MALR* 271.

Meagher, Dan, 'The Protection of Political Communication Under the Australian Constitution' (2005) 28 *UNSWLJ* 30.

Miller, Toby, 'A Short History of the Penis' (1995) 43 *Social Text* 14.

Millon, David, '*Circumspecte Agatis* Revisited' (1984) 2 *Law and History Review* 105.

Moretti, Barbara, 'Outing: Justifiable or Unwarranted Invasion of Privacy? The Private Facts Tort as a Remedy for Disclosures of Sexual Orientation' (1993) 11 *Cardozo Arts and Entertainment LJ* 857.

Nicholson, Marlene Arnold, 'McLibel: A Case Study in English Defamation Law' (2000) 18 *Wisconsin International Law Journal* 1.

O'Malley, Pat, 'From Feudal Honour to Bourgeois Reputation: Ideology, Law and the Rise of Industrial Capitalism' (1981) 15 *Sociology* 79.

Ozdowski, Sev, 'The Content of an Australian Bill of Rights' (2003) 9 *AJHR* 29.

Patfield, Fiona, 'The Origins of a Company's Right to Sue for Defamation' (1994) 45 *NILQ* 233.

Peonidis, Filimon, 'Freedom of Expression, Autonomy and Defamation' (1998) 17 *Law and Philosophy* 1.

Pollack, David H., 'Forced out of the Closet: Sexual Orientation and the Legal Dilemma of "Outing"' (1992) 46 *University of Miami LR* 711.

Post, Robert C., 'The Social Foundations of Defamation Law; Reputation and the Constitution' (1986) 74 *California LR* 691.

Potter, Richard, 'Development of Freedom of Speech Defences to Defamation in Australia' (1998) 3 *MALR* 82.

Pound, Roscoe, 'Interests of Personality: Part II' (1915) 28 *Harvard LR* 445.

Rimmer, Matthew, 'Gossip We Can Trust: Defamation Law and Non-fiction' (2004) 9 *MALR* 37.

Schaffner, Joan E., 'Protection of Reputation Versus Freedom of Expression: Striking a Manageable Compromise in the Tort of Defamation' (1990) 63 *S Cal LR* 433.

Schultz, Julianne, 'Stars, Lies and Propaganda' (2004) 5 *Griffith Review: Addicted to Celebrity* 7.

Simons, Margaret, 'Life without Reputation' (2004) 5 *Griffith Review: Addicted to Celebrity* 67.

Skolnick, Jerome H., 'The Sociological Tort of Defamation' (1986) 74 *California LR* 677.

Slaughter, M. M., 'The Development of Common Law Defamation Privileges: From Communitarian Society to Market Society' (1992) 14 *Cardozo LR* 351.

Stone, Adrienne, '*Lange, Levy* and the Direction of Freedom of Political Communication' (1998) 21 *UNSWLJ* 117.

Stone, Adrienne and Williams, George, 'Freedom of Speech and Defamation: Developments in the Common Law World' (2000) 26 *Monash ULR* 362.

Stuckey, Michael, 'A Consideration of the Emergence and Exercise of Judicial Authority in the Star Chamber' (1993) 19 *Monash ULR* 117.

Tingley, Charles, 'Reputation, Freedom of Expression and the Tort of Defamation in the United States and Canada: A Deceptive Polarity' (1999) 37 *Alberta LR* 620.

Treiger Bar-Am, Leslie Kim, 'Defamation Law in a Changing Society: The Case of *Youssoupoff v Metro-Goldwyn-Mayer*' (2000) 20 *Legal Studies* 291.

Veeder, Van Vechten, 'The History and Theory of the Law of Defamation: Part I' (1903) 3 *Columbia LR* 546.

Veeder, Van Vechten, 'The History and Theory of the Law of Defamation: Part II' (1904) 4 *Columbia LR* 33.

Walker, Sally, 'Regulating the Media: Reputation Truth and Privacy' (1994) 19 *Melb ULR* 729.
Walton, Michael, 'Human Rights: What's Been Left Out of Australia's First Bill of Rights?' (2004) 29 *Alt LJ* 195.
Ware, Hilary E., 'Celebrity Privacy Rights and Free Speech: Recalibrating Tort Remedies for "Outed" Celebrities' (1997) 32 *Harvard Civil Rights-Civil Liberties LR* 449.
Watterson, Ray, 'What is Defamatory Today?' (1993) 67 *ALJ* 811.
Wick, Ronald F., 'Out of the Closet and Into the Headlines: "Outing" and the Private Facts Tort' (1991) 80 *Georgetown LJ* 413.
Williams, Daryl, 'Recognising Universal Rights in Australia' (2001) 24 *UNSWLJ* 771.
Williams, Daryl, 'Against Constitutional Cringe: The Protection of Human Rights in Australia' (2003) 9 *AJHR* 1.
Williams, George, 'Human Rights and the Second Century of the Australian Constitution' (2001) 24 *UNSWLJ* 782.
Williams, George, 'The Victorian *Charter of Human Rights and Responsibilities*: Origins and Scope' (2006) 30 *Melbourne University Law Review* 880.
Winterton, George, 'The ACT Bill of Rights' (2004) 7 *CLPR* 47.
Yatar, Eric K. M., 'Defamation, Privacy, and the Changing Social Status of Homosexuality: Re-Thinking Supreme Court Gay-Rights Jurisprudence' (2003) 12 *Law and Sexuality* 119.
Yeates, Helen, 'The League of Men: Masculinity, the Media and Rugby League Football' (1995) 75 *Media Information Australia* 35.

Book Chapters

Lee, H. P., 'The Implied Freedom of Political Communication' in H. P. Lee and George Winterton (eds), *Australian Constitutional Landmarks*, Cambridge University Press, Cambridge, 2003, 383–411.
Lumby, Catharine, 'Real Appeal: The Ethics of Reality TV' in Catharine Lumby and Elspeth Probyn (eds), *Remote Control: New Media, New Ethics*, Cambridge University Press, Cambridge, 2003, 11–24.

Conference Papers

Gleeson, Kate, 'Castration Anxieties in the Age of ET: Does a Man Own his Penis?', 'Law in a Changing World', Faculty of Law, University of Sydney, University of Sydney Postgraduate Law Conference, 31 October – 1 November 2003.
Levine, Hon Justice David, 'Does Our Defamation Law Strike the Right Balance?', Judicial Commission of New South Wales, Supreme Court Annual Conference 2002, 16–18 August 2002.

Parliamentary Papers

Commonwealth of Australia, House of Representatives, *Hansard*, 11 February 1975.
Commonwealth of Australia, House of Representatives, *Hansard*, 14 October 2003.
Commonwealth of Australia, Senate, *Hansard*, 14 October 2003.
New South Wales Legislative Assembly, *Hansard*, 26 October 1994.
New South Wales Legislative Assembly, *Hansard*, 2 December 1994.
New South Wales Legislative Assembly, *Hansard*, 8 August 2000.
New South Wales Legislative Council, *Hansard*, 29 November 1994.

Law Reform Documents

Attorney-General's Taskforce on Defamation Law Reform, *Defamation Law: Proposals for Reform in New South Wales*, July 2002.
Australian Government Attorney-General's Department, *Revised Outline of a Possible National Defamation Law*, July 2004.
Australian Law Reform Commission, *Unfair Publication: Defamation and Privacy*, Australian Government Publishing Service, Canberra, 1979.
Faulks Committee, *Report of the Committee of Defamation*, HMSO, London, 1975.
Government of Western Australia, *Committee Report on Reform to the Law of Defamation in Western Australia*, September 2003.
Standing Committee of Attorneys-General Working Group of State and Territory Officers's *Proposal for Uniform Defamation Laws*, July 2004.

Newspaper Articles

'Apology to Paul Hasleby', *The West Australian*, 14 May 2003, np.
'Ball's firmly in Hasleby's court', *The Sunday Tasmanian*, 18 May 2003.
'Cairns aide sacked in row over Morosi', *The Australian*, 20 February 1975, 1.
'Cruise wins libel case', *The Australian*, 31 October 1998, 18.
'Footballer miffed at overexposure', *Deutsche Presse-Agentur*, 14 May 2003.
'Hasleby's anguish over penis picture', *The Mercury*, 14 May 2003, 56.
'Hollywood stars win libel damages', *The Financial Times*, 30 October 1998, 1.
'Kidman agrees libel damages', *The Times* (London), 15 October 2003, 6.
'Kidman wins affair case', *The Times* (London), 1 August 2003, 6.
'Lemon twist to Jason hearing', *The Herald Sun*, 1 April 1992, np.
'Player unhappy at photo of tackle', *Courier-Mail*, 13 May 2003, 7.
'So Sorry Old Man', *The Daily Star*, 18 May 2003, 34.

Ackland, Richard, 'Relax, MPs are still fair game', *The Sydney Morning Herald*, 12 March 1999a, 17.

Ackland, Richard, 'Being branded gay isn't the insult it used to be', *The Sydney Morning Herald*, 11 November 2003, 11.

Ackland, Richard, 'High price to pay for a deflated ego', *The Sydney Morning Herald*, 21 May 2004, 11.

Alexander, Peter, 'Publish and be damned by absurd defamation laws', *The Sydney Morning Herald*, 30 November 2000, 20.

Armitage, Liz, 'Ellis book did no damage to careers: QC', *The Canberra Times*, 10 November 1998a, 3.

Armitage, Liz, 'Abbott-Costello libel case a watershed, court told', *The Canberra Times*, 11 November 1998b, 3.

Armitage, Liz, 'Ministers, wives win $277,500 in libel damages', *The Canberra Times*, 6 March 1999a, 1.

Armitage, Liz, 'Publisher appeals against Abbott, Costello damages', *The Canberra Times*, 1 April 1999b, 3.

Askew, Kate, Wainwright, Robert, Chessell, James and McClymont, Kate 'We dropped in, Rene, but you were out', *The Sydney Morning Herald*, 14 November 2003, 1.

Associated Press, 'Tom Cruise wins $10m defamation judgment', 16 January 2003.

Baird, Julia, 'Women, take a hint from Junie Morosi', *The Sydney Morning Herald*, 18 October 2003, 43.

Barker, Geoffrey, 'Funnell vision and a game of Hayden seek', *The Australian Financial Review*, 23 October 1998, 3.

Barkham, Patrick, 'Shaffer mistress facing eviction', *The Times* (London), 12 February 2004, 6.

Barrett, Patrick, 'The Face hopes for 11th-hour saviour', *The Guardian*, 23 March 2004, 19.

Beacham, Digby, 'Hasleby to decide', *The Sunday Times* (Perth), 25 May 2003.

Blackhurst, Chris, 'The "mistress" fighting for a share of the Shaffer legacy', *The Evening Standard*, 10 July 2002, 5.

Bolt, Andrew, 'The real legacy of Jim Cairns', *The Herald Sun*, 16 October 2003, 19.

Borham, Susan, 'Hughes farewells ACP with $350,000 victory', *The Sydney Morning Herald*, 13 February 1993a, 2.

Borham, Susan, 'Vinnie prepares to dismount and disrobe', *The Sydney Morning Herald*, 16 February 1993b, 2.

Borrill, Rachel, 'TV stars sues magazine over "outing" poster', *The Independent*, 31 March 1992a, 2.

Borrill, Rachel, 'Pop star explains a "male tart"', *The Independent*, 1 April 1992b, 2.

Borrill, Rachel, '"Face" editor apologises for picture', *The Independent*, 2 April 1992c, 2.

Borrill, Rachel, 'Damages for actor "should nail gay lie"', *The Independent*, 3 April 1992d, 3.

Borrill, Rachel, 'Donovan awarded £200,000 damages for "queer" libel', *The Independent*, 4 April 1992e, 1.

Borrill, Rachel, 'Triumph of the blue-eyed boy next door', *The Independent*, 4 April 1992f, 3.

Boseley, Sarah, 'Editor "cut libel" from outing story', *The Guardian*, 2 April 1992a, 2.

Boseley, Sarah, 'Jury urged to nail "gay slur"', *The Guardian*, 3 April 1992b, 2.

Boseley, Sarah, 'Expensive outing could smother The Face', *The Guardian*, 4 April 1992c, 3.

Boseley, Sarah, 'Future of the Face in balance after lawyers talk', *The Guardian*, 7 April 1992d, 2.

Botsman, Peter, 'Grassroots intellectual's ideas not so loopy now', *The Australian*, 16 October 2003, 13.

Bowers, Peter, 'The Morosi time-bomb ticks away …', *The Sydney Morning Herald*, 27 February 1975, 7.

Brent, Peter, 'Now for press gallery closets', *The Canberra Times*, 5 July 2002, 12.

Brown, James, 'Shame about "The Face" – a great magazine stifled by its past', *The Independent on Sunday*, 21 March 2004, 15.

Button, Simon, 'Jason Donovan – "I don't regret my career going off the rails"', *The Sunday Mirror*, 1 February 2004, 38.

Byrnes, Holly, Grant, Sarah and Jackson, Steve, 'Making A Woman's Day', *The Daily Telegraph*, 'Sydney Confidential', 24 May 2007, 32.

Cameron, Michael, 'Rivkin settles defamation case', 'Media', *The Australian*, 8 July 2004, 18.

Campbell, Roderick, 'Abbotts and Costellos win more costs', *The Canberra Times*, 22 June 1999a, 4.

Campbell, Roderick, 'Ellis's words "vulgar but not defamatory"', *The Canberra Times*, 31 August 1999b, 1.

Casimir, Jon and Squires, Tony, 'Capper finds bottom line', *The Sydney Morning Herald*, 'Stay in Touch', 9 February 1993a, 20.

Casimir, Jon and Squires, Tony, 'HQ goes for a duck', *The Sydney Morning Herald*, 'Stay in Touch', 11 February 1993b, 24.

Casimir, Jon and Squires, Tony, 'Celebrities' new clothes', *The Sydney Morning Herald*, 'Stay in Touch', 26 March 1993c, 26.

Casimir, Jon and Squires, Tony, 'Nude trend continues', *The Sydney Morning Herald*, 'Stay in Touch', 15 April 1993d, 20.

Charlton, Peter, 'Jim gives up secret of heart', *The Courier-Mail*, 17 September 2002a, 3.

Charlton, Peter, 'An affair to remember', *The Courier-Mail*, 17 September 2002b, 9.

Chenoweth, Neil, 'It's a bad business', *The Australian Financial Review*, 21–22 February 1998, 1.

Chenoweth, Neil, 'Costs next battle in Rivkin-Fairfax case', *The Australian Financial Review*, 19 May 2004, 12.

Chenoweth, Neil, Elma, Shraga and Graffagnini, Rosemarie, 'Rivkin's Swiss bank scandal', *The Australian Financial Review*, 30 October 2003, 1, 10–11.

Clancy, Ray, 'Donovan wins damages of £200,000 for gay slur', *The Times* (London), 4 April 1992, np.

Coghlan, Scott, 'No longer a private matter for Hasleby', *The Australian*, 13 May 2003a, 18.

Coghlan, Scott, 'Hasleby reaches settlement', *The West Australian*, 17 May 2003b, 48.

Colman, Elizabeth, 'Rivkin lets his health do the talking', *The Australian*, 24 December 2003, 1.

Colman, Elizabeth, Milligan, Louise and Sandrejko, Nick, 'No excuses left, Rivkin goes to jail', *The Australian*, 7 February 2004, 1.

Cook, Trevor, 'Blogging: a personal medium is now the message', *The Australian Financial Review*, 20–21 March 2004, 22–3.

Corbett, Bryce, 'Jase dressed for gay abuse contest', *The Daily Telegraph*, 29 May 1996, 13.

Corbett, Bryce and Symons, Emma-Kate, 'Jason bares all for gays', *The Daily Telegraph*, 8 November 1996, 13.

Cornford, Philip, 'Walk on the mild side: Saffron out of step with council', *The Sydney Morning Herald*, 21 December 2004, 3.

Cosgrove, Stuart, 'Making the Face Fit', *The Guardian*, 7 March 1994, 14.

Crabb, Annabel, 'Cairns admits Morosi affair', *The Age*, 16 September 2002, 3.

Crisp· Lyndall and Margo, Jill, 'Sex and power', *The Australian Financial Review*, 6 July 2002, 24.

Curtin, Jennie, 'ET case was "over the top"', *The Sydney Morning Herald*, 14 October 1993, 3.

Curtis, Maree and Wilson, Sarah, 'Wise guy – Jason Donovan earns a little respect – Don't look back in anger', *The Sunday Telegraph* (Sydney), 4 May 2003, 1.

Dean, Anabel, 'Fergie's sister awarded $300,000 for "slut" reports', *The Sydney Morning Herald*, 28 November 1990, 3.

Dean, Anabel, 'Makim's payout delayed for appeal', *The Sydney Morning Herald*, 19 February 1991, 6.

Dean, Anabel, 'E.T. describes years of ridicule', *The Sydney Morning Herald*, 31 January 1995a, 6.

Dean, Anabel, 'E.T. happy after $100,000 damages for nude photo', *The Sydney Morning Herald*, 2 February 1995b, 2.

Debelle, Penelope, 'Goodbye South Australia – Ellis's latest tome in tomb', *The Sydney Morning Herald*, 28 September 2002, 2.

Devine, Frank, 'Credibility in tatters – so what's new?', *The Australian*, 16 November 1998, 13.

Dixon, Robyn, '$350,000 price tag on a man's privacy', *The Age*, 12 February 1993, 3.

Dore, Christopher, 'Crucified in Jerusalem, Mrs Costello's agony', *The Australian*, 20 October 1998a, 1.

Dore, Christopher, 'Costello stands and delivers', *The Australian*, 21 October 1998b, 1.

Dore, Christopher, 'Sex claims did no damage to ministers – QC', *The Australian*, 10 November 1998c, 3.

Dore, Christopher, 'Punish or our "politicians are damned"', *The Australian*, 11 November 1998d, 7.

Dore, Christopher, '$277,500 to heal minister's wounds', *The Australian*, 6 March 1999, 5.

Editorial, '$350,000 out of the shadows', *The Sydney Morning Herald*, 12 February 1993, 10.

Editorial, 'Abbott and Costello: time to change the law', *The Canberra Times*, 6 March 1999, 3.

Editorial, 'A blow to online freedom', *The New York Times*, 11 December 2002, 34.

Editorial, 'Down (Under) with the Internet', *The Wall Street Journal*, 11 December 2002, 18.

Elam, Shraga and Chenoweth, Neil, 'Offset Alpine: ASIC widens Swiss probe', *The Australian Financial Review*, 13 August 2004, 1.

Ellingsen, Peter, 'Just as he did in 1970, in death Jim Cairns still draws a crowd', *The Age*, 18 October 2003, 6.

Ellison, Michael, 'Tom Cruise sues wrestler for gay "slur"', *The Guardian*, 4 May 2001a, 12.

Ellison, Michael, 'Cruise sues over second gay claim', *The Guardian*, 6 June 2001b, 10.

Este, Jonathan and Leak, Bill, 'Ellis scotches rumour with dry toast', *The Australian*, 31 October 1998, 12.

Fabro, Allesandra, 'Regulator may broaden Offset probe', *The Australian Financial Review*, 17 November 2003, 5.

Faulk, Tina, 'Pulp and be damned the preferred choice', *The Canberra Times*, 7 July 2001, 8.

Gare, Shelley, 'Hot air clouds in egosphere', *The Australian*, 24 October 1998, 24.

Gentleman, Amelia, 'Erotic thriller Hollywood couple sue over sex claims', *The Guardian*, 24 April 1999, 6.

Gerard, Ian, 'Cruisy life is over for the ship of cools', *The Weekend Australian*, 27–28 March 2004, 5.

Giles, Darrell, 'Cruise sues porn star', *The Herald-Sun*, 4 May 2001, 7.

Glendinning, Lee, Tomas, Juan-Carlo and O'Malley, Nick, 'Cell door finally swings shut after Rivkin abandons last-ditch appeal', *The Sydney Morning Herald*, 7 February 2004, 1.

Gordon, Michael, 'How politics got into the gutter', *The Age*, 24 October 1998, 1.

Grattan, Michelle, 'Morosi: pressure on PM: Whitlam told he should step in', *The Age*, 21 February 1975, 1.

Grattan, Michelle, 'Costello's catastrophe or the politicians' revenge', *The Australian Financial Review*, 24 October 1998a, 26.

Grattan, Michelle, 'Confessions of a romantic', *The Australian Financial Review*, 7 November 1998b, 24.

Green, Penelope, 'Ellis judge out of step on sex – QC', *The Australian*, 31 August 1999, 5.

Hardy, Rebecca, 'Love and redemption for the boy next door', *The Daily Telegraph* (Sydney), 24 January 2004, 4 at 5.

Harris, Tony, 'Cairns's Lasting Legacy', *The Australian Financial Review*, 28 October 2003, 70.

Harvey, Adam, 'A gap in the truth and a life cut short: A new inquest into the death of a Sydney model aims to find the facts behind a tragic mystery', *The Sunday Telegraph*, 23 November 2003, 14–15.

Hattenstone, Simon, 'Prisoner of his fame', *The Guardian*, 5 October 1996, 6.

Henderson, Gerard, 'Bob Ellis, let me introduce Frank Hardy', *The Sydney Morning Herald*, 27 October 1998, 13.

Hickie, Kathleen, 'Nudity not on for ET the "sex symbol"', *The Sydney Morning Herald*, 3 February 1993a, 5.

Hickie, Kathleen, 'Rugby league star "repulsed" by ET's nude shower shot', *The Sydney Morning Herald*, 4 February 1993b, 7.

Hickie, Kathleen, 'Editor "careless" in printing ET's photo', *The Sydney Morning Herald*, 5 February 1993c, 5.

Hickie, Kathleen, 'Photographer says "no denying" ET exposure', *The Sydney Morning Herald*, 6 February 1993d, 5.

Hickie, Kathleen, 'ET case a storm in a teacup: QC', *The Sydney Morning Herald*, 10 February 1993e, 5.

Hickie, Kathleen, 'Judge defends payout to ET', *The Sydney Morning Herald*, 13 February 1993f, 7.

Hickie, Kathleen, 'Justice miscarried in ET case: QC', *The Sydney Morning Herald*, 19 August 1993g, 3.

Hickie, Kathleen, 'ET's award justified, QC tells court', *The Sydney Morning Herald*, 20 August 1993h, 2.

Hills, Ben, 'I'll talk when I'm out of this mess', *The Age*, 6 December 1974, 1, 3.

Hills, Ben, 'Caroline's world and the Rivkin link', *The Sydney Morning Herald*, 25 February 1998, 1.

Hoffmann, Bill, 'Weird but true', *The New York Post*, 16 May 2003, 33.

Holland, John, 'Don't blame me, says Miss Junie', *The Age*, 12 December 1974, 5.

Hudson, Phillip, 'Tanya Costello free to boast of a new age husband', *The Age*, 15 April 2000, 4.

Iley, Chrissy, 'Jason tells: love and me', *The Sunday Mail* (Adelaide), 28 July 1991a, np.

Iley, Chrissy, 'Jason: not "outed" … just outraged', *The Herald Sun*, 3 August 1991b, 19.

Iley, Chrissy, 'Sexuality, love and me', *The Sunday Mail* (Brisbane), 4 August 1991c, 8.

Jackson, Sally, Dore, Christopher and Sutherland, Tracey, 'The 33 words that sank Jerusalem', *The Australian*, 24 October 1998, 1.

Jardine, Cassandra, 'Narcissism drove me to drugs hell', *The Sun Herald*, 3 May 1998, 56.

Jenkins, Lin, 'Blonde hair claim vindictive, says Jason Donovan', *The Times* (London), 1 April 1992, np.

Jost, John, Skelton, Russell and McCarthy, Phillip, 'Juni's husband gets Govt job', *The Age*, 5 December 1974, 1.

Jost, John, 'Morosi storm rocks Govt: Revoke her job: MPs and Hawke tell Cairns', *The Age*, 6 December 1974, 1.

Jurman, Elizabeth, 'Right of reply may end big defamation payouts', *The Sydney Morning Herald*, 7 September 1993a, 1.

Jurman, Elizabeth, 'End big libel awards: lawyers', *The Sydney Morning Herald*, 24 November 1993b, 7.

Kelly, Paul, 'Morosi must go, many Labor members believe: Cairns backs aide's honor (sic) and integrity', *The Australian*, 21 February 1975, 1.

Kelso, Paul, and White, Michael, 'Magazines might sue over Major-Currie affair', *The Guardian*, 30 September 2002, 1.

Kent, Paul, 'Life beyond the tryline', *The Sydney Morning Herald*, 1 February 2000, 24.

Kent, Simon, 'Jason bares all on gay jibe', *The Sun Herald*, 17 November 1996, 31.

Kirby, Terry, 'After 20 years of being cool, "The Face" has fallen out of fashion', *The Independent*, 13 March 2004, 21.

Knox, Malcolm, 'Defamation abuse has stifled criticism – author', *The Sydney Morning Herald*, 26 April 2003a, 9.

Knox, Malcolm, 'He wrote with a joint in his hand', *The Sydney Morning Herald*, 'Spectrum', 26 April 2003b, 4.

Koch, Phillip, 'Chris's other life', *The Sunday Telegraph* (Sydney), 8 September 1996, 69.

Lampe, Anne, 'Kennedy and Rivkin facing criminal and corporate charges', *The Sydney Morning Herald*, 4 March 2004, 23.

Lawson, Valerie, 'Playwright's lover wins damages in second act of court drama', *The Sydney Morning Herald*, 13 February 2004, 10.

Legge, Kate, 'Junie's shadow over the Cairns clan', *The Weekend Australian*, 18 October 2003, 1.

Leith, William, 'Jason Donovan: the amazing technicolour nightmare', *The Observer*, 17 November 1996, 6.

Lewis, Daniel, 'Fairfax lawsuit settled', *The Sydney Morning Herald*, 27 July 1991, 6.

Loane, Sally, 'In her own right', *The Sydney Morning Herald*, 23 October 1998, 13.
Macdonald, Emma, 'Howard's bovver boy', *The Canberra Times*, 28 April 2001, 1.
Maclean, Sheena, 'Truth pulls plug on spin cycle', *The Australian*, 24 February 2005, 23.
Main, Andrew, 'Sick note keeps Rene out of jail', *The Australian Financial Review*, 5 November 2003, 1, 8.
Main, Andrew, 'DPP weighs charge against ex-Rivkin PA', *The Australian Financial Review*, 11 March 2004, 9.
Manly, Chris, 'Jason is a new man', *The Sunday Telegraph* (Sydney), 18 April 1999, 24.
Mapstone, Naomi, 'Costellos regain privacy with court victory', *The Canberra Times*, 6 March 1999, 1.
Marr, David, 'Pulped fiction: Abbott and Costello want justice', *The Sydney Morning Herald*, 20 October 1998a, 1.
Marr, David, 'Abbott saw "six figures" in grubby tale', *The Sydney Morning Herald*, 21 October 1998b, 2.
Marr, David, 'Psst, Bob, heard the latest from Hayden?', *The Sydney Morning Herald*, 22 October 1998c, 1.
Marr, David, 'The day lawyers used the magic word at Random', *The Sydney Morning Herald*, 23 October 1998d, 1.
Marr, David, 'The price of honour', *The Sydney Morning Herald*, 24 October 1998e, 35.
Marr, David, 'After the break, who's playing Banquo now?', *The Sydney Morning Herald*, 10 November 1998f, 4.
Marr, David, 'Can "reckless" words hurt a politician?', *The Sydney Morning Herald*, 11 November 1998g, 6.
Marr, David, 'Unchaste: the slur that cost $277,500', *The Sydney Morning Herald*, 6 March 1999a, 1.
Marr, David, 'Abbott-Costello case becomes a trial of attrition', *The Sydney Morning Herald*, 3 April 1999b, 3.
Marr, David, 'That's not quite all, folks: Abbott, Costello in rerun', *The Sydney Morning Herald*, 30 August 1999c, 3.
Marr, David, 'Little people and big questions', *The Sydney Morning Herald*, 31 August 1999d, 4.
Marr, David, 'Butt out, boys, this case is Tanya's and Margaret's', *The Sydney Morning Herald*, 1 September 1999e, 4.
Marr, David, 'It's goodbye Jerusalem, and it's goodbye Bob', *The Sydney Morning Herald*, 11 November 1999f, 3.
Marr, David, 'Pulp friction', *The Sydney Morning Herald*, 27 November 1999g, 37.
Marr, David, 'Costello pulps another book', *The Sydney Morning Herald*, 2 June 2000, 3.

Marr, David, 'A law unto themselves, or so they hope', *The Sydney Morning Herald*, 14 April 2005, 15.
Martin, Chelsey, 'Court awards Costellos and Abbotts $277,500', *The Australian Financial Review*, 6 March 1999, 7.
McClymont, Kate, 'Culpable error turns Ellis book into pulpable fiction', *The Sydney Morning Herald*, 28 April 2001, 1.
McClymont, Kate, 'A passing glimpse of Rene Rivkin's former café society', *The Sydney Morning Herald*, 24 March 2004, 1.
McClymont, Kate and Cornford, Philip 'Rivkin and The Gap fugitive', *The Sydney Morning Herald*, 20–21 March 2004, 1.
McClymont, Kate and Fray, Peter, 'When Rivkin held court', *The Sydney Morning Herald*, 3–4 April 2004, 31.
McGavin, Harvey, 'Presses stop rolling on Eighties style guide', *The Guardian*, 24 April 2004, 18.
McGregor, Richard, 'Unspeakable lies', *The Australian*, 6 March 1999, 27.
McGregor, Richard, 'Treasured times with Peter: Liberals face the future', *The Australian*, 15 April 2000, 7.
McLachlan, Miranda and Skulley, Mark, 'Last march of idealist Cairns', *The Australian Financial Review*, 18 October 2003, 8.
McRae, Toni, 'Junie: my story', *The Sun* (Sydney), 9 December 1974a, 1, 3, 26.
McRae, Toni, 'Life with Junie', *The Sun* (Sydney), 20 December 1974b, 1, 5.
McRae, Toni, 'Tragedy – and hopes for another baby', *The Sun* (Sydney), 23 December 1974c, 7.
McRae, Toni, 'Junie about the house', *The Sun* (Sydney), 24 December 1974d, 5.
McRae, Toni, 'My love for Junie: Cairns slams gossips', *The Sun* (Sydney), 7 February 1975, 1.
McRae, Toni, 'How wrong I've been: Jim Cairns tells about his changed life and philosophy', *The Sun* (Sydney), 10 May 1976, 7.
Milligan, Louise, and Saunders, Megan, 'Rivkin eludes jail for six more weeks', *The Australian*, 5 November 2003, 4.
Milliken, Robert, 'Stiff judgment on nude picture', *The Independent*, 13 February 1993, 12.
Millington, Andrew, 'Musical star tells of disgust over gay slur', *The Guardian*, 31 March 1992a, 2.
Millington, Andrew, 'Donovan not homosexual, magazine says "unreservedly"', *The Guardian*, 1 April 1992b, 2.
Milmo, Cahal, 'Major threatened with legal action over four-year affair with Currie', *The Independent*, 30 September 2002, 3.
Milmo, Cahal, 'Mail pays damages to Kidman over Law affair claim', *The Independent*, 1 August 2003, 7.
Milmo, Dan and Martinson, Jane, 'Axe hangs over The Face as falling sales force Emap titles review', *The Guardian*, 12 March 2004, 23.
Milne, Glenn, 'Their crime? Being unhip, according to the media mafia', *The Australian Financial Review*, 26 October 1998, 13.

Mitchell, Alex, 'Jason will save paper that shamed him', *The Sun Herald*, 5 April 1992a, 3.

Mitchell, Alex, 'Gays turn on Jason', *The Sun Herald*, 29 November 1992b, 28.

Mitchell, Neil, 'Junie must go, say unions', *The Age*, 26 February 1975, 1.

Moore, Des, 'Astounding economic naivety of Jim Cairns', *The Australian Financial Review*, 21 October 2003, 63.

Morgan, Hugh, 'Attack on integrity lacks moral standing', *The Australian Financial Review*, 5 April 2005, 63.

Morris, Sophie, 'Howard axe hangs over ACT's landmark bill of rights', *The Australian*, 3 March 2004, 3.

Morris, Steven, 'Currie's revelation of affair with Major puts libel case in new light', *The Guardian*, 1 October 2002, 2.

Myers, Paul, 'Jason Donovan offers to forgo up to 70pc of libel damages from magazine', *The Guardian*, 8 April 1992, 2.

Nicholls, Sean, 'Rules may let Rivkin avoid prison indefinitely', *The Sydney Morning Herald*, 20–21 December 2003a, 5.

Nicholls, Sean, 'It's time for a second opinion on run of medical certificates, Rene told', *The Sydney Morning Herald*, 23 December 2003b, 3.

O'Brien, Natalie, 'Rene's boys before it all went up in smoke', *The Australian*, 24 March 2004, 1.

O'Brien, Natalie and Colman, Elizabeth, 'Europe-wide hunt for Rivkin driver', *The Australian*, 10 March 2004, 3.

O'Brien, Natalie, Sexton, Jennifer and Saunders, Megan, 'Mystery letter casts new light on Offset fire', *The Australian*, 17 March 2004, 3.

O'Donoghue, Craig, 'Parker faces fitness test – Western Bulldogs v Fremantle', *The West Australian*, 10 May 2003, 181.

O'Loughlin, Toni, 'ASIC net tightens on Rivkin', *The Australian Financial Review*, 7 November 2003, 1.

O'Malley, Nick, 'Rivkin's great escape ends with order to proceed directly to jail', *The Sydney Morning Herald*, 30 January 2004, 3.

O'Neill, Anne-Marie, 'Public exposure', *Courier-Mail*, 13 February 1993, np.

O'Neill, Sean, 'Publicity threat haunts secret gays', *The Independent*, 3 August 1991, 3.

Pearson, Christopher, 'Trouble in topsy-turvyland', *The Australian Financial Review*, 26 October 1998a, 13.

Pearson, Christopher, 'Rafferty's rules OK in media offensive', *The Australian Financial Review*, 9 November 1998b, 17.

Pelly, Michael, 'Abe Saffron down – and uttering cross words', *The Sydney Morning Herald*, 2 December 2004, 25.

Pheasant, Bill, 'Police raid Rivkin and Kennedy', *The Australian Financial Review*, 14 November 2003, 1.

Plane, Terry, 'New Ellis book, new court case', *The Australian*, 26 September 2002, 3.

Price, Matt, 'Photo shows Dockers champ is indeed formidable footballer', *The Weekend Australian*, 17 May 2003a, 48.
Price, Matt, 'End of a romantic tragedy', *The Sunday Herald Sun*, 19 October 2003b, 28.
Quinn, Sue, 'Tom and Nicole sue over "sex sessions"', *The Sun Herald*, 25 April 1999, 3.
Reeves, Richard, 'Why the Face didn't fit any more', *The Observer*, 4 July 1999, 14.
Reynolds, Mark, 'People may claim I'm gay, but I really don't care, says Nicole – Star opens her heart over broken marriage and the rumours surrounding it', *The Daily Mail*, 6 November 2002, np.
Ross, Deborah, 'Fame and misfortune', *The Independent*, 12 January 2004, 2.
Rush, George and Molloy, Joanna, 'They cruise straight to libel win', *The New York Daily News*, 30 October 1998, 14.
Ryan , Kelly, 'Proud farewell for Labor great', *The Herald Sun*, 18 October 2003, 15.
Salusinszky, Imre, 'For those national symbols that mean most, think local', *The Australian*, 19 May 2003, 10.
Schermerhorn, Terry, 'Cruise files second sex suit', *The New York Post*, 5 June 2001, 7.
Sexton, Michael, 'Sex, politics and a tale of two cities', *The Australian Financial Review*, 20 March 1999, 23.
Sheehan, Paul, 'Publisher is not ready to say goodbye', *The Sydney Morning Herald*, 2 April 1999, 11.
Simons, Margaret, 'Power and a little glory', *The Sydney Morning Herald*, 'Spectrum', 8 November 2003, 4.
Smark, Peter, 'Morosi: trial by smear and reporting', *The Age*, 22 February 1975, 2.
Smith, Heather, 'Revealing displays', *The Sydney Morning Herald*, 'Sport', 13 May 1996, 26.
Snow, Deborah, 'Absolute Abbott', *The Sydney Morning Herald*, 11 March 2000, 1.
Stannard, Bruce, 'I'll survive, a cool Junie tells the press', *The Australian*, 12 December 1974, 1.
Stavro, Andrew, 'Ellis unpulped on sale', *The Australian*, 21 May 2001, 6.
Steger, Jason, 'Publisher pulls plug on Bob Ellis profile', *The Age*, 28 April 2001, 5.
Stephens, Tony, 'Junie and me: Cairns concedes a very real kind of love', *The Sydney Morning Herald*, 17 September 2002, 2.
Strangio, Paul, 'Charismatic folk hero', *The Herald Sun*, 27 October 2003, 76.
Strong, Geoff, 'What's worth 6 fat bums or 7 hands?', *The Sunday Age*, 14 February 1993, 1.
Sullivan, Caroline, 'Jason gets sorted', *The Guardian*, 19 October 2000, 6.

Sullivan, Jane, 'Publish and be damned? Not these days', *The Age*, 6 April 2001, 17.

Sutton, Candace and Benns, Matthew, 'New Caroline inquest: Richardson, Rivkin could be asked about Wood's alibi', *The Sun-Herald*, 9 November 2003, 9.

Taylor, Lenore, 'The provocateur', *The Australian Financial Review*, 30 April 2004, 28.

Timms, Daryl, 'Keeping it under wraps', *The Herald Sun*, 12 May 2003a, 42.

Timms, Daryl, 'Photograph irks Docker', *The Herald Sun*, 13 May 2003b, 67.

Toy, Naomi and Connolly, Fiona, 'Face-saving move tipped', *The Daily Telegraph* (Sydney), 29 March 2004, 18.

Trioli, Virginia, 'Fallen Idol', *The Age*, 8 June 1996, 21.

Verkaik, Robert, 'Kidman wins libel action against Sun', *The Independent*, 15 October 2003, 4.

Vincent, Sally, 'Pills and soap', *The Guardian*, 22 May 1999, 24.

Wainwright, Robert, 'Chiselled charmer', *The Sydney Morning Herald*, 29 April 2004a, 11.

Wainwright, Robert, 'Wood link to printing firm reopens fire investigation', *The Sydney Morning Herald*, 6 May 2004b, 3.

Waldren, Murray, 'Abbott and Costello roll on, and Bob's your uncle', *The Australian*, 11 November 1999, 4.

Walker, Lisa and Gale, Alan, 'I slept with Junie, Cairns admits at last – Confession after 27 years', *The Daily Telegraph* (Sydney), 17 September 2002, 11.

Wallace, Richard, 'Cruise in £6m gay slur win', *The Daily Mirror* (London), 17 January 2003, 26.

Walsh, Brian, 'The Selling of ET', *The Sun-Herald*, 8 March 1992, 68.

Walter, Natasha, 'Are Tom and Nicole's eyes wide shut?', *The Independent*, 26 April 1999, 4.

Waugh, John, 'Morosi says no truth in sexual innuendoes', *The Sydney Morning Herald*, 12 December 1974, 1, 15.

Webb, Honey, 'Boyfriend denies killing model', *The Sydney Morning Herald*, 5 March 1998, 7.

Wells, Matt, 'New Statesman to sue Major for libel case costs', *The Guardian*, 5 October 2002, 13.

Whittaker, Paul, 'Rivkin's factory fire was a "set-up"', *The Weekend Australian*, 6–7 March 2004, 1.

Whitworth, Damian, 'Losing face over libel bill', *The Times* (London), 4 April 1992, np.

Will, Iron, 'Always keep a positive attitude – Andrew Ettinghausen', *The Daily Telegraph*, 18 March 1997, 32.

Williams, Nadine and Hurt, Jessica, 'Footy club upset at revealing photo', *The Advertiser*, 13 May 2003, 20.

Williams, Thea, 'Also Rann books a voyage around Bob Ellis', *The Australian*, 10 January 2003, 2.

Wilmoth, Peter, 'Jason, seriously', *The Sunday Age*, 'Agenda', 23 April 1995, 1.
Wright, Tony, '$277,500 for Abbotts and Costellos', *The Age*, 6 March 1999, 6.
Yeaman, Simon, 'Law and disorder', *The Hobart Mercury*, 27 July 2002, 37.

Magazine Articles

'Centrefold', *Australian Women's Forum*, March 1993, np.
'Centrefold', *Australian Women's Forum*, May 1993, 28.
'Centrefold', *Australian Women's Forum*, June 1996, np.
'The Sexiest Man Alive', *Cleo*, August 1992, 96.
Craig, Ailsa, 'Junie Morosi: her own story', *Woman's Day*, 17 February 1975a, 4.
Craig, Ailsa, 'My three husbands – and my business career', *Woman's Day*, 24 February 1975b, 19.
Craig, Ailsa, 'Why I defended Dr Cairns', *Woman's Day*, 3 March 1975c, 15.
Gambotto, Antonella, 'Prince Andrew', *Cleo*, November 1991, 98.
Gow, Michael, 'In bed with Jason', *(Not Only) Blue*, 1996, No. 6, 44.
James, Peter S., 'The power and the glory', *(Not Only) Blue*, Issue 00, 1995, np.
Kerr, James and Cochrane, Brett, 'Hunks', *H.Q.*, April 1991a, 96.
Lord, Gillian, 'A league of his own', *(Not Only) Blue*, Issue 24, 1999, 64.
McKew, Maxine, '"To she who lunches well, much will be given: Those words of wisdom augured well the dejeuner demolition of many an unwary lunch companion', *The Bulletin*, Vol. 121, No. 50, 16 December 2003, np.
Moore, Tony, 'Soppy and stroppy: How suing and self help has made our nation softer than a soggy sao', *Strewth*, Issue 9, 2002, 6.

Internet Articles

Ackland, Richard, 'Devastating verdict for Jeff Kennett' (1999b) 76 *Gazette of Law and Journalism* (http://www.lawpress.com.au/genews/ge76.html) (accessed 19 April 2004).
Ackland, Richard, 'Fallout from Kennett case' (1999c) 77 *Gazette of Law and Journalism* (http://www.lawpress.com.au/genews/ge77b.html) (accessed 19 April 2004).
Good, Ron, '"Despicable plotter" imputations defamatory' (1999) 63 *Gazette of Law and Journalism* (http://www.lawpress.com.au/genews/ge63.html) (accessed 4 January 2004).
Kux, Y. C., 'Plaintiff not a happy camper: Rene Rivkin loses his defamation case against Fairfax' (2001) 127 *Gazette of Law and Journalism* (http://www.lawpress.com.au/genews/ge127_Rivkin_Fairfax.html) (accessed 3 January 2004).
Kux, Y. C., 'Charlotte is a shocker – ex-model defamed by *Woman's Day*: *Dawson v ACP Publishing Pty Ltd*' (2003a) 149 *Gazette of Law and Journalism* (http://

www.lawpress.com.au/genews/ge149_7ADawson_ACP.html) (accessed 7 June 2004).

Kux, Y. C., 'Jury finds former Gadens senior partner defamed – but *not* because he was portrayed as a homosexual exhibitionist' (2003b) 153 *Gazette of Law and Journalism* (http://www.lawpress.com.au/genews/ge153_Kelly_Fairfax.html) (accessed 8 November 2003).

Kux, Y. C., 'Hodge successful with three "cunningly" drafted imputations: *Gregory Hodge v TCN Channel Nine Pty Ltd and Nine Network Australia Pty Ltd*' (2004a) 154 *Gazette of Law and Journalism* (www.lawpress.com.au/genews/ge154_Hodge_7A.html) (visited 3 March 2004).

Kux, Y. C., 'Football hero "Sparkles" defamed by *Today Tonight*: *McGaw v Channel Seven Sydney Pty Ltd*' (2004b) 157 *Gazette of Law and Journalism* (http://www.lawpress.com.au/genews/ge157_McGaw_Channel7.html) (accessed 8 July 2004).

Kux, Y. C., 'Abe Saffron defamed by crossword puzzle' (2005a) 166 *Gazette of Law and Journalism* (http://www.lawpress.com.au/genews/ge166_Saffron_GCP_280705.html) (accessed 19 December 2007).

Kux, Y. C., 'Abe Saffron defamed by inclusion in "unique compendium of Australian villains"' (2005b) 165 *Gazette of Law and Journalism* (http://www.lawpress.com.au/genews/ge165_Saffron_Silvester_300605.html) (accessed 19 December 2007).

Reucassel, Craig, 'Rivkin gets his "homosexual" imputation up: *Rivkin v Amalgamated Television Services Pty Ltd*' (2001) 128 *Gazette of Law and Journalism* (http://www.lawpress.com.au/genews/ge128_Rivkin_ATVS.html) (accessed 2 January 2004).

Whitton, Evan, 'Libel law based on lies distributes cash to liars: Now Ruddock wants to let criminals sue from the grave' (2004) 111 *Justinian* (www.justinian.com.au/subscribers/je111_EWhitton171104.html) (accessed 18 November 2004).

Websites

Australian Story: http://www.abc.net.au/austory/content/2004/s1147959.htm.
Escape With ET: http://www.escapewithet.com.
Men For All Seasons: http://www.menforallseasons.com.au/index2.html.

Videos

The E.T. Story: The Life and Career of Andrew Ettingshausen.

Reference Works

The Macquarie Dictionary, 3rd edn, The Macquarie Library Pty Ltd, Macquarie University, 1997.

The Oxford English Dictionary, 2nd edn, Vol. II, Clarendon Press, Oxford, 1989.

The Oxford English Dictionary, 2nd edn, Vol. IV, Clarendon Press, Oxford, 1989.

The Oxford English Dictionary, 2nd edn, Vol. VIII, Clarendon Press, Oxford, 1989.

Index

Basically, looks at how Post's concepts are evident in Aust^n case law,

- Nice job on comp. damages 77-81

cf.

Occasionally a tendency to recount/recite the law (eg 69-74) to make a simple point (71, 74) – but note 61 intro.

- Recount/recite strategy: 105-117 Morosi & Abbott Costello, then analysis

The claims appear as assertions looking fwd (eg 40, 74) and these are the things I want to see.

Qn Is there a diff in the way concepts are encoded in damages, as opposed to the elements of the cause of action?

- The limited case study makes this an int'g possibility (Crampton)
- See also 117-8 on Abbott & Cost., ; 136 on homosexuality
- Maybe also 101 on celeb.

- Abb & Cost = 5pp descrip of case, + less than 2 of the media stuff
  - Not clear the 5 pp was necessary, and the 2 pp is more int'g.

Curious omission: Marsden ?!?
- control of repn
- re-stating of libel!
- sexuality
- celebrity ??

Could have looked at Packer ?!?

OED definitions, where the lit might offer richer findings.
eg 172

Empirical project -> divorces with non-celebrities?

Chp 7 - curious view of status 156, 158
- 165 - lasting impact?

[LM] Repn as celeb does not work, maybe. Celeb status is a diff motivn, + allows control over repn (p.4 + d), but not clear if is

37 – with Gibbons

Mode of comm^n is imp^t : 40

[But] It is page 118 before we really start to see this.

- "control" 119 – maybe not quite control, though 'attempt to control' (....) could be a better phrase.

REP AS CELEB (given the title, should be more of it!!)

121

124 – but needs more!! And, needs a closer analysis.

138–141 → gets better on Rivkin.

Liberace & Cruise not so good.

143–6 → Donovan well done

[But] no conclusion to chp 6 ?!!?

147

161

Mitchell

Ralph

Milo → 1 + 2

Baker

Kenyon

REFERENCING

(*) 71-2, 122 : almost unreadable

(*) 63 - just not as smooth as with notes

Mix of Quote + Harvard - eg: p7.

We share concerns → lack of att[n] to report[n] is a prob

→ we both look only at pf's case

What of pf motivations? 107 cf. 117

OVERALL

(-) Aust[n] focus heavy

(+) Media coverage

eg. 81 87 10

"Encoded" 77, 67, 7

84